D1264688

# Attack from the Sea

# Attack from the Sea

A History of the
U.S. Navy's Seaplane
Striking Force

William F. Trimble

Naval Institute Press
Annapolis, Maryland

Naval Institute Press
291 Wood Road
Annapolis, MD 21402

Library of Congress Cataloging-in-Publication Data

Trimble, William F., 1947–
    Attack from the sea : a history of the U.S. Navy's seaplane striking force / William F.
Trimble.
        p. cm.
    Includes bibliographical references and index.
    ISBN 1-59114-878-2 (alk. paper)
    1. P6M (Jet seaplane)—History.   2. United States. Navy—Aviation—History.
3. Naval research—United States—History.   4. World War, 1939–1945—Naval
operations, American.   5. Cold War.   I. Title.
    UG1242.B6T75 2005
    359.9'4834—dc22
                                                                    2004027342


Printed in the United States of America on acid-free paper ∞
12 11 10 09 08 07 06 05     9 8 7 6 5 4 3 2
First printing

To Paul, Harriet, and Jonathan

# Contents

# Acknowledgments

Robert C. Alberts, a fine writer, biographer, and historian, once told me that every book has a story behind it. The story behind this book began when a friend of mine, George Cully, and I were in my office talking about various things—not all of them history related. George has a deep knowledge of and enthusiasm for aviation history; at one point in our conversation he asked me if I knew anything about the Martin P6M SeaMaster. Pretty cool airplane, but what did the navy plan to do with it? What was its mission? I told him I had no idea. Then I went to my shelves and pulled out an edition of *Jane's Fighting Ships* from the late 1950s. In it was an official navy artist's rendering of a converted LSD with a P6M on the stern and another being serviced from a boom extending from the ship's starboard side. It looked as if the navy was serious about deploying the airplane using existing auxiliary vessels. Subsequently I discovered that the P6M was to have been a component of a Seaplane Striking Force, which George suggested might have been an alternative to the aircraft carrier and Polaris ballistic missile submarine in the strategic role. Without George's questions and prodding at a crucial early stage, this book would not have happened.

By the spring of 1999 I was a visiting professor at the Air War College, where I finally had time to investigate new research and writing projects. With the Seaplane Striking Force still in mind, I contacted people who knew more about naval aviation in the 1950s than I did, among them Dave Rosenberg and

Jeff Barlow. Both replied promptly to my inquiries, encouraging me in the belief that the sources were available and that the Seaplane Striking Force might be a good subject for study, if placed in the right technological and strategic context. My boss at the Air War College, Col. Chuck Holland, generously gave me the time and resources to travel to Washington, DC, to talk to people and scout out the materials at the National Archives and Naval Historical Center. Then came an overture from Mike Neufeld, one of the curators at the National Air and Space Museum (NASM), to apply for the museum's Charles A. Lindbergh Chair of Aerospace History. With the encouragement and support of my department chair at Auburn, Larry Gerber, I sent in a proposal, offering the Seaplane Striking Force as my research and writing project. Much to my delight, the museum accepted me as the Lindbergh Chair for 1999–2000.

I cannot say enough good things about the help, advice, and support I received from everyone in Washington that year, during which time I substantially finished the book manuscript. The chair of the Aeronautics Division at NASM, Dom Pisano, made me feel at home in his shop, as did others on the staff, including Peter Jakab, Alex Spencer, Rick Leyes, John Anderson, Tom Crouch, and Bob van der Linden. Just ending his tour as Ramsey Fellow in Naval Aviation History at the museum was Tom Wildenberg. We knew each other from our common research interests and struck up a friendship that continues to this day. He read the manuscript, providing critical comments and asking hard questions that demanded thoughtful answers. I am forever grateful to him. Through Tom I met Ed Miller, who suggested I look more closely at the navy's prewar efforts to develop a seaplane striking force. At NASM, too, were Hal Andrews and Dick Knott, both of whom know more about naval aviation history than I ever will, and whose advice and help came at the most opportune times. Tom's successor as Ramsey Fellow, Bill Althoff, was another of the naval aviation experts at the museum whom I came to rely on during and after my year there.

No one was more helpful to me during this project than Al Raithel and Stan Piet, coauthors of a well-written and well-researched study of the Martin P6M, which appeared in 2001. I lent them materials that I had found and they reciprocated, going the extra mile by reading and critiquing my manuscript in its early form. Without their supreme knowledge of the P6M I would have overlooked many fruitful avenues of research and committed any number of grievous errors of fact and interpretation.

During many days and weeks at the National Archives, Barry Zerby and Vern Smith at Archives II and Rick Peuser and Becky Livingston at the "downtown" building dug out Bureau of Aeronautics and other records that form the core of this book. I cannot say strongly enough how indebted I am to all of the National Archives and Records Administration people, overworked and underpaid public servants who daily perform the thankless jobs that make everything else possible. At the Naval Historical Center I relied heavily on Mike Walker at the Operational Archives Branch and Roy Grossnick at the Naval Aviation History Branch. At the San Diego Air and Space Museum, A. J. Lutz and Bob Bradley led me through the voluminous Convair collection, a treasure trove for everyone in aerospace history.

Where to begin and end the long list of others who contributed to this book is a challenge. Tom Hughes at the Air War College stands out among those trying to make sense out of naval aviation during and after World War II. Tom Hone is one of the most gifted and insightful scholars in the field today; for some reason he thinks my work is noteworthy enough to warrant publication. David Arnold at Auburn led me to important Defense Technical Information Center materials that historians need to be aware of and tap into. Bob Hunter lent me many of the Bureau of Aeronautics materials he had harvested from the National Archives during intensive research on navy postwar lighter-than-air units. Adm. Charles S. Minter Jr. (USN-Ret.), made time in his busy schedule to talk about his experiences as P6M program manager. At Auburn, Amy Foster, Jim Hansen, and Kristen Starr provided specific information just when I needed it. I greatly appreciate the time Lys Ann Shore devoted to copyediting the manuscript and extend my thanks to Paul Wilderson, Mark Gatlin, and Kristin Wye-Rodney at the Naval Institute Press for shepherding the book through the production stages. My sincere apologies go to anyone I have overlooked who deserves recognition for helping with this book.

In Washington, Paul and Harriet Sirovatka and their son Jonathan again welcomed me into their home and family. My indebtedness to them goes back decades and knows no bounds. And my own family—wife Sharon, and sons Will and Mike—steadfastly and patiently stood with me on this project, which, with a long absence in Washington, was particularly stressful for family life. To them, as always, go my deepest feelings of gratitude and love.

# Attack from
# the Sea

# One

# Naval Aviation in Crisis

Joe Evans, commander of the U.S. submarine *Neptune,* anxiously scanned the early morning sky around the rocky island of Moab in the western Pacific. "It was nine o'clock before they started coming in. We could hear them long before they could be seen. Then there was a tiny dot high up in the blue, dropping down, coming in, getting bigger and bigger every second, until the first plane landed on the water and taxied into the bay." Looking for all the world like giant airborne sea monsters, the big flying boats settled onto the water one after another. They were late. Evans soon learned that they had missed the island on their first approach just before sunrise and had had to reverse course and initiate a standard search pattern to find it. He was relieved when he saw them "drop down out of the sky in such a marvelous display of power and skill and assurance" after their exhausting night flight, and he wanted to get on with the job of refueling and arming them for the next stage of their carefully timed mission.

Evans's submarine was one of three assigned to supply a squadron of flying boats en route to attack a Japanese troop staging area three thousand miles from the nearest Allied air base. At this critical point early in World War II, the U.S. carrier forces had been stretched beyond their limits in blunting multiple Japanese naval offensives, and no one wanted to risk the precious ships and their aircraft so far from home. But a coordinated attack by flying boats, replenished at a remote site close enough to allow them to haul their maximum payloads yet out of range of enemy land-based air power, had great appeal. A resounding success, the raid caught the Japanese totally by surprise and destroyed key elements of their invasion force. The U.S. aircraft returned to the island having suffered the loss of only a single one of their number to antiaircraft fire, although another had been damaged and had been obliged to land at sea to make emergency repairs before limping home.

Thrilling stuff, but entirely fictional. The story sprang from the fertile imagination of Cdr. Wilford Jay ("Jasper") Holmes, who wrote using the pseudonym Alec Hudson. First published as "Rendezvous" in *The Saturday Evening Post* in August 1941, the piece reappeared a year later in a collection of short stories about submarine warfare. Holmes based his narrative on prewar attempts to find ways to use big, long-range seaplanes in the attack role, augmenting land-based and carrier aircraft. As an intelligence officer at Pearl Harbor during the war, Holmes was among the elite group of navy cryptanalysts who played a critical part in deciphering Japanese naval codes.[1]

American naval officers who read Holmes's stories were intrigued by the concept of dispatching a seaplane unit on a long-range attack mission supported by submarines or surface vessels at an advanced position. They were not alone, apparently. On 3–4 March 1942, in the Japanese "K Operation," two four-engine Kawanishi H8K "Emily" flying boats flew from Wotje in the Marshall Islands 1,900 miles to Hawaii, refueling from submarines stationed at French Frigate Shoal west of Midway. Weather problems thwarted the strike, forcing the aircraft to jettison their ordnance at sea and on a mountainside in Oahu, but the seaplanes eluded Hawaii's defenders and returned safely to their base.

In the aftermath of the raid, Adm. Chester Nimitz, the Commander-in-Chief, Pacific Fleet (CINCPAC), believing that the Japanese had no aircraft capable of making such a long-range attack, called in Cdr. Edwin T. Layton and other intelligence officers to get an explanation. Layton told him that he thought the Japanese had borrowed a page from Holmes in planning and executing the strike. Whether that was the case or not is beside the point, because the attack left a lasting impression on American naval officers. In the late 1940s, when the service struggled to redefine its strategic functions and grappled with what seemed to be insurmountable political and technological problems in waging a war with the Soviet Union, they returned to the potential long-range strike capabilities of big seaplanes.[2]

As historian David R. Mets points out, the navy faced an "institutional identity crisis" following World War II. Victory over the Japanese in the Pacific seemed to validate the navy's long-held conviction that the path to victory was to meet and defeat the enemy's military forces; there might be cause to modify how force was applied, but there was no reason to make radical changes to the nation's military organization or to redirect national strategy. The navy's thinking was at variance with that of most officers in the army air forces (later the air force), who believed just as firmly that their brand of warfare—centered on the long-range strategic bomber, preferably armed with the atomic bomb—had been the winning weapon during the war and was destined to transform how all conflicts would be fought and won in the future. Naval officers considered nuclear warfare of the kind the airmen envisaged not only to be a threat to their service's traditional strategic role, but to be savage and fundamentally immoral.[3]

Against the backdrop of this dichotomy in strategic thinking and inter-service conflict, the navy struggled through the late 1940s and early 1950s to bolster its relevancy by acquiring a viable strategic strike capability against the Soviet Union, a vast land power frustratingly beyond the navy's reach. Despite air force opposition, executive hostility, and congressional skepticism, the service pursued several tracks to achieve its objective. An obvious course, and the one with the most appeal to admirals fresh from the Pacific war and the triumph of the fast carrier task forces in a strategic role against Japan, was to acquire aircraft and weapons compatible with existing ships while agitating for a "supercarrier" more suitable for the long-range, heavy attack mission. Another road—less desirable from the point of view of carrier aviators—led toward unmanned, ship-launched guided weapons with the range and pay-load capacity to reach into the heart of Russia. Yet each of these alternatives at the start of the new decade had glaring technological, operational, economic, and political shortcomings.

From an unexpected and often overlooked corner of naval aviation came a third possibility, which for a time seemed to have none of the disadvantages of the first two and offered the prospect of a dispersed, mobile force capable of performing a range of strategic missions. After the war, Vice Adm. Robert B. ("Mick") Carney, Deputy Chief of Naval Operations (DCNO) (Logistics), and his staff submitted reports demonstrating that a sea-based force could give the navy the advantages of strategic surprise and mobility. He articulated this in testimony before the House Armed Services Committee in its unification and strategy hearings in the fall of 1949, but his ideas received little attention in the midst of the heated debate over carriers and big bombers.[4] Carney's proposal took on more relevance in 1951, when the navy awarded a contract to the Glenn L. Martin Company in Baltimore for the P6M SeaMaster, a high-performance, four-engine jet flying boat, and sought ways to integrate it into the Seaplane Striking Force (SSF), a system using a family of advanced water-based aircraft in attack, defense, and supply roles, backed by inexpensive surface tenders and submarines, to complement carrier-based attack airplanes in strategic and tactical missions. At the center of the force was the P6M, with the Consolidated Vultee Aircraft Corporation (Convair) F2Y-1 fighter providing air defense of advanced bases, the Convair R3Y Tradewind serving as logistical support, and the Martin P5M Marlin and Convair P6Y antisubmarine warfare (ASW) seaplanes defending the force from enemy submarines.[5]

An independent sea-based strike force such as the SSF was far from a novel idea. The concept went back at least to the early 1930s, when American strategic planners sought solutions to the problem of mounting an assault across the Pacific with minimum air support and limited ability to attack long-range targets. Adm. Ernest J. King, chief of the Bureau of Aeronautics (BuAer), despaired that the Consolidated PBY Catalina, which in many ways solved the navy's problem of long-range scouting for the fleet, was wasted unless it was also used in the attack role. Moreover, he and others saw the big flying boat as a crucial adjunct to carrier aircraft in making possible the advanced base strategy that lay at the heart of War Plan Orange, the navy's blueprint for war against Japan.[6]

Later, in the wake of the crisis of 1949–50, the navy's attempts to develop a sea-based strike force reflected the service's quest to maintain or enhance its funding and political influence, as well as to counter air force claims of exclusivity in the strategic role. Enticed by promises of "breakthroughs" in seaplane technology, the navy thought at last that it could meet the air force on a level playing field, only to discover that the technology could not deliver on promises as either a strategic or a tactical platform. In the end, the big carrier staved off encroachments from the air force and helped keep naval aviation viable in the nuclear era, while the combination of the nuclear-powered submarine and Polaris intermediate range ballistic missile provided the navy with a second-strike strategic capability.[7] And, as everyone knows, the big carrier since the mid-1960s has time and again demonstrated its capabilities in a variety of roles short of general war.

Throughout the program's existence, the navy studiously avoided enmeshing the SSF in interservice disputes. Well aware that the SSF had ingredients that duplicated the "natural" strategic mission of the air force, the navy cast the P6M within the acceptable framework of its mission in the next world war, stressing that its job was low-level, precise mining of Russian harbors and the narrow seas that Soviet submarines had to transit to get to Allied sea lanes. It did not take long, though, for navy planners to recognize that a large, long-range airplane capable of carrying a heavy payload of mines could also haul an equivalent tonnage of bombs, some of them nuclear, far inland against strategic targets. When the administration of Dwight D. Eisenhower adopted its "New Look," which emphasized nuclear deterrence as a means of curbing both Soviet aggression and defense expenditures, the SSF became even more alluring. Although always referred to as the airplane's "secondary" mission, the strategic nuclear delivery potential of the P6M on at least one occasion provoked the air force to make a public appeal for the navy to give up or at least share such sea-based strategic weapons.

Just how important the SSF became as a potential strategic force is shown by the early, largely unsatisfactory efforts of the navy to adapt the atomic bomb to existing aircraft carriers. Most of the navy's attack carriers were of the *Essex* class, World War II veterans too small to carry out the strategic mission effectively. Even though Secretary of Defense Louis A. Johnson had agreed to the navy's plans to upgrade the ships under the so-called 27A conversion program of 1947, it was obvious that they alone could not do the job. The three biggest carriers in the fleet, the 45,000-ton *Midway* class, could under certain circumstances operate heavy attack aircraft, but not in a way designed to maximize their performance potential.

So the navy staked nearly everything on a new supercarrier designed from the keel up to operate the largest and most capable strategic aircraft. Johnson's abrupt cancellation of the ship in 1949 left the navy, as historian Jeffrey Barlow writes, at "sixes and sevens," even though optimists in the service held out hope that under different circumstances they might still get their supercarrier if they played a careful political game and deemphasized the ship's strategic capabilities. The optimists turned out to be right. In June 1951, only one month after BuAer submitted outline specifications for the high-performance seaplane, the Bureau of Ships finished its initial characteristics for a new supercarrier, completed four years later as *Forrestal*.[8]

The long, dark shadow the atomic bomb cast over the navy is most apparent in the service's efforts after 1945 to develop nuclear-capable carrier aircraft. In an attempt to achieve a nuclear delivery capability—an attempt that in retrospect looks nothing short of desperate—the navy modified Lockheed P2V maritime patrol aircraft to carry the MK 4 atomic bomb. Tests in April 1948 with the *Midway*-class *Coral Sea* showed that the airplane could be launched from the large conventional carriers using rocket assistance (known as "jet-assisted takeoff," or JATO) to get up to takeoff speed, but attempting to land back aboard was another proposition entirely, even though the airplane was equipped with an arresting hook. Plans called for the airplanes to be lifted aboard the carriers in port, and after completing their missions, they were to find bases ashore at which to land, or somehow ditch close enough to the task force for their crews to be rescued. Even more advanced aircraft, such as the North American AJ-1 Savage, specifically designed for the nuclear strike mission, suffered from limitations in range and payload, and other performance-related shortcomings. Not until the fleet received the Douglas A3D Skywarrior jet bomber in 1956 did it finally enjoy a true all-weather, high-speed heavy attack capability.[9]

Guided weapons offered little more than potential in the 1950s, hampered by primitive propulsion and guidance systems. The abortive Taurus was to use radio-controlled carrier bombers to haul nuclear weapons on one-way flights into the Soviet Union. Triton was a ship-launched cruise missile with a 2,000-nautical-mile range that looked promising but never got far in the development phase. Regulus, a much smaller shipboard cruise missile, fared better, only to encounter problems with reliability, range, and payload after being put into service in 1955. Although its supersonic sibling Regulus II was much better all around, the navy canceled the program in late 1958 for budgetary reasons.[10]

In addition to highlighting the navy's strategic and political dilemma, the SSF program and its history illustrate how the navy went about research and development in the 1950s. Although defense budgets grew steadily after the surge caused by the Korean War, there was intense competition for each dollar, both among the services and within them. During the decade, the navy experimented with the concept of the "weapon system" in an effort to contain costs and maximize results. As developed by Martin and other airframe manufacturers, the concept encompassed not only the discrete weapon, but also its many component parts, electronic equipment, payloads, logistical support network, training programs, and other elements—all integrated and coordinated with the airplane. Historian Glenn E. Bugos, in his study of the McDonnell F-4 Phantom II fighter, viewed the airplane as the culmination of an iterative process of bringing together parts into systems. The weapon system idea, in addition, emphasized the need for centralized program management within a carefully defined organizational "matrix."[11] Both Martin and the navy wagered that the weapon system concept applied to the SSF would be an efficient and cost-effective solution to a complex strategic and tactical requirement.

Divergent factors within the navy also shaped the program. In the navy's tradition-haunted caste system, aviation occupied the top echelon, within which those flying seaplanes lived in the shadow of carrier aviators, who tended to regard their colleagues as able but a notch below their own exalted status. George A. Rodney, Martin's chief test pilot, was not alone when he recalled that "in truth, there was hardly a key Naval aviator that was willing to give up a single carrier fighter for a whole fleet of P6M's." Even worse, seaplane advocates perceived carrier aviators to be as closed-minded as the aviators thought the battleship "gun club" had been during the interwar years. Capt. Robert B. Greenwood of BuAer recalled that at the time he "rather naively believed that the naval aviation leaders were open minded in the search for new developments. . . . I realized that the fight for research funding for seaplanes was not easy, but the thought that carrier proponents had become the 'Status quo' advocates was beyond belief at the time."[12]

Those perceptions and the profound cultural differences that lay behind them might not have been much of a problem, particularly with Adm. Arleigh A. Burke, a nonaviator, as Chief of Naval Operations (CNO), except that in the zero-sum fiscal environment of the 1950s, any money diverted from carrier aviation to seaplanes was in effect money lost. It did not help, either, that those responsible for operations sometimes seemed out of touch with the technological and fiscal deficiencies of the program and demanded more of the weapons than could realistically be expected.

On the purely technological level, the aircraft earmarked for the SSF pushed the state of the art in the early 1950s. It was a daunting task to design a flying boat to perform well both aerodynamically and hydrodynamically; generally, seaplanes lagged behind landplanes in maximum lift-drag ratios and other performance criteria, although the gap narrowed in the 1940s.[13] Two of the airplanes, the P6M and the Convair XF2Y, were powered by turbojet engines with afterburners. At the time the navy (and the air force, for that matter) was feeling its way with the new power plants, which presented challenges in the development of high-temperature materials, in addition to the operational problems related to their unique power characteristics. As if that were not enough, Martin with the P6M explored the use of titanium and aluminum alloy honeycomb sandwich structures, plastics, precision inertial guidance systems, aerial refueling, and electronic digital computers. Convair was generally more conservative; still, the XF2Y was radical in concept and operations if not materials and electronics, the company's R3Y-1 transport pioneered the application of geared turboprops in large flying boats, and the stillborn P6Y ASW seaplane was to bring a new dimension to antisubmarine warfare in support of the P6M attack force.

There are times when new technologies, or variations on older ones such as the SSF, suddenly materialize to threaten established ways of doing things. Often inferior in performance to its competition, a new technology can stimulate investment due to a few distinct advantages, then rapidly improve to the stage where it is poised to supersede or "disrupt" the old order.[14] At this point, though, decision makers must learn to curb their enthusiasm, because it is equally possible for the older technology to evolve and adapt to meet the new challenge while the usurper falls short of expectations. The SSF can serve as a cautionary tale for defense procurement, showing that technology forecasting remains an unpredictable exercise.

Finally, the navy's sea-based strike system provides further amplification of one of the verities of technological change: it does not occur in a linear manner from conception to innovation. Rather, as historians have discovered, technological change is a complex, interactive process that defies easy rationalization. Although the concept of a mobile attack force existed in the minds of a few forward-thinking officers well before the P6M came on the scene, the idea did not reach full maturity until after most of the hardware was well along the development curve. In other words, the airplane and its potential capabilities helped crystallize ideas about delivery capacity and flexibility. Other, nontechnical factors were at work, too, not the least of which were the political and economic circumstances of the 1950s and the drive and influence of such key personalities as Arleigh Burke, who survived the 1949 "revolt of the admirals" to became CNO at a crucial stage in the airplane's gestation.

The chapters that follow chronicle the proverbial "path not taken," an alternative paradigm that offers a glimpse of a notional weapon system that showed great promise first as a means of extending the navy's conventional reach, then as a complement to both the carrier and the land-based long-range bombers that were the backbone of the air force's strategic nuclear deterrent. Despite skepticism about the viability of the SSF, there grew within the highest levels of the service a belief that it would help restore the navy to its former status as the nation's first line of defense. By 1954 elaborate proposals called for phasing out the fleet's heavy attack aircraft and phasing in the SSF as a less costly and more effective alternative. Far from a relic of naval aviation's romantic past, the SeaMaster and its kin promised the realization of the dream of securing the future of naval aviation through a largely invulnerable nuclear force sufficient to deter any rival. As the focal point of the program, the P6M for a short time became in the eyes of some the airplane for every occasion: reliable, flexible, and competitive in cost with land-based and carrier aircraft. That the airplane never achieved the goals set for it or that the SSF had conceptual and operational flaws does not diminish the validity of the idea of a mobile weapon system capable of long-range attack from the sea.

# Seaplanes and Strategy

Throughout most of the 1930s, some naval officers looked at the big flying boat (VP) as a long-range patrol and reconnaissance aircraft that also had a significant attack capability. After 1921 War Plan Orange, the navy's guide to fighting a Pacific war against Japan, centered on what historian Edward S. Miller refers to as the "Through Ticket," advocated by "thrusters" who wanted a swift and massive counterattack across the ocean, securing a "Western Base" and defeating the Japanese in a decisive fleet engagement in the vicinity of the Philippines. By the early 1930s the "cautionaries" in the navy began to gain more credence in the planning process. They foresaw a more arduous campaign, with the "sequential occupation" of key islands in the central Pacific as advanced bases, wearing the enemy down until U.S. forces could defeat the Japanese fleet, invest the home islands, and effect Japan's capitulation following a merciless blockade.[1]

Aircraft played an important part in defending the mid-ocean bases, the first of which would most likely be located in the Marshall Islands, held by the Japanese as a League of Nations mandate following World War I. Only patrol flying boats capable of searching out at least 1,000 miles and staying in the air for a minimum of twenty-four hours could provide security against attack by Japanese carrier strike forces. Landplanes could not do the job, nor was it anticipated that carrier aircraft, short-legged and essential for defense of the fleet, could be diverted for such missions. VP squadrons, on the other hand, needed protected waters for safe and efficient operations and enough tenders and auxiliaries to support them indefinitely at the advanced bases.[2]

BuAer's Plans Division stressed big, long-range flying boats as a component of the air forces the navy would need to implement its Pacific strategy. In the fall of 1929 the Plans Division recommended that heavy VPs be self-sustaining "for a considerable period" away from bases and be equipped to carry bombs and torpedoes for attacks against enemy ships. The following year, the bureau began looking into designs for three- and four-engine flying boats with maximum takeoff weights (MTOW) between 36,000 and 43,000 pounds and a range of at least 3,000 miles.[3]

In April 1931, as the navy neared a decision on a new flying boat to replace the venerable biplane PN series, Capt. Frederick J. Horne, commander aircraft, scouting force, aboard the seaplane tender *Wright*, wrote to the CNO about the need for higher speed, longer range, and greater endurance than the VPs then in service. He wanted airplanes that could stay in the air for twenty-four to twenty-eight hours and cruise at 100 knots or more. Fully aware of the strategic picture in the Pacific, Horne called for an airplane that could be sent out at midnight, reach its patrol sector 600 miles out at dawn, stay on station throughout the daylight hours, and return after dark. He also recommended that the aircraft "carry some bombs for offense against surface craft and submarines" as the opportunity arose, and that under some circumstances they might want to concentrate for more deliberate attacks on enemy fleet units. Finally, and most intriguingly, Horne saw that the long-range flying boats could be "rigged as heavy bombers by substituting bomb loads for a part of the fuel loads required for distant patrols."[4]

A few weeks later, Rear Adm. William A. Moffett, chief of BuAer, underscored Horne's thinking about the potential attack role of the long-range flying boat. Endurance, cruising speed, and range were the most important criteria in determining the requirements for a new generation of flying boats, which should be designed to carry heavy bombs for attack missions. Moffett believed further that seaplanes, supplementing carriers in the strike role, would acquire additional significance as the navy's carrier force reached its treaty-limited plateau in the 1930s. "The Bureau's plan is to provide VP planes primarily for patrol," Moffett wrote, "but so armed that the responsible commanders may use them for as many different purposes as may be required in war." As the navy entertained proposals for a new flying boat, Moffett kept the attack mission in mind. He urged rejection of Martin's entry, which he said had inadequate provision for 500-pound and 1,000-pound bombs. Consolidated's

XP2Y-1, in contrast, was a "fully developed airplane" that was almost sure to be a success in operation. The new Consolidated flying boat went into service in 1933 as the P2Y-1 Ranger. A good airplane, it could carry up to 2,000 pounds of ordnance and stay in the air as long as twenty-five hours, and early in its career it set nonstop distance records of more than 2,000 miles.[5]

Long-range flying boats were on Horne's and Moffett's minds that spring in part because the General Board, an advisory body made up of senior officers, had just initiated studies of a new carrier design. Tonnage limits imposed by the 1922 Washington Treaty forced planners into tough design choices as they tried to combine the largest offensive air complement and maximum speed within a ship of about 20,000 tons.[6] The design, which after many iterations culminated in *Yorktown* and *Enterprise,* nevertheless was a compromise of striking power, protection, and speed. Furthermore, two 20,000-ton ships used up all but 15,000 tons of the total U.S. treaty allotment. Within the treaty's qualitative restrictions individual ships would not have optimum performance characteristics, while the treaty's quantitative limits would determine the fleet's total striking capacity.

Faced with these realities, even the staunchest carrier advocates came to the understanding that the long-range flying boat was an offensive asset. Vice Adm. Joseph Mason Reeves, commander battleships, battle force, had been the central figure during the 1920s in the development of carrier doctrine. One of the "cautionaries," Reeves thought that longer range aircraft and Japanese bases in the Mandates would complicate U.S. plans for the Pacific offensive. He wanted at least five VP squadrons to protect the U.S. force as it advanced from the Marshalls to the Philippines. By the end of 1933 OP-12, the War Plans Division in the office of the CNO, and Reeves's own staff had included VPs in their planning for the central Pacific offensive, although the range of existing flying boats limited their usefulness west of the Marshalls.[7]

Almost providentially, in 1933 the industry provided the flying boat the navy needed for the central Pacific campaign. From Consolidated Aircraft (Convair's predecessor) came an airplane that represented little short of "an aeronautical design breakthrough"—the XP3Y-1, better known as the Catalina, a name it acquired when it went into service with the British early in World War II. Consolidated received a contract for the prototype in October 1933, winning out over rival Douglas with a proposal for an airplane that had a range of at least 2,000 miles. It was an inspired design, the most aerodynamically efficient flying boat to date. Characterized by a 104-foot cantilever wing mounted high on a pylon above the hull, and with an MTOW of just under 20,000 pounds, the twin-engine airplane had superb endurance for scouting and patrol, and with reduced fuel could haul enough heavy ordnance to be attractive as a long-range bomber.[8]

Working with BuAer, Consolidated engineers, led by Isaac M. ("Mac") Laddon, refined the design over the next year. In March 1935 Consolidated delivered the XP3Y-1 from the company's Buffalo, New York, plant to Hampton Roads, Virginia, for its first test flights. It was all the navy could want, meeting or exceeding every one of the manufacturer's performance guarantees. In June 1935 the navy awarded the company a production contract. The aircraft carried two 1,000-pound bombs in internal racks on either side of the center of the wing, and 1,200 pounds of smaller bombs externally. The MTOW went up to more than 22,000 pounds, range exceeded 2,100 miles, and top speed was 175 miles per hour. The high-tech MK 15 Norden bombsight, combined with the Stabilized Bombing Approach Equipment, supposedly gave pinpoint accuracy in level bombing attacks.[9]

As a strike aircraft, the new Consolidated flying boat had to be able to deliver torpedoes if it were to play a role in the decisive fleet action envisaged as the culmination of the U.S. Pacific offensive. In October 1933 BuAer looked at the problem of carrying a 1,400-pound MK VII torpedo under each wing of the airplane. Engineers found no clearance or other problems to preclude carrying or launching the torpedo, although the wing structure had to be strengthened. Range fell off to less than 1,000 miles, and the top speed went down by more than 20 miles per hour; estimated performance with the new and heavier MK XIII torpedo was even lower. Tests with the XP2Y-2 at the Naval Torpedo Station in Newport, Rhode Island, in 1935 did not go well. Of twenty-four MK XIIIs launched, only ten ran well. In one experiment, when two torpedoes were launched simultaneously, they collided with one another and exploded. Nor were things much better with the XP3Y-1 equipped with two MK XIII torpedoes. By 1936 BuAer concluded that for the interim the airplane would have to use the old MK VII.[10]

In the meantime BuAer concentrated on the development of a seaplane intended exclusively to launch torpedoes against enemy capital ships. The nature of the ordnance and the method of delivery dictated the basic configuration: a twin-float monoplane with the torpedoes carried within or under the fuselage between the floats. BuAer issued detail specifications in March 1934 for a seaplane with an MTOW of about 25,000 pounds and a top speed of 150 miles per hour, powered by two 800-horsepower Pratt and Whitney radial engines and capable of hauling two 1,850-pound MK XIII torpedoes or four 1,000-pound bombs more than 1,000 nautical miles. On 30 June 1934 Hall-Aluminum Aircraft Corporation signed a contract for $309,000 to design and build the airplane.[11]

Work on the new airplane, designated XPTBH-1, did not get off to an auspicious start, as Hall and the navy quickly became mired in technical details and interpretations of contractual fine print. Delays ensued when the company relocated from Buffalo to a new plant in Bristol, Pennsylvania. Then, well before the completion of the mockup in December, it became apparent to BuAer that Hall's proposal for carrying the weapons in an open bay within the fuselage was not feasible and that the airplane would fail to meet even minimal performance objectives. Consequently, Rear Adm. Ernest J. King, Moffett's successor as BuAer chief, ordered Hall to work with the bureau on a revised design.[12]

Still a mid-wing, twin-float monoplane, the resulting XPTBH-2 bore only a passing resemblance to the earlier Hall effort. MTOW had been reduced to about 20,000 pounds, maximum speed increased to 190 miles per hour, number of crew members cut from five to four, and range increased to 1,500 nautical miles. Payload was now a single MK XIII torpedo or two 1,000-pound bombs. The mockup inspection in May 1935 generally went well, but not much else did, as Hall struggled with subcontractors and a shortage of skilled laborers. Finally the airplane was ready for flight tests in February 1937, during which it failed to meet contract performance criteria for top speed and minimum speed for launching torpedoes. After taking delivery in the summer of 1937 and dispatching press releases about the revolutionary capabilities of the torpedo plane, BuAer quietly relegated the airplane to testing duty at the Naval Torpedo Station in Newport and turned its attention back to advanced flying boats for fleet strike missions.[13]

In the meantime, congressional legislation brought into question the purpose and mission of the navy's new long-range flying boats. On 27 March 1934 President Franklin D. Roosevelt signed into a law a naval bill jointly sponsored by Rep. Carl Vinson (D-Ga.), chairman of the House Naval Affairs Committee, and Sen. Park Trammell (D-Fla.), chairman of the Senate Naval Affairs Committee. Its express purpose was to procure sufficient ships and aircraft to bring the navy up to its treaty limits.

As the Vinson-Trammell bill wended its way through the legislative maze, CNO Adm. William H. Standley asked Rear Admiral King to come up with ideas about a naval air force adequate for a treaty navy. King saw an opportunity and took it. On 6 March 1934 he sent to the CNO a proposal for 2,184 aircraft, of which no fewer than 590 were large, long-range patrol planes, organized into 32 squadrons, 15 in the Atlantic and 17 in the Pacific. To King, "the development of long range seaplanes into an effective striking arm of the fleet will be definitely established with the types of airplane now in the process of being laid down for purchase under the Treaty Navy." Hauling bombs and torpedoes, these new airplanes "will make available to the Commander-in-Chief a very powerful offensive weapon capable of being concentrated at any desired point on very short notice." Eleven tenders, of which ten were new construction or conversions of older ships, gave the seaplane forces unprecedented mobility.[14]

Standley, hoping to get the cost of such a massive program down to a more "reasonable basis," recommended that the General Board study the proposal before committing himself to the numbers and types of airplanes BuAer wanted. In response to the board's request for clarification of BuAer's proposal, King explained that major considerations in determining its aircraft requirements were geographical factors, the location of permanent and temporary advanced bases, and the demands imposed on the naval air arm by the transpacific offensive called for in War Plan Orange. BuAer had based its estimates on an extrapolation from the performance of the P2Y-2, finding that "a certain minimum number of airplanes is required to cover efficiently a given area," even if a newer airplane had greater range and speed than an older one. King hoped the board understood that his bureau regarded the flying boats as key ingredients in "mobile units, available to the Fleet as powerful striking forces," in addition to their traditional scouting mission. "There is no conflict between these functions," he insisted, "and there is no duplication involved in providing sufficient maintenance, overhaul, and supply bases, as well as sufficient tenders for mobile base operations and concentration of units." Because the need for the airplanes and supporting ships was "unquestioned," it was "the unqualified opinion of this Bureau that these functions are entirely Naval in character and that the Navy must make proper provision for their fulfillment."[15]

General Board hearings in the spring and summer of 1934 centered on the numbers and types of aircraft, bases, and support facilities needed under the Vinson-Trammell legislation. Before the board on 21 March King took the opportunity to emphasize the flexibility of the SSF, which could be quickly "concentrated in the area of operations . . . as part of the Fleet." An "alarming" shortage of tenders limited the mobility of the force. He urged the board to provide an adequate number of new ships, which he considered as important as carriers in a Pacific air offensive. In July, Cdr. Newton H. White Jr., who had spent the last year with the patrol forces, testified that a striking force was a necessity and that it required that the support ships be able to concentrate in enough time to launch an attack. Representing BuAer, Cdr. Alva D. Bernhard told the board later in the month that the flying boats "must take the offensive" if the navy were to be able to have any success in a Pacific war.[16]

Standley was unmoved and called on King to cut the size of the patrol plane force. Under pressure, King admitted that the 590 he had called for originally had been put out for negotiation purposes and that he was willing to reduce his request to 354, still "too big" for Standley but at least closer to what he wanted. There was no meeting of the minds between the two on the use of seaplanes in the attack role: Standley knew the importance of long-range reconnaissance for the fleet but had no proof that flying boats could accomplish strike missions; in the absence of such verification he insisted that there was no room in the budget for two strike forces, one from carriers and the other using seaplanes. He told King he "doesn't believe [the] striking force [is] reasonable," and refused to approve it other than as an adjunct to the normal patrol duties of the aircraft.[17]

Pugnacious as always, King was not about to give in without a fight. To show that carrier-based aircraft by themselves could not bear the total offensive burden, especially in a treaty-limited navy, the bureau forwarded data to the General Board on the performance of the Douglas XTBD-1 torpedo bomber and the Consolidated P2Y-3 and XP3Y-1 flying boats. At least as far as BuAer was concerned, it was clear that the XTBD-1, with a maximum range of 662 miles carrying 1,500 pounds of bombs or a single torpedo, was greatly inferior to the P2Y-3, with a range of 2,000 miles carrying 2,000 pounds of ordnance. The XP3Y-1 was even better, able to haul 2,000 pounds for 2,200 miles, and new four-engine flying boats, then being considered by the bureau, could exceed 2,500 miles with 4,000 pounds of bombs or torpedoes.[18]

Continuing his efforts to sway the board into endorsing the maximum number of seaplanes and retaining their strike role, King wrote on 9 August 1934 that in a future Pacific war the commander-in-chief would want to have as many long-range patrol planes as possible to cover the fleet as it steamed west from Hawaii and to protect the advanced bases the fleet would establish in the Mandates. Adding a persuasive new argument to his advocacy of seaplanes as a "powerful striking force," King stressed that they could be manufactured regardless of international agreements, as opposed to carrier aircraft, whose numbers were circumscribed by the carrier tonnage permitted under the Washington Treaty.[19]

Admiral Reeves added his eloquent voice to the growing chorus singing the praises of the SSF as a mobile component of the fleet. Now commander-in-chief of the U.S. Fleet, Reeves told the General Board on 14 August that the big flying boats were useful in any capacity and that it was impossible for a fleet commander to have too many of them. He estimated that 590 would be needed at the outset of a Pacific war, and many more as the conflict intensified. They were most useful as "combatant units of the Fleet," which "just like squadrons on the carrier, should be free to move from one base to another," and to operate as needed from tenders at advanced positions removed from fixed support facilities. The flying boats' ability to carry heavy bomb loads made them a "very valuable offensive unit where that work is required." If he had to establish priorities between patrol planes and carrier aircraft, Reeves said that the big, complex flying boats needed to come first, because they required a longer gestation period than most carrier planes.[20]

In the end, Standley got what he wanted. The General Board wound up its inquiry at the end of August and reported its findings to the secretary of the navy and CNO on 5 September 1934. BuAer's reduced demand for 354 flying boats was still excessive; the board estimated that 204, including 24 for training, would suffice, reasoning that after many years of neglect, the type was likely to undergo rapid development and that the navy did not want to be left with large numbers of obsolescent aircraft. Following Standley's lead, the board disputed King's arguments about the seaplane in the attack role. The "primary function" of the flying boat was scouting, with bombing a secondary mission coincidental to reconnaissance. "So far the effectiveness of patrol planes as a striking force has not been demonstrated. The employment of this type of plane in an attack against enemy shore objectives or in attack against an enemy approaching the coast can be visualized, but it is practically impossible to coordinate an attack of such planes with a Fleet action held at any great distance from their base." Put another way, the board could not see dispersed, mobile seaplane forces delivering blows at great distances against enemy fleet units or strategic targets ashore. The board also rejected King's pleas for tenders, conceding that only one new ship was needed in addition to *Wright* and that it should be built only after all other ship classes had been brought up to treaty ceilings.[21]

King must have been seething at what he could only conclude was a short-sighted rejection of a novel means of projecting power from the sea. In a letter to Standley on 27 September, he charged that the navy had "under-estimated the usefulness of patrol planes as bombers," comparing them to cruisers, which in addition to reconnaissance were expected to augment the offensive capability of the fleet. With range and payload capacity comparable to that of the latest air corps bombers, the flying boat, even in its older versions, brought flexibility and options that "any Commander-in-Chief would welcome and which any enemy would dislike." The conclusion seemed obvious: "In an Orange war in the area of the Mandated Islands and in the Philippine area, the possibilities inherent in the concentrated use of patrol planes as a striking force are apparent."[22]

BuAer proceeded in the fall of 1934 on the assumption that there would be sufficient numbers of new flying boats to employ some on offensive missions, even if the CNO and the General Board regarded the strike mission as secondary to patrol and reconnaissance. Design studies by the bureau's Engineering Division included a new generation of four-engine flying boats with a maximum range of 3,200 statute miles (reduced to 2,700 miles with a 4,000-pound bomb load), a top speed of 190 miles per hour, and a service ceiling of 20,000 feet. Finally, in November 1934, under pressure from King and the secretary of the navy, Standley reluctantly acceded to King's 354 patrol planes.[23]

In January 1935 Standley turned his attention to how the patrol planes would be used, calling upon the operating forces for ideas about flying boats, their estimated combat range, whether they could perform in the open ocean, what kinds of support ships they would need, and the shore bases necessary to support them. He had in mind an airplane that could fly from the advance base somewhere in the Mandates to a secondary location and remain there, with a minimum of support, for three or four days flying 600-mile patrols. Would a twin-engine or a larger four-engine airplane similar to those coming out of the Sikorsky and Martin companies be the better choice as a successor to the XP3Y-1? Or would a smaller airplane, which could be broken down and shipped in component form to the advanced base in the Mandates for "local defense," be more feasible?[24]

Standley's request prompted a close look at the attack role of present and future flying boats. Capt. George J. Meyers, director of OP-12 in the CNO's office, cast his response in light of the capabilities of the XP3Y, soon to join the fleet as the PBY-1, the *B* denoting "bomber." The flying boats' primary missions were patrolling the nation's coastal areas and the seas around the Philippines, as well as protecting advanced bases and the fleet as it took the offensive in the western Pacific. A secondary function was strike, carried out as the opportunity arose during patrol and scouting missions. War Plans estimated that a minimum of 180 VPs would be needed for the movement of the fleet from Hawaii to the Philippines. The airplanes would come from new production as well as the shifting of squadrons from bases in the Canal Zone and the West Coast to Pearl Harbor.[25]

King responded with an examination of the strategic situation in the Pacific in view of the current and anticipated VP situation and what he considered to be the shortsightedness of the CNO's office. He acknowledged that the primary purpose of the big flying boats was scouting and reconnaissance. Nevertheless, he had not given up on attack, stressing that "it appears that the possibilities of patrol planes as a striking force have not been sufficiently recognized," and warning that "this failure to consider the offensive capabilities of patrol planes" might have a negative effect on the way planners considered using them in a Pacific war.

To King, the long-range bomber was a "certainty" and would undergo "unlimited development," and the sooner the navy came to grips with its reality the better. Consolidated's new PBY-1 pointed the way to the future. A squadron of twelve flying boats could deliver up to 48,000 pounds of ordnance, only 10,000 pounds less than all of *Lexington's* and *Saratoga's* bombing aircraft. Mindful of air power propaganda and the army's commitment to strategic bombing, King believed the navy ignored the potential of the long-range flying boat at its peril. "It is hardly conceivable," King wrote, "that squadrons of these planes, based at strategical naval centers, are not distinctly a naval weapon for use over the sea against naval objectives." The long-term risk was that "if the Navy relinquishes to the Army the use of the long range bomber as a striking force over the seas, it is relinquishing the most promising development in the future of Aviation," forever impairing the navy's strategic capability and jeopardizing the nation's defense.

It was not necessary or even desirable at this point, with the PBY-1 coming into service, to fix the size of the navy's "Patrol-Bombing Force," as King liked to call it. He still held out hope that Congress would pay for at least 310 patrol planes, 135 assigned to 9 squadrons based on the West Coast and at Pearl Harbor, and 60, organized into 4 squadrons, going to the fleet based on tenders. Everything possible should be done to ensure that there were enough shore facilities and tenders to support a force of this size.[26]

Standley could not have been surprised at King's response. On 1 April he recast his original request for information in more general terms and forwarded it to people in his own office and the fleet for their ideas about the number and types of VPs and their potential use in wartime. He made it clear that the principal purpose of the flying boats was patrol, particularly from bases in Hawaii and the Philippines, and protection of the fleet as it moved from Pearl Harbor to its first base in the eastern Marshalls. Once the enemy had been located, an air offensive could be mounted, but only with forces available and not with any dedicated attack squadrons. In general, he believed that the advanced flying boat squadrons, rather than posing a threat to the enemy, would be vulnerable to attack and would have to be protected by shore-based and carrier aircraft.[27]

Meyers took Standley's new overture as an opportunity to educate his boss about the pros and cons of flying boats as a striking force. He disagreed with King on several points, the foremost being the limited numbers of VPs he estimated would be available at the start of a war and the need to use virtually all of them for long-range scouting for base and fleet security. Additionally, he did not want to see scarce and valuable carrier aircraft diverted from their normal duties with the mobile fleet, and he doubted whether there would ever be enough tenders to provide the logistical support to mount major strikes by VPs early in the war. If BuAer were really serious about using flying boats as attack aircraft, he thought Standley should ask the bureau to put together a comprehensive plan. It would include the numbers of tenders required, and would cover issues of fuel, ordnance, base defense, pilot training, and ground personnel. It would also address a host of other questions that needed to be answered before fielding a viable force: What targets lent themselves to attack by VPs? What tactics would the aircraft and crews employ—level or dive bombing? Based on present data, how accurate was the bombing likely to be and what results could be expected?[28]

Others were more optimistic about the SSF as a component of the air offensive in the western Pacific. A principal adherent continued to be Reeves, who thought a squadron of "the longest range, highest performance flying boats" needed to be created at Pearl Harbor as soon as possible. He wanted the airplanes to have a minimum range of 3,000 nautical miles carrying 2,000 pounds of bombs, preferably ship-killing 1,000-pound bombs rather than a greater number of smaller weapons. Reeves also urged the CNO to form two squadrons of torpedo-equipped flying boats. Finally, he reminded Standley of the need for more tenders, which he considered essential to maximize the mobility and offensive capabilities of the airplanes. Meyers's relief as director of OP-12, Rear Adm. William S. Pye, agreed with Reeves on the effectiveness of big, long-range flying boats, especially if they were outfitted with torpedoes as well as bombs, although he preferred to hold off on forming attack squadrons until BuAer had made a decision about a four-engine flying boat.[29]

Capt. Alan G. Kirk in the Ships Movements Division of the CNO's office hit the nail on the head with his analysis of the basing and logistical problems associated with VPs, regardless of their mission. Current facilities at Coco Solo in the Canal Zone, San Diego, and Pearl Harbor were "taxed now to the saturation point," and could not handle even the relocation of existing squadrons, let alone the numbers of new units King and others wanted. Even worse was the shortage of seaplane tenders, which Kirk thought was "the most serious deficiency in the U.S. Fleet at the present time," and a situation "which is becoming more and more serious as the VP procurement program materializes." Under ideal circumstances, ten new large seaplane tenders (AVs) would be needed to support the squadrons on the West Coast and Hawaii. But only four new tenders were likely to be funded, and they needed to be given top priority in the shipbuilding program.[30] In emphasizing the importance of logistical support for effective seaplane operations, Kirk highlighted a problem that arose time and again as the navy sought to integrate the flying boat into an operational striking force.

His tour as BuAer chief ended in June 1936, and King returned to the fleet as commander aircraft, base force, taking the opportunity to see what big flying boats could do. Four VP squadrons and forty aircraft, supported by the tender *Wright* and eight smaller vessels, participated in exercises in the vicinity of Hawaii in the fall of 1936. Some of the aircraft successfully carried out "concentrated bombing attacks" against towed targets. High winds and rough seas at French Frigate Shoal challenged the crews and support personnel who serviced and armed the aircraft, but Johnston Island, about 700 miles to the southwest, proved to be a more suitable prospective anchorage. King deemed the lessons "invaluable" in showing what patrol planes—old P2Y-2s and P2Y-3s—could accomplish in supporting the fleet from advanced bases.[31]

For the next few years, flying boats continued to figure as a major part of U.S. plans for war in the Pacific. Even though the Boeing B-17 long-range heavy bomber entered the army air corps inventory in 1937, it was obvious that there would never be enough of them and that captured island bases would not have the capacity to handle the numbers needed to deliver decisive blows against such Japanese strongholds as Truk in the Carolines. Nor could carrier aircraft do the job, because many of them would be occupied providing air cover for the fleet or defending advanced bases.[32] By default, a portion of the attack responsibility fell on the navy's VP force.

In Fleet Problem XIX, held in March and April 1938, the new PBYs saw action in the strike role, scoring some notable successes while suffering losses that raised the question of their vulnerability to antiaircraft fire and fighter cover. As the fleet approached within 600 miles of the California coast with the two carriers *Lexington* and *Saratoga,* PBYs from San Diego attacked *Lexington* with 500- and 1,000-pound bombs, damaging the ship enough in the minds of the umpires that they took it out of the exercise. Later, off Hawaii, PBYs from Pearl Harbor attacked *Saratoga* and *Ranger,* severely damaging *Ranger* but at the cost of thirty of the big flying boats. PBY strikes on the carriers as they returned to the West Coast at the end of the exercise resulted in the loss of additional aircraft and minimal damage to the big ships.[33]

For the mobility considered essential to realize the full advantages of long-range flying boats in either the attack or the reconnaissance mission, tenders were a necessity, and they were hard to come by in the late 1930s. King, Kirk, and others had for years urged the construction of new tenders or the conversion of older ships. The General Board had reluctantly agreed to one new ship and one conversion in 1934, but Capt. Royal E. Ingersoll, the director of OP-12 in the summer of 1937, estimated that there was "an immediate need" for five more large tenders within two years. To make up for the existing and estimated deficiency, BuAer looked at using any type of ship, including submarines. From the bureau in June 1937 came a proposal for the emergency servicing of patrol planes by a submarine, which could refuel up to six aircraft and under some circumstances could submerge under a flying boat and lift it clear of the water for maintenance and minor repairs. Adm. James O. Richardson, then acting CNO, agreed with the bureau's recommendation for trying out the idea "as soon as practicable" and designated *Nautilus* for the conversion during its regular refit in 1938. No funds, however, were available to test the concept.[34]

To a certain extent the lack of tenders became a moot point after 1940, when all but the most ardent seaplane enthusiasts recognized that a technological gap between flying boats and landplanes made it highly unlikely that they would ever see front-line service as attack aircraft. Adm. Arthur B. Cook, former BuAer chief, reported that a joint exercise with the army in the San Francisco Bay area in early 1940 "again demonstrated that the primary function of patrol planes is the service of information and their use as attack forces is questionable except as a last resort." Only in "desperate circumstances" should flying boats be used for daylight torpedo attacks, where they would be sitting ducks for fighters and anti-aircraft fire. King, too, gave up on the fly-ing boat, acknowledging that the VPs might be good only as a defensive force to protect a limited area of the north Pacific from a Japanese offensive.[35]

On the eve of Pearl Harbor, CNO Adm. Harold R. Stark cut to the heart of the matter. "There is an inherent difficulty in incorporating in seaplanes performance characteristics comparable to those of landplane types now and prospectively available," he said. "The range, ceiling, maneuverability, and speed of seaplane patrol bombers suffer greatly by comparison with landplanes of about the same size." Flying boats still had a role to play as patrol planes in areas where enemy air opposition was light and where airfields were not imme-diately available, but they were "unsuitable for bombing objectives having strong antiaircraft defenses, or for operations involving combat with fighter aircraft."[36] One of the most thoughtful and articulate men in uniform at the time, Stark seemed to have written the epitaph for the SSF.

The PBY was well along the road to obsolescence when the country went to war in 1941. Like Stark, few thought it would be suitable for offensive mis-sions, yet under some circumstances it proved surprisingly effective in attack-ing Japanese shipping and land targets. There were some hard lessons at first. On 27 December 1941, PBYs from the island of Ambon off New Guinea flew 800 miles to bomb the Japanese base of Jolo. Lethal antiaircraft fire and dense fighter defenses led to heavy losses and convinced those in charge that mass level bombing by the flying boats was "suicide." At the Battle of Midway in June 1942, PBYs located elements of the Japanese invasion fleet and managed to damage a tanker in a daring night torpedo attack. Despite intensive searches, the flying boats were never able to find the main Japanese carrier force, whose fighters and antiaircraft guns most likely would have destroyed them had they tried to drive home torpedo and bombing attacks.[37]

Far to the north in the forbidding Aleutians, where air bases were few and far between and antiaircraft defenses relatively light, the PBYs fared better. Beginning on 11 June 1942 and lasting three days, PBYs mounted a round-the-clock bombing "blitz" against Japanese ships and shore installations on the island of Kiska. Only one flying boat was shot down, but half of the twenty aircraft participating in the raids were damaged. More forays against Kiska came in late July and early August, with the Japanese losing a freighter in one of the attacks. In December 1943 and January 1944, PBYs from Unmak staged night bombing raids on the Japanese base at Paramashiro in the Kurile islands, experiencing no losses and causing minimal damage.[38]

Better known were the operations of the famous "Black Cat" squadrons in the south and southwest Pacific in 1942 and 1943. Needing only a patch of sheltered water and flying mainly at night, radar-equipped PBY-5s constantly menaced Japanese transports and warships during the long and bloody Guadalcanal campaign; two Japanese cruisers were victims of PBY torpedo attacks, although both ships survived. As the U.S. offensive shifted northward from Guadalcanal toward Bougainville, PBYs struck the Japanese stronghold of Rabaul in late 1943 and early 1944. Wewak was another target of PBY bombing raids in February 1944. PBYs also supported the 1943–44 offensive by the southwest Pacific command along the northern coast of New Guinea, and by the summer of 1944 they were regularly bombing targets in the southern Philippines. Australian Catalinas were equally aggressive in bombing raids on Truk and Rabaul, and later in the war laid mines in Manila Bay and in Japanese-held ports along the China coast. The war revealed the strengths and weaknesses of the flying boat in the strike role in the most dramatic way possible. Historian Richard C. Knott concluded that "never in history has an aircraft so ill-designed for combat wreaked so much havoc on such a dangerous and merciless adversary."[39] If such an outdated design as the Catalina could contribute to the maritime offensive in the Pacific, there was reason to believe that a new generation of high-performance flying boats, benefiting from the most recent technological advances, could give the navy a strategic and tactical alternative to the aircraft carrier in the event of another war.

# Three

# The Carrier Conundrum

Secure in their thinking that the aircraft carrier would continue as the navy's dominant weapon, most in the service did not look for alternatives to the big ships in the years immediately after the war. Certainly no one anticipated a catastrophic series of events that threatened not only the future of the aircraft carrier but also naval aviation itself. That all changed in the spring of 1949. On an official trip to Corpus Christi, Texas, on Saturday, 23 April, Secretary of the Navy John L. Sullivan received a long-distance phone call telling him that Secretary of Defense Louis A. Johnson had just sent him a memorandum reporting the cancellation of the navy's supercarrier *United States*. The message struck Sullivan like a body blow, but it was not unanticipated. Earlier in the week, he had spoken with Johnson, taking the opportunity to explain the importance of the ship to the navy, only to be abruptly cut off when Johnson said that he had to get to another important meeting right away. Johnson did not respond to a memorandum from Sullivan on the subject the next day. Back from his weekend trip on Monday, 25 April, Sullivan unsuccessfully tried to talk to Johnson and went over the implications of the cancellation with his close advisers and the navy's top leadership. He was convinced that the incident left him no choice but to resign as secretary.

Sullivan's letter of resignation emphasized how much the navy had at stake in the new carrier, which had first been proposed by Adm. Marc A. Mitscher shortly after the end of the war. In 1947 Sullivan had set aside more

than $300 million in scarce shipbuilding funds for the vessel, whose con-
struction subsequently received approval from the armed services committees
of both houses of Congress. Just a week before Johnson's decision, the ship's
keel had been laid at Newport News. Sullivan deplored Johnson's heavy-
handedness, "which so far as I know represented the first attempt ever made
in this country to prevent the development of a powerful weapon," and por-
tended "a renewed effort" by forces hostile to naval aviation to eliminate the
navy's air arm. "However," he went on, "even of greater significance is the
unprecedented action on the part of a Secretary of Defense in so drastically
and arbitrarily changing and restricting the operational plans of an Armed
Service without consultation with that Service. The consequences of such a
procedure are far-reaching and can be tragic."[1]

In the aftermath of the supercarrier cancellation came doubts that the
navy would be able to fulfill its strategic role in the postwar era and even questions about the viability of the service as a separate entity in the fledgling
national military establishment. Sullivan's successor, Francis P. Matthews, a
Nebraska businessman with little experience in national affairs, was unwilling
to stand up for the navy in the face of Johnson's assaults. Problems worsened
when a document drafted by Cedric Worth, special assistant to the undersecretary of the navy, and Cdr. Thomas D. Davies, assistant head of BuAer's
Patrol Design Branch, highlighted some of the irregularities in the procurement for the air force of the Consolidated B-36 long-range heavy bomber.
Mostly based on hearsay and gossip, the memo found its way anonymously
to Rep. James E. Van Zandt, a western Pennsylvania Republican and a navy
veteran who was skeptical about air force claims for the strategic bomber. The
document finally led Carl Vinson, one of the navy's staunchest advocates, to
launch a House Armed Services Committee investigation of the B-36 in
August. Much to the navy's consternation, the hearings became a forum for
the air force, whose generals rebutted the navy's allegations and successfully
defended the strategic importance of the big bomber while presenting a public image of Worth and other members of the navy leadership as disgruntled
and subversive troublemakers.[2]

Things got even worse for the navy that fall. In September the testing by
the Soviet Union of an atomic bomb heightened the public's attention to
national defense and brought up once more on Capitol Hill the old issue of
integrating the navy's air arm into the air force. In October the naval leadership got a chance to make its case during hearings on defense unification and
strategy held by Vinson's committee. Technical experts debated the vulnera-

bility of the B-36 to enemy interceptors and the effectiveness of strategic bombing. CNO Adm. Louis E. Denfeld reminded the committee of the centrality of sea power and questioned the Joint Chiefs of Staff (JCS) in favoring the air force and the B-36 over the navy's new carrier. Denfeld's testimony earned him the ire of Secretary Johnson and cost him what support he may have had among his fellow officers of the JCS, who now considered him untrustworthy and disloyal. Johnson reacted swiftly to what the press termed the "revolt of the admirals," and with Matthews's consent and the approval of President Truman, Johnson fired Denfeld and replaced him as CNO with a more pliable choice, Adm. Forrest P. Sherman.[3]

A near-casualty of the sorry affair was Capt. Arleigh A. Burke, who headed OP-23, a group within the office of the CNO charged with studying service unification and related issues. During the B-36 controversy, Burke and his organization came under fire from the press as a "secret publicity bureau" whose purpose was to malign the air force. Not long after taking over from Denfeld, Sherman eliminated OP-23, and Matthews directed that Burke's name be removed from the list of officers in line for promotion to flag rank. Only timely intervention by Truman's naval aide convinced the president to restore Burke to the list before the end of the year.[4]

The Vinson committee's report on unification and strategy, which appeared in March 1950, was generally favorable to the navy and aviation. It pointed out that air power encompassed more than long-range strategic bombing and emphasized the navy's position as an equal partner in the nation's defense. Yet the report did not advocate resurrecting the supercarrier, critical as a physical expression of the navy's strategic role. Nor was more money forthcoming from Congress for naval aviation, which continued to limp along under severe budget constraints. Stung by recent events and wary of further congressional or public controversy, Rear Adm. John H. Cassady, the assistant CNO (Air), suggested in a memo only a few days after Sullivan's resignation that "we should immediately *lay off any* mention of 'strategic bombing' and should also lay off any mention of 'long-range' aircraft" in any policy documents or other statements of mission or purpose.[5]

Of the many problems facing the navy in the immediate postwar years, none seemed as difficult as developing the aircraft and the aircraft carriers for the service to compete, even as a junior partner, with the air force in the strategic strike role. With the air force nuclear capability hanging over it, the navy at first denied that atomic weapons could win wars while simultaneously attempting to develop its own means of delivery. The divided thinking ran deeper. As navy planners focused on using nuclear-capable carrier aircraft against traditional naval targets, some of the more vocal members of the service publicly advocated expanding the navy's role to include strategic objectives far from the enemy's coastline, which appeared to duplicate army air forces (and later air force) roles and missions. To make matters worse from the air force point of view, navy research and development programs included carrier-launched heavy attack aircraft capable of delivering atomic bombs. Even more serious, Project Jupiter, a 400,000- to 600,000-pound, multi-role, land-based airplane carrying six or more parasite fighters for defense, looked on paper like a navy B-36.[6] Simultaneously, fiscal constraints, the limits of technology, and opposition from air force officers and civilian leaders seemed to conspire against even the navy's most reasonable and modest postwar aspirations for a nuclear mission.

In late July 1946, following Operation Crossroads, the atomic bomb tests at Bikini atoll in the Pacific, Secretary of the Navy James V. Forrestal, with the tacit approval of President Truman, agreed to a request from the Special Weapons Division (OP-06) in the office of the CNO (OPNAV) that carriers and carrier aircraft be modified to handle and deliver atomic bombs. At the time, the navy already had under way the design and development of a new flush-deck carrier, from which aircraft large enough to deliver atomic bombs could operate. As for the airplanes, the service had let contracts to North American Aviation for the XAJ-1 Savage, which could be equipped to carry an atomic bomb, and had plans for heavier aircraft specifically designed for the nuclear role.[7]

In an effort to gain internal and external support for its nascent nuclear capability, the navy tried to tailor its forces to accomplish distinct maritime missions and to integrate its ideas of force projection into contemporary strategic plans. Based in part on World War II experiences where the army air forces had been reluctant to divert aircraft to maritime missions, navy planners wanted to ensure that they had the resources to support any future naval efforts. In particular, naval officers scarred by the Battle of the Atlantic viewed with alarm the huge Soviet submarine fleet and formulated plans in 1946 that emphasized neutralizing the threat by targeting submarine bases for attack with nuclear and conventional weapons. Offensive mining campaigns would simultaneously bottle up Russian submarines in port or block their access to the Allied sea lanes in the Atlantic and Pacific. A year later, the navy's Strategic Plans Division (OP-30) in Naval Strategic Planning Study (NSPS) 3 suggested the use of carrier aircraft to engage Soviet fighters and to attack transportation and logistical networks to slow a Soviet offensive in western Europe before land-based aircraft could be brought to bear.[8]

In June 1948 the General Board completed a comprehensive study of the problems the navy was likely to face and how it might fight a war with the Soviet Union within the next ten years. The board concluded that strategic bombing would be important in waging the war, but cautioned that bombing alone was not likely to be decisive, if only because large parts of the country could not be attacked, even by long-range heavy bombers operating from advanced bases. The navy and its aircraft carriers were essential for performing such traditional missions as securing the sea lines of communication and supporting amphibious operations out of range of land-based air power. In addition, nuclear-capable carrier aircraft could be used against Soviet submarine facilities and in certain instances could strike targets in the Soviet Union beyond the reach of air force bombers.[9]

Four months later, on 18 October 1948, Vice Adm. Arthur W. Radford, the vice CNO, elaborated on the navy's ideas for the next war in testimony before the Commission on Organization of the Executive Branch of the Government, chaired by Ferdinand Eberstadt, a dedicated public servant and former business partner of Secretary of Defense Forrestal. Radford looked first at air force plans to win a war against the Soviet Union by strategic bombing and concluded that the "known technical limitations of present day aircraft leads to something more than a reasonable doubt of our abilities to carry out such a program." More likely was a longer and more costly war, fought in phases with a variety of weapons, nuclear and conventional. It would start with attrition of the enemy's forces, followed by an Allied buildup, and then a counteroffensive to bring the war to a conclusion. Bombing would be part of the attrition phase of the war, as well as of the war's final stages. Carrier aviation—the "one weapon the United States now has wherein our superiority is so marked that it cannot be matched"—was critical to blocking the Soviet offensive, reducing the Soviet air force, preventing the invasion and occupation of Britain, and keeping the vital Atlantic lifelines open. Less optimistic, the commander-in-chief, Eastern Atlantic and Mediterranean, Adm. Richard L. Conolly, worried that putting carriers forward to assault the Soviet Union meant there would not be enough ships available for sea control in the Atlantic.[10]

The JCS 1949 war plan "Dropshot" incorporated some of Radford's and the navy's concepts, envisaging an offensive by a combined American-British carrier task force against Soviet naval facilities and land-based naval aviation in the Black Sea and the Barents Sea around the port of Murmansk. In addition to Allied assaults on surface and air forces, some 40,000 mines would be sown in the first six months of the war as part of the effort to contain Soviet submarine forces.[11]

Ordinarily such carefully defined naval nuclear roles would not have earned the opposition of the air force, but they did exactly that in the highly charged political atmosphere of the late 1940s. Fleet Adm. Chester W. Nimitz, former commander-in-chief, Pacific Fleet, and a World War II hero, contributed to the controversy. In December 1947, following his retirement as CNO, Nimitz called for the navy to concentrate on developing the offensive capability to strike at the vital centers of enemy power. That same month, Rear Adm. Daniel V. Gallery, assistant CNO (Guided Missiles), penned a memorandum to Vice Adm. Donald B. ("Wu") Duncan, DCNO (Air), expressing doubts about the effectiveness of air force strategic bombers and outlining a scenario in which the navy became the major force for attacking the Soviet Union with nuclear weapons. Meant as an internal "think piece," the Gallery memorandum eventually became known to the air force and found its way into the newspapers in 1948.

Official reassurances that the navy did not intend to usurp the air force's principal responsibility for strategic bombing did nothing to allay fears among air force leaders, who took the Gallery memorandum, coupled with the "Nimitz Valedictory," as it came to be known, as evidence of the navy's duplicity in developing new weapons for strategic purposes while officially denying that it was doing so. In response, the air force started chipping away at navy credibility. Beginning in 1948, a series of air force studies showed that carriers were severely circumscribed in their ability to mount and sustain a nuclear offensive, while themselves being vulnerable to attack by submarines and land-based aircraft.[12]

Increasingly, the focus of air force attention became the navy's plans to incorporate a long-range nuclear delivery capability in its present and future carriers. Of the most immediate importance were the three 45,000-ton, *Midway*-class CVB "battle carriers." As the biggest and newest carriers in the fleet, the *Midway*-class vessels were a natural choice for modifications. In November 1946 the CNO authorized a conversion program encompassing stronger flight decks to accommodate the planned AJ-1 attack aircraft and the necessary bomb hoists, storage, and handling equipment for atomic weapons.[13]

Next was conversion of nine World War II *Essex*-class carriers to fly heavier aircraft loaded with nuclear weapons. Begun in 1947 under what was known as the 27A program, the updates included strengthening the flight decks and installing new arresting gear to handle aircraft up to 40,000 pounds. Six of the ships in the 27A program received new magazines, larger bomb hoists, and the assembly shops needed for atomic bombs. Even with modifications, the elevators of the *Essex*-class vessels could not bring fully laden attack aircraft to the flight deck, and the airplanes could not fit through the hangar deck fire doors.[14]

Understanding that even with the anticipated modifications, existing carriers would never be fully up to the task of launching and landing large attack aircraft, navy planners began looking at entirely new carrier designs. Based on studies of the strategic bombing offensive in Europe, BuAer determined that bombs in the range of 4–6 tons were needed to ensure the destruction of a wider variety of targets. Not coincidentally, the World War II–vintage MK III fission bomb, at 10,300 pounds, fell in the middle of the weight range being considered by the bureau. Whether conventional or nuclear, such ordnance meant heavier airplanes, some up to 100,000 pounds MTOW, which in turn meant bigger carriers.[15]

Following up on the recommendation of Vice Adm. Marc A. Mitscher, the DCNO (Air), who knew from his experience in World War II that carriers operating long-range aircraft were better equipped to counter land-based air attacks, Sullivan, then undersecretary of the navy for air, approved design studies of a new ship. In May 1946 the Bureau of Ships responded with the CVB-X, a 69,000-ton carrier that could accommodate twenty-four ADR-42s—100,000-pound aircraft specifically intended for nuclear attack. Over the next year the carrier design, now renamed Project 6A, evolved in response to aviators' desires for a flush-deck ship devoid of any obstacles that might inhibit the operation of large aircraft and in response to political worries that a special-purpose ship was likely to raise the ire of the air force. The result by the summer of 1947 was a multi-purpose ship displacing nearly 80,000 tons and operating eighteen ADR-42 and eighty fighter aircraft. Bureau of the Budget approval for inclusion in the 1949 shipbuilding program did not come until Sullivan, now secretary of the navy, agreed to delete a battleship and a large cruiser to offset the expense of the carrier.[16]

With the navy's carrier building and conversion programs well under way, prominent air force officers wasted no time in taking the offensive. Gen. James H. ("Jimmy") Doolittle, who in April 1942 had led the famous B-25 raid on Tokyo from the carrier *Hornet,* wrote to Carl Hinshaw, vice chairman of the Congressional Aviation Policy Board, on 14 February 1948 to say that even though the aircraft carrier had done a "magnificent job" during the war, it had limitations countering a land power like the Soviet Union. Doolittle considered the use of carrier aircraft to assault the Soviet Union or to slow a Soviet attack on western Europe to be "wholly unrealistic," largely because of the carrier's vulnerability to attack by land-based aircraft. In any case, Doolittle concluded, the large carrier was too much, too soon, and the navy was likely to fail in its effort to combine a new ship and untried jet-powered aircraft. "The chance of realizing a strategic carrier any time in the practical future is, therefore, remote and the value in case of realization at least questionable. On the other hand, proven long range land based aircraft will surely be available long before large carriers could possibly be ready."[17]

Further indications of trouble came later in the year. When the Joint Chiefs of Staff took up the matter of the 6A carrier on 26 May 1948, the air force member of the JCS, Gen. Hoyt S. Vandenberg, objected, stating that he could not go along with the navy's plans without a full study of the budgets of all three services. Moreover, Sullivan himself balked at the CNO's idea of building three additional carriers—one each in fiscal years 1950–52—forcing the navy to designate the 6A ship as a prototype. Nevertheless, an appropriation for the carrier, now designated CVA 58 and named *United States,* followed in June, along with President Truman's approval of the additional funding. Most in the navy thought that after a long battle they had at last secured an important strategic role for their service.[18]

Optimism in the navy ranks proved short-lived when Johnson canceled the new carrier in April 1949, precipitating Sullivan's resignation and generating fear and uncertainty about the service's future role in the country's defense. During the summer of 1949, Johnson continued to assail naval aviation. For fiscal year 1951 he proposed reducing the navy's budget to $3.8 billion, a cut of about $400 million from that of the previous year. In contrast, the air force was to receive $4.5 billion, up about $100 million from 1950. Johnson's moves followed a disturbing trend. In fiscal year 1948 the navy had received about 40 percent of the total defense budget; this fell to 35 percent in fiscal year 1949 and to about 30 percent in 1950. Meanwhile, the air force soared from only 13 percent of the defense budget in 1948 to 32 percent in 1950. For a perspective on how much things had changed in a little over a decade, the navy had received $472.5 million in fiscal year 1935, or more than 49 percent of the total military expenditures, compared to the army air corps' $30 million, amounting to 3 percent of the total budget. As late as 1939, the navy, at $768.4 million, had 53 percent of total expenditures, and the air corps, at $83.1 million, accounted for only 6 percent of the total.[19]

The proposed budget cuts for 1951 were nothing short of crippling. Anticipated were the elimination of four of the eight *Essex*-class carriers, slicing carrier air wings in half; a cut of 8–10 percent in aviation personnel; and equally devastating reductions in marine air units, and sea- and land-based antisubmarine and patrol squadrons. At the same time, the air force agitated for even more funding to support a seventy-group bomber force and appeared to have gained the upper hand in the political battle of Washington.[20] The subsequent "revolt of the admirals" and Denfeld's dismissal were evidence of the turmoil that enveloped naval aviation by the end of 1949.

Building the flush-deck carrier and converting existing carriers were only part of the navy's challenge in establishing a foothold in the long-range strategic mission. Finding aircraft suitable for the role and showing that they could operate from existing carriers proved to be equally demanding. In 1946 the ADR-42 was little more than a gleam in BuAer's eye, and the XAJ-1 program had just been authorized. Under political pressure to show that it could contribute something right away to a strategic air campaign, the navy cast about for an airplane with the necessary range and payload capacity for nuclear delivery.

That airplane was the Lockheed P2V-1 Neptune, a twin-engine ASW patrol bomber that entered the inventory in the summer of 1946. By any definition, the Neptune was a remarkable airplane. With an MTOW of 61,000 pounds, it could haul a bomb load of up to 4,000 pounds, and it had the "legs" needed for long-range missions. In September 1946 a P2V-1 nicknamed "Truculent Turtle" and piloted by Cdr. Thomas D. ("Tom") Davies flew nonstop without refueling from Perth, Australia, to Columbus, Ohio, staying in the air more than fifty-five hours and covering a distance of 11,236 miles. Some officers saw the potential propaganda value of the Neptune in the struggle with the air force over the strategic role. When Rear Adm. Thomas H. Robbins Jr. read in February 1947 of a plan by the army air forces to make a record flight from Honolulu to New York with a P-82 jet fighter, he talked to a friend in BuAer about the P2V. The arithmetic told the tale: the P-82 could average 239 miles per hour, whereas the Neptune could average 292 miles per hour. "May I suggest the desirability that a P2-V be in Honolulu awaiting favorable weather for a ferry flight to New York and accidentally time its departure within a half hour or so of the P-82, and thus beat the P-82 to New York by three or more hours."[21]

No one followed up on Robbins's proposal, but the point had been made that the navy had in the P2V an airplane with extraordinary capabilities.

The issue at hand, though, was whether the P2V-1 could fly from the 27A *Essex*-class carriers and those of the *Midway* class. Cdr. John T. ("Chick") Hayward, an aviator and director of plans and operations for the Armed Forces Special Weapons Project, believed the airplane could do so, and in the spring of 1947 he received authorization to put together crews and airplanes to try out the concept. Early tests demonstrated that the P2Vs could take off from the carriers using JATO, but that getting back aboard was more problematic. Rather than have the ship at risk of being put out of commission in the event of a landing accident, Hayward determined that in the event of war the aircraft would ditch near the ship or make their way to Allied land bases. Altogether, twelve airplanes underwent modifications that included auxiliary fuel tanks and arresting-gear hooks, radar bombing systems for high-altitude attacks against land targets, and bomb bays fitted for the 3,300-pound MK 8 gun-type atomic bomb. Redesignated as P2V-3Cs, the Neptunes were ready for service in the spring of 1949.[22]

In the meantime, Hayward's team culminated months of intensive training on 28 April 1948 with the first carrier takeoffs. At sea off Norfolk, a modified P2V-2 flown by Tom Davies took off using JATO from the *Midway*-class carrier *Coral Sea* and flew ashore to the Norfolk Naval Air Station. Within minutes a second P2V flew from the ship to Norfolk. Composite Squadron 5 (VC-5), with Hayward as the commanding officer, was created at Moffett Field in September 1948, receiving its first P2V-3Cs a couple of months later.[23]

Once Hayward had shown the feasibility of operating P2Vs from carriers, Vice Adm. John Dale Price, the DCNO (Air), thought he knew how they could be used to upstage the newly independent air force. To celebrate its first anniversary, the air force in the fall of 1948 planned to launch B-29s from bases outside the continental United States to fly over selected cities as a demonstration of their long-range capabilities. Price suggested that on Navy Day, 13 October, six P2Vs be launched from *Midway* off Cape Hatteras and fly to six cities in the Midwest and on the West Coast. "Publicity in connection with these flights," Price wrote, "could emphasize the fact that this is done with planes and carriers *now in existence,* thus dispelling the idea now prevalent in some quarters that our real reason for building the 6A carrier is to invade the Air Force field of strategic bombing."[24]

The airplanes were not ready for such a sensational demonstration of the navy's long-range prowess until the following spring. On 7 March 1949 Hayward, now a captain, flew a P2V-3C, overloaded to a weight of 74,000 pounds and carrying a dummy MK 8 bomb, from *Coral Sea* across the country to Muroc, California (later Edwards Air Force Base), released the bomb, and then flew back to the Naval Air Test Center at Patuxent River, Maryland. From *Midway* off the coast near Norfolk on 7 April, a Neptune took off on a flight of 4,000 miles to the West Coast, then continued on to the Gulf of Alaska and back to Naval Air Station Moffett Field in Sunnyvale, California. In February 1950 another P2V-3C launched from *Franklin D. Roosevelt* off the coast of Florida covered more than 5,000 miles, its route taking it to San Francisco via the Panama Canal.[25]

Additional operational units and a rigorous training program marked the navy's heavy attack program over the next year. Composite Squadron 6 (VC-6) came together on 6 January 1950 under Cdr. Frederick L. Ashworth. A naval aviator who had specialized in ordnance, Ashworth was the crew member responsible for arming the "Fat Man" plutonium weapon dropped on Nagasaki. He had also participated in the Operation Crossroads atomic tests in 1946. Hayward's VC-5 successfully completed a number of missions to Hawaii and back before the end of the year in preparation for deployment to the Sixth Fleet in the Mediterranean. Neptunes from Ashworth's squadron gained experience on missions to Alaska and Hawaii, and participated in a mock nuclear attack as part of Operation Convex 1 in November 1950. A third heavy attack squadron, VC-7, was formed in November 1950. In the meantime the navy labored to perfect the North American AJ-1 Savage, which was better suited to the carrier delivery of nuclear weapons.[26]

All airplanes are bundles of compromises, but the Savage had more than its share—largely due to the limitations of engine technology at the time. The AJ-1 had its origins in BuAer analyses of long-range carrier aircraft shortly after the war. One of the studies called for an airplane with an MTOW of 45,000 pounds, a combat range of 1,000 miles, a bomb load of 8,000 pounds, and a top speed of 500 miles per hour. At the time, the only way to get the requisite range was to use piston engines, but they did not give the bomber the necessary speed. Conversely, turbojet engines provided the airplane with better high-speed performance, but being exceptionally "thirsty," they seriously compromised its combat range. The result was a hybrid: North American's winning design for the XAJ-1 in 1946 incorporated a pair of Pratt and Whitney R-2800 radial engines for cruising, augmented by an Allison J33 turbojet for swift, high-altitude run-ins to the target. The navy ordered fifty-five of the airplanes.[27]

Initially the AJ-1 was not configured to carry atomic weapons. Ashworth and Capt. Joseph N. Murphy of BuAer made an unofficial trip to the West Coast to take a close look at the mockup of the XAJ-1 at North American to see if changes could be made to accommodate the atomic bomb. Relying on his experience with the Nagasaki bomb, Ashworth determined that the airplane's design could be changed without too much trouble, and he recommended that the navy approve the modifications. After inexplicable delays Forrestal gave the go-ahead, and in June 1946 North American received a contract to make the necessary modifications to the layout and equipment of the XAJ-1 bomb bay for the MK III bomb. The navy's atomic weapons unit at Sandia National Laboratories, in Albuquerque, New Mexico, evaluated the installation.[28]

The XAJ-1 flew for the first time in July 1948 and went to Hayward's VC-5 for tests on 1 September 1949. The airplane met most of BuAer's criteria for a carrier bomber with an MTOW of 54,000 pounds, a maximum bomb capacity of 12,000 pounds, and a 1,000-mile range using wingtip tanks, but its top speed of 400 knots was well below original expectations. In April 1950 Hayward made the first carrier takeoff of the airplane, followed by landings in August. Prematurely rushed into service, the airplanes ran into problems. The first twelve examples suffered from inadequate cabin pressurization and structural deficiencies, and had to go back to North American for rectification of the problems. In August 1950 one of the airplanes crashed during testing by North American at Edwards Air Force Base. Three months later, at the end of October, a VC-5 AJ-1 went down after taking off from *Franklin D. Roosevelt,* and still another AJ-1 out of Patuxent River crashed two weeks later in the Chesapeake Bay. Engine and hydraulic problems proved to be the reasons for the rash of accidents, demanding immediate remediation to keep the airplanes flying, and the Savage never shook its temperamental reputation.[29]

Not only was it necessary to ensure that the AJ-1 could reliably deliver the atomic bomb, the navy also had to mold the airplanes, their weapons, the ships, and their crews into a fully integrated system. A team from Sandia worked with *Coral Sea* in Norfolk in late February and early March 1950 to determine what the ship and crew would need to handle both the 10,800-pound MK 4 implosion weapon and the MK 8 gun-type bomb. Additional tests on 16–18 March took place at sea. Navy special weapons units and their equipment flew from Kirtland Air Force Base to Norfolk in the navy's big Lockheed R60-1 Constitution transport. After arriving at dockside, they transferred a MK 4 and a MK 8, which had arrived by rail, to *Coral Sea.*[30]

At sea the teams and the ship's crew experimented with loading a MK 4 bomb on an AJ-1 using the airplane's internal hoist, while the carrier went through various maneuvers and generated winds over the deck approaching 50 knots. Even though nearly everything worked as expected, the exercise showed how cumbersome it was to store and secure the separate components of the weapons, assemble them in spaces designated for that purpose, and load the completed bombs into the airplane. Beginning in the summer of 1950 and continuing through the end of the year, thirty-eight MK III and MK 4 nonnuclear bomb assemblies were shipped to Norfolk for use in training the attack squadrons' air and ground crews in the storage and assembly of the weapons. Some of the assemblies and twenty-four-man teams went aboard *Midway*-class carriers bound for the Mediterranean. Should there be a crisis, the navy's plan was to have the bombs ready at sea to receive nuclear cores delivered by air across the Atlantic and then by AJ-1 to the carriers in theater. VC-5 completed its training and successfully passed its carrier qualifications at the end of August.[31]

The squadrons deployed overseas for the first time in February 1951. Making up VAH-1, VC-5's Neptunes and Savages flew from Norfolk to Port Lyautey (now Kenitra) in French Morocco, previously established as the advanced base and support facility for the unit in North Africa. The P2V-3Cs stayed at the Port Lyautey airfield, but the AJ-1s flew out to the *Midway*-class CVBs as they operated in the Mediterranean. The deployment did nothing to enhance the AJ-1's reputation, as the craft suffered a number of accidents and were temporarily grounded for safety modifications. Starting in 1952 the P2V-3Cs were withdrawn from frontline duty as more AJ-1s reached operational status. The training and deployment schedule called for a minimum of two twelve-plane units to be "war ready," a difficult proposition given the need for intensive technical instruction of flight crews and other personnel in handling nuclear weapons aboard carriers and the inherent problems of operating the big, multi-engine aircraft.[32]

Deployments of the heavy attack units to the Pacific took some time because of the limited number of aircraft and trained crews. In February 1952, in response to a request from the commander-in-chief of the Pacific Fleet, CNO Adm. William M. Fechteler could promise only to dispatch four AJ-1s from VC-6 to San Diego by the middle of July, followed by the full deployment of the squadron to Japan with nine AJ-1s and two P2Vs in January 1953. After VC-6 left for the Pacific, a new squadron, VC-9, was to replace it in the Atlantic. Fechteler expected that the numbers of aircraft and crews would be increased over the next two years, allowing more flexibility in the assignment of the heavy attack units, but for the time being the navy was stretched thin.[33]

Not much could be done to improve the navy's strategic nuclear capability in the early 1950s. Advocates of heavy attack pinned their hopes on the North American XA2J-1, which was scheduled to fly in July 1951. Powered by two Allison turboprops, the airplane had an MTOW of 58,000 pounds and could lift a payload in excess of 10,000 pounds. With an 8,000-pound payload, the A2J had a range of more than 1,000 nautical miles and a cruising speed of 410 knots. The navy expected that it could operate from both the 27A *Essex*-class and the *Midway*-class vessels, but it could not be handled on the ships' elevators with a full bomb and fuel load. The program ran into delays, and the first airplane did not take off until January 1952. From Douglas, the navy ordered two XA2D-1s, followed by a preproduction order for ten more airplanes in January 1950. The first XA2D-1 made its initial flight in March 1950, only to be lost in a crash in December. There was a delay of more than a year before the second airplane flew in April 1952, and the program bogged down amid gearbox and control system problems in its turboprop engines. Lighter than the XA2J-1, the Douglas had an MTOW of 23,000 pounds and could deliver a 4,000-pound payload over a distance of 660 nautical miles. The XA2D-1 was the first of the light attack aircraft the navy thought would be compatible with the more compact, high-yield nuclear weapons then under development.[34]

In 1950, though, the Douglas A3D Skywarrior seemed to offer everything the navy wanted in the long-range strike role. It was free of the limitations of the two North American models and compared well with the medium jet bombers then coming into the air force inventory. With two J40 turbojets (later Pratt and Whitney J57s), a 6-ton bomb capacity, and a range of 1,000 miles, the 68,000-pound airplane cruised at more than 500 knots at altitudes above 40,000 feet. The big bomber flew for the first time in October 1952 and reached Heavy-Attack Squadron (VAH) 1 in late March 1956. It, too, had its share of "teething" problems before being accepted as one of the most reliable and versatile aircraft in the fleet.[35]

After suffering so much at the hands of the civilian and military leadership in 1949 and 1950, the navy turned the corner on funding and carriers in 1951. A major break came with the firing of Louis Johnson as secretary of defense in September 1950 and his replacement by the highly regarded George

C. Marshall. Then Denfeld's successor as CNO, Forrest Sherman, showed how adept he could be at working within the system and convincing his fellow members of the JCS that the navy was willing to cooperate and not compete with the air force in the strategic mission. When Sherman pointed to the need for more forces afloat in the western Pacific, he got the JCS to agree to an additional carrier for fiscal year 1951. The Korean War demonstrated the value of the carrier in conflicts other than all-out nuclear war and loosened the purse strings for the navy and the other services. With carriers playing a major role in supporting the air campaign in Korea, the navy felt confident that it had finally made its case for the flexibility of the carrier and its aircraft complement in taking the war to an enemy at the outset of a conflict and remaining in the theater indefinitely.[36]

Equally important, the Truman administration reversed course on the big carrier, finally granting the navy its cherished big-deck ship. The ship remained uppermost in the minds of many in the navy after the CVA 58 cancellation. In the same secret memo of April 1949 recommending that the navy downplay the strategic role of its carriers, Rear Admiral Cassady had argued that existing ships, no matter how much they were improved, could not meet the need for sustained, all-weather conventional operations in a hostile environment, especially if they had to fly a mix of new jet interceptors, airborne early warning aircraft, and ASW aircraft. Only the big flush-deck ship could satisfy the multi-mission requirement. A year later, in May 1950, Cassady expanded on these views, suggesting that the navy "should, when the time is ready, agitate for a flush deck carrier," something that he considered vital to realize the full potential of the new airplanes coming into service.[37]

Cassady had to wait until October to see a new carrier added to the fiscal year (FY) 1952 budget. Another three years passed before the Bureau of Ships completed plans for CVA 59, which carried over some of the general concepts of the *United States.* At 60,000 tons it was smaller than the previous ship, but it incorporated the new angled deck, an island superstructure, steam rather than hydraulic catapults, and other improvements. Most important, the ship would be fully capable of operating the entire range of existing and planned fleet aircraft.[38]

Despite the reversal of the navy's carrier fortunes by 1951, the service was not much better off than it had been before the *United States* cancellation. The navy's aviation budget was significantly larger, due mostly to the Korean War buildup, but the increase did not automatically mean more money for the kinds of airplanes and ships the navy needed to stay in the strategic game with the air force. Moreover, *Forrestal* and its sibling *Saratoga* (CVA 60) were built using money diverted from other shipbuilding programs.[39]

Questions about the carrier's role in a major war with the Soviet Union remained unanswered. Even though the carrier had many proven capabilities, the ship remained singularly unsuited to launch a retaliatory blow in the event of general nuclear war—the so-called second strike, considered vital to a credible nuclear deterrent. Joint exercises with the British in northern Europe in 1952 and 1953 demonstrated that carriers might be lost in attacks by land-based aircraft and that in bad weather carrier air units could have their effectiveness cut by up to 80 percent. Readiness issues also bothered navy planners. Carrier deployment cycles were notoriously slow; at any given time, one-third of the nation's carrier force was likely to be going through overhaul and training, and the odds were that most of the carriers that were ready for action would be in port or in transit when a surprise nuclear attack began. In contrast, the air force's Strategic Air Command provided the only capability for a quick and devastating response.[40]

Another problem was the reliance on forward basing. Considered essential for supporting the heavy attack squadrons, such advanced bases as Port Lyautey were expensive and vulnerable, tying down the carriers and their air units, and largely negating the independence and mobility the navy touted as advantages the carrier held over the air force and its land-based bombers. Finally, the navy rightly stressed the carrier as a multi-use weapon, suitable for fighting limited conventional conflicts as well as more general wars, while downplaying the carrier's nuclear retaliatory capabilities. Wounded in the interservice battles of the late 1940s, the navy had resigned itself to playing a narrowly defined strategic role secondary to that of the air force.[41] When an alternative came along for a promising new concept in an independent, mobile, sea-based strategic force, it found a receptive audience within BuAer and the office of the CNO.

# Four

# Seaplane Reborn

By the end of World War II, the four-engine landplane appeared to have pushed the seaplane into an obscure corner of aviation's closet. With sleek aerodynamic shapes, retractable landing gear, and more reliable power plants, landplanes were without peer in range, speed, and payload. Most aeronautical engineers agreed the flying boat suffered because of its inherent mass in comparison to its land-based cousins. The flying boat had a large frontal area, sharp steps (transverse breaks between the forebody and the afterbody of the hull), and chines (angled intersections of the hull bottom and hull sides), as well as a deep, bulky hull, essential for the engines, propellers, and control surfaces to stay clear of the water and spray. Because of this, its fuselage had a larger surface area than that of a landplane, which gave it relatively lower lift-drag ratios and cruising speeds than a landplane. To be sure, the flying boat had the advantage of virtually unlimited-length "runways" around the globe, but as engineers belatedly discovered, concrete was cheap, and more airports and bases were built with runways to accommodate the weight and long take-off runs of the largest landplanes.[1]

Aerodynamic and hydrodynamic research also seemed to conspire against the seaplane. A critical limiting factor in seaplane design was hull loading. Roughly analogous to wing loading (a variable of the airplane's total weight and its wing area expressed in pounds per square foot), hull loading is usually represented as a coefficient incorporating the width of the hull, its weight, and the density of water. Exceeding the hull loading at low speeds caused problems ranging from excessive spray and cockpit visibility restrictions to flooding of the engines and loss of directional control. At higher speeds—notably the critical "hump" where the aircraft transitioned to planing—resistance factors changed dramatically, and other stability and control problems occurred.[2]

Because the width or beam of the hull was a primary variable, decades of experience with seaplane design had resulted in relatively low length-to-beam (l/b) ratios, usually on the order of 5:1 or 6:1. Attempts by designers to improve hull loading by increasing the l/b ratio (also known as the fineness or aspect ratio) caused the hydrodynamics to deteriorate even more, a problem that could not be alleviated without decreasing the weight of the airplane and negating any potential hull loading gains. Especially worrisome was the problem of "porpoising," an oscillation in pitch that occurred above the hump speed and that could cause loss of control. Many knowledgeable engineers concluded by the mid-1930s that seaplane design had reached an unresolvable "technical impasse."[3]

Hints that the technological deadlock might be broken came from across the Atlantic. In 1935 at the Royal Aircraft Establishment (RAE) in Farnborough, Lawrence P. Coombes, W. G. A. Perring, and L. Johnston used dynamically similar models to study the aerodynamics and hydrodynamics of seaplanes. These free-flying scale models allowed engineers to vary fuselage and wing configurations and to record hydrodynamic and aerodynamic data impossible to obtain using wind tunnels and towing tanks separately. The British researchers developed new equations that included hull and beam dimensions along with hull loads and hydrodynamic resistance in predicting high-speed, waterborne performance.[4]

From Germany came promising theoretical information and test data that also appeared to give new life to the flying boat. As early as 1935, Walter Sottorf at the Deutsche Versuchsanstalt für Flugwesen Luftfahrt (DVL) outside Berlin found that a seaplane hull with a high l/b ratio had aerodynamic properties comparable to those of a landplane while demonstrating more favorable hull loading than previously supposed. Publication of an abridged version of Sottorf's work by the National Advisory Committee for Aeronautics (NACA) in 1938 stimulated renewed interest in the flying boat in the United States.[5]

Among those who thought that the work at RAE and DVL pointed the way to a potential breakthrough in seaplane technology was Ernest G. Stout of Convair. A Kansas native born in 1913, Stout received his bachelor's and master's degrees in aeronautical engineering from New York University. His

1939 master's thesis was on calculating seaplane performance. After a year at the Glenn L. Martin Company, Stout joined Convair in November 1936, where he specialized in aerodynamics and flight testing. Through him, Convair obtained the detailed reports of Sottorf's experiments from DVL and, beginning in July 1938, initiated a series of tests using dynamically similar models towed next to a speedboat. Sometimes referred to as the "seaplane admiral," Stout was an enthusiastic convert and eloquent spokesman for water-based aircraft.[6]

During World War II the immediate and anticipated requirements for long-range military aircraft stimulated comparisons of the flying boat and the landplane. In April 1943 BuAer's Preliminary Airplane Design Section completed a study of the performance of seaplanes and long-range, land-based aircraft as bombers. Using data extrapolated from existing aircraft and engines, BuAer found that flying boats were not as "clean" aerodynamically as landplanes with similar power and wing loadings. The flying boats paid a penalty in rate of climb and ceiling but compared well in range. At MTOWs from 150,000 to 250,000 pounds, and l/b ratios of 9:1, the difference between the flying boat and the landplane narrowed. In part, the flying boat was at a disadvantage due to overly conservative wing loadings and a tendency to pack the spacious hull with more equipment. BuAer recommended that the navy focus on four- and six-engine flying boats up to 250,000 pounds as future long-range bombers and that additional studies investigate the potential of even larger, eight-engine seaplanes with MTOWs of 300,000 pounds.[7]

Some also saw the potential of flying boats in transoceanic commercial air travel. During the 1930s Sikorsky, Martin, and Boeing pioneered long-range, four-engine seaplanes, and Pan American established regular transpacific and transatlantic flying boat passenger service before the decade was out, only to have the war intervene. Aviation pioneer Glenn L. Martin wrote in September 1944 that when the war ended, "friendly battle lines of international competition will be drawn up quickly along the world air trade routes." Landplanes had attributes "so obvious that there is no necessity to detail them"; so did the large flying boat, not the least of which were its range and payload capacity, and its ability to take off and land nearly anywhere.[8]

In a more hopeful atmosphere for the military and commercial possibilities of large seaplanes, Convair engineers collaborated with their NACA counterparts at the Langley lab in Hampton, Virginia, and at Stevens Institute of Technology in Hoboken, New Jersey, to gather data on the aerodynamics and hydrodynamics of flying boats. Using Langley's towing tank, experimenters refined their techniques and designed more sophisticated apparatus to allow greater freedom of movement of test models, some of which provided their own power through electric motors and adjustable-pitch propellers. At the Stevens towing tank a specially designed carriage allowed rapid calculation of more general aerodynamic and hydrodynamic data.[9]

In June 1943 Convair engineers began experiments using free-flight, radio-controlled, dynamically similar models on an extension of San Diego Bay near the Convair factory. Outdoors, a wide variety of operating conditions could be found, including wind speeds from a dead calm up to scale velocities of 30–40 knots. Waves and swells could be generated to add to the realism of the tests. The experiments involved one-eighth-scale flying models of the four-engine, 40,000-pound XPB2Y-4 Coronado and the twin-engine, 48,000-pound Model 31, later designated the XP4Y-1 Corregidor, which featured the highly efficient Davis wing.[10]

By August 1943, Stout and Convair's Hydrodynamic Research Laboratory had prepared a study of flying boat designs that showed them to be generally competitive with landplanes. With a hypothetical 180,000-pound airplane as a starting point, the Convair engineers looked at the performance of ten different combinations of hull forms, determining which hydrodynamic and aerodynamic characteristics provided the optimum foundations for a "sound development program." Among the designs Convair analyzed were single and double (catamaran-type) hulls, hydrofoils (for some time regarded by the navy as a means of improving the waterborne stability and reducing the hydrodynamic drag of high-performance seaplanes), and Ventnor arrangements, which channeled water at high speed through a tunnel on the bottom of the hull. The outstanding discovery, though, was verification that hulls with a high l/b ratio, on the order of 10.5:1, provided good stability and high load coefficients.[11]

The report concluded that much could be done to improve flying boat performance and that only design practices rooted in the latest theories and backed by solid research would realize those gains. It recommended a "thorough research program" to investigate hydrofoils, high l/b ratio hulls, and the use of turbojet engines, at least during takeoff. By mid-1944 Convair had invested nearly $250,000 of its own funds in advanced seaplane research. For the short term, the Convair tests pointed the way to modifications of the XP4Y-1 that allowed an increase of nearly 60 percent in its MTOW. For the long term, the experiments reinforced the company's faith in dynamic modeling and established Convair as the leader in the field, well positioned to take advantage of renewed navy interest in high-performance flying boats.[12]

Following discussions with engineers from BuAer and NACA, Convair submitted a proposal in July 1944 to expand its investigations into high l/b ratio flying boat hulls and other advanced seaplane designs. The company suggested breaking down the project into stages, beginning with a reexamination of DVL studies of hulls with l/b ratios of 10.5:1 and continuing through free-flight tests of dynamically similar models with hull l/b ratios ranging from 6:1 to 10:1. For the free-flight tests Convair employed its one-eighth-scale model of the PB2Y-4, modified so that it could be fitted with interchangeable hulls of varying dimensions and configurations. Towing tank tests at NACA and Stevens Institute complemented the dynamically similar experiments. Convair also included studies of hydrofoils in the proposal, although there was no mention of turbojet engines. The navy contract, signed on 1 September 1944, included all elements of the Convair proposal with the exception of the hydrofoil investigations.[13]

Convair completed the analytical portion of the program by April 1945, reporting favorably on the hydrodynamic characteristics of high l/b ratio hulls and indicating that a solution to the performance shortcomings of seaplanes might be in the offing. The dynamically similar model tests did not go as smoothly, due to delays in completing the free-flight model and a strike that held up work on the 10:1 l/b hull. To make matters worse, blustery winds and high waves in the bay pushed the flight schedule back into the spring of 1946.[14]

To back up its commitment to advanced seaplane designs, Convair compared the performance of a flying boat to a similarly sized landplane. For the study, completed in August 1945, the company chose its Model 37, a transport version of the B-36 strategic bomber with an MTOW of 320,000 pounds. The flying boat used the same engines, wing, and tail assembly as the transport, although the wing and horizontal stabilizer were raised to clear the water and tractor rather than pusher propellers were used. Hampered by higher structural weight than the landplane, the flying boat still compared well, having slightly more range and payload than the landplane and falling only marginally short in top and cruising speeds.[15]

That August, too, Stout traveled to Germany as part of a navy mission to acquire aerodynamic and other technical data from captured German documents. Returning with a trove of information on flying boats, Stout proposed a supplemental test program designed to wring as much information as possible from the latest German developments. He was particularly interested in obtaining and translating design data on the Blohm and Voss BV-222 "Wiking" (Viking), a six-engine flying boat with an MTOW of 108,000 pounds, and the even larger, six-engine, 200,000-pound BV-238. Of most significance to Stout and Convair was that the BV-222 had an unusually slender hull, with an l/b ratio of 9:1. Moreover, the Germans had employed a large, dynamically similar model to evaluate the aerodynamic and hydrodynamic properties of the BV-238. Stout wanted to build a one-eighth-scale, dynamically similar model of the BV-222 for experiments in the Langley towing tank, and possibly for powered free-flight tests in San Diego. Finally, he sought to investigate the application of turbojet power and radical hull forms for high-Mach-number aircraft using both towing tank and free-flight tests. In June 1946 the navy awarded Convair a $220,000 fixed-price contract for the additional research.[16]

In BuAer, Convair found a strong supporter of its advanced seaplane research in Capt. Walter S. Diehl. A graduate of the University of Tennessee, Diehl was commissioned in the navy in 1917, completed MIT's aeronautical engineering program a year later, and worked in the Aircraft Division of the Bureau of Construction and Repair from 1918 to 1921. As an engineer in BuAer after 1921, he was actively engaged in aerodynamic and hydrodynamic research with NACA, including studies of skin friction, pressure coefficients on airfoils, and seaplane characteristics and performance. Diehl was one of the navy's brightest and most experienced technical officers, and he took a personal interest in Stout's and Convair's seaplane research. Virtually all the correspondence pertaining to the company's 1944 contract and subsequent agreements passed over Diehl's desk, often eliciting incisive handwritten comments on route slips.[17]

Further indicators of the navy's commitment to advanced seaplane research were the acquisition of one of the BV-222 flying boats for evaluation at Naval Air Station Patuxent River and the decision to bring Walter Sottorf to the United States under Operation Paperclip, the American effort to round up German scientists and engineers. The BV-222 was one of two captured by the Americans at the end of the war and flown to the United States. Sottorf, meanwhile, worked at the David Taylor Model Basin outside Washington, where he continued his prewar studies of high l/b ratio hulls and other aspects of advanced flying boat design.[18]

The contract took Convair's research in several different directions. The BV-222 studies, which included a towing tank model and a flying scale model, confirmed the advantages of high l/b ratio hulls and led directly to the hull design of the Model 117, powered by four turboprop engines. In June 1946 Convair received a contract to build two of the aircraft, designated XP5Y-1, heavily armed for long-range antishipping and ASW missions. With an MTOW of 123,500 pounds, a hull loading far in excess of what had been thought possible before the war, and an l/b ratio of 10:1, the airplane incorporated much of what Convair had learned about flying boat design over the last decade. Convair started in the spring of 1948 with a one-tenth-scale model of the airplane, carrying out intensive hydrodynamic tests that showed it to be superior to earlier designs in directional stability and takeoff performance. The company proclaimed in December 1948 that the XP5Y-1 had "more than doubled the hydrodynamic efficiency of any previous seaplane design and again placed water-based designs on an equitable basis with contemporary land-based aircraft." Stout saw the XP5Y-1 as a harbinger of a brave new world for water-based aircraft.[19]

After delays, Convair rolled out the airplane in December 1948, though it still lacked engines because the complex Allison T40 turboprops were not yet ready. The airplane flew for the first time on 18 April 1950. Thereafter, persistent problems with the geared engines buried in the wing limited the number of hours the aircraft could fly. Yet for all the XP5Y-1's troubles, its hydrodynamic characteristics were excellent; even overloaded to 150,000 pounds, the airplane demonstrated admirable water-handling properties. It also did well in the air, exhibiting speeds unheard of in the world of flying boats. Stout proclaimed in 1951 that the XP5Y-1 had performance comparable to some of the best piston-engine fighters of World War II.[20]

Promising studies of high-performance, turbojet-powered, waterborne aircraft capable of transonic and supersonic speeds also came from Convair's June 1946 development contract. Along with eliminating propellers, turbojet power promised lower hull height, less frontal area, reduced aerodynamic drag, and greater stability on takeoff and landing. At the same time, engineers had to find solutions to spray problems and ensure that the airplane incorporated all of the aerodynamic features needed for flight at high Mach numbers. Challenges loomed, but the vision was a beguiling one: if the company succeeded with a rational, scientifically based research program, it could offer a family of aircraft combining the speed of the best land-based fighter and attack airplanes with the flexibility of sea basing. Stout led a team at Convair that concentrated first on the ideal aerodynamic configuration and then, using dynamically similar models, worked backward toward a fuselage/hull shape

that gave hydrodynamic qualities equal to those of the XP5Y-1 and other flying boats.

Among the many problems they encountered in the tests was ensuring
similarity of the model tests with the expected results at full scale. As aerody-
namicists, Stout and his colleagues had to grapple first with the Reynolds
number. In experiments with water moving around objects in pipes, Osborne
Reynolds, a nineteenth-century, Irish-born mechanical engineer, had determined that the flow over a scale model and a full-size object was identical
provided the researcher adhered to a mathematically derived ratio of density,
velocity, viscosity, and diameter of the object. That ratio—the Reynolds
number—provided a correlation between the results of wind tunnel testing
with models and the performance of full-scale aircraft; the higher the
Reynolds number, the more accurate wind-tunnel figures were in predicting
the real performance of an airplane or airship.[21]

Turning their attention to hydrodynamics, the Convair team encountered
the Froude number. Named for British engineer William Froude, who in 1867
had built the first modern towing tank, the number was useful for establishing the similitude of water resistance between models and full-scale ship (or
flying boat) hulls. Froude found that dividing the full-scale speed by the square
root of the scale of the model yielded a number (the Froude number) equal
to the resistance expected in a full-scale ship (or flying boat) if its dimensions
were divided by the scale of the model cubed. Both the Reynolds and Froude
numbers are dimensionally constrained, only coinciding at full scale, so the
size of the test models was crucial to the accuracy of the results, especially as
flying boat speeds increased into the transonic range. Dynamic modeling
eased the Convair engineers' task of dimensional analysis by allowing them to
integrate multiple variables and obtain results that promised greater accuracy
than more conventional experimental methods.[22]

Project Skate, Convair's high-Mach-number seaplane program, began
in June 1946, using the company's elegant XB-46 four-jet bomber to provide baseline aerodynamic data. Armed with that information and confident
that a "new viewpoint" would break through conventional thinking about
seaplane performance, Convair engineers completed what they referred to as
a "blended" wing-hull design, incorporating a moderately high l/b ratio of
8.76:1 and a low-aspect-ratio swept wing smoothly integrated into the fuselage by large fillets. In some ways it resembled experimental lifting-body
shapes developed in the 1960s and 1970s for space reentry vehicles. Due to
the low center of gravity of the design, wingtip floats were unnecessary. Spray

dams to minimize water ingestion into the engines could be retracted into the hull for increased aerodynamic efficiency. A retractable step on the bottom of the hull improved waterborne stability and takeoff characteristics and reduced drag at transonic and supersonic speeds. Not only did Convair engineers believe the airplane would display superb rough-water capabilities, they also thought it would be able to operate from snow and ice with a minimum of modifications.[23]

Preliminary tests of one-twentieth-scale and one-tenth-scale dynamically similar models of the airplane confirmed the soundness of the concept and encouraged BuAer about high-performance seaplanes. The bureau's representative in San Diego reported on 14 May 1947 that the experiments had yielded "data which is worthy of serious consideration. . . . It appears entirely feasible that a high speed flying boat can be designed and constructed which would be comparable in performance to land based aircraft and still retain all the tactical advantages of a flying boat." At a conference three weeks later, BuAer officers set out the characteristics for a seaplane incorporating the features of the Skate and forwarded them to Convair to help the company refine its test program. In general, BuAer wanted a single-seat, turbojet-powered fighter aircraft with a maximum speed at sea level of 550 knots, a ceiling of 40,000 feet, a 200-mile combat range, four 20-millimeter (mm) guns, and a full suite of the latest electronic equipment.[24]

The concept of a jet-powered seaplane interceptor was not unique to BuAer or Convair. Starting in 1943, Arthur Gouge and Henry Knowler of the Saunders-Roe company, one of Britain's leaders in flying boats, began design work on a high-performance, twin-jet seaplane. The company won a contract to build three of the aircraft, the first of which, designated SR.A/1, flew in 1947. Exhibiting a good mix of hydrodynamics and aerodynamics, the 16,000-pound airplane met expectations in test flights over the next two years. The third example achieved a speed of more than 500 miles per hour in 1949 before being lost in a landing accident; the destruction of the second prototype in a crash that same year led the British to discontinue the program.[25]

In May 1948 Convair received a $202,000 navy contract that included translation of additional captured German seaplane data, tests of large flying boat designs with extreme l/b ratios up to 16:1, and more detailed studies of jet-powered seaplanes. Over three years, Convair built and tested six Skate models, varying from one-twentieth to one-eighth scale; all were unpowered, used for high-speed, open-water towing tests and catapult launches and for wind tunnel experiments. BuAer also issued outline specifications for subsonic and supersonic water-based attack planes, with a range of 1,700 nautical miles, as alternatives to carrier aircraft in the delivery of atomic bombs. Following the bureau's specifications, Convair incorporated into its program preliminary studies of a 152,000-pound, supersonic, water-based strike aircraft, referred to as the Betta. Convair proposed having the three-engine bomber sortie from an advanced base, land offshore to refuel, and fly on to its target. In addition to the Skate and Betta series, Convair undertook experiments with small models of the Cudda, a swept-wing, twin-jet-powered transonic bomber. About halfway through the seaplane project in October 1949, Convair reported to the navy that it was satisfied with the results of its high l/b ratio studies and proposed altering the contract to permit it to concentrate exclusively on the high-performance designs.[26]

Meanwhile, the Skate program had moved into its next phase, involving free-flight tests of radio-controlled models. Skate Number 7 was a one-thirteenth-scale model equipped with two small pulsejets. A pair of pulsejets also powered a one-fifteenth-scale model of Skate 9; four were podded to simulate the thrust of two Westinghouse J40 turbojets in a larger, one-tenth-scale version of Skate 7. Early tests were encouraging, despite problems keeping the miniature engines up to operating temperature and finding ways to shut them off at the end of their test runs.[27]

Believing that the point of diminishing returns had been reached in Convair's Skate research, BuAer recommended to the CNO's office in April 1948 that it was time to move forward with a real airplane or terminate the program. OP-55 (Air Warfare Office) responded that a high-performance seaplane fighter similar to the Skate would be useful in providing expanded all-weather defense of advanced bases, which were always considered vulnerable to air attack, and the CNO agreed to set aside funds from the FY 1949 budget to begin the program. In a series of conferences in the summer of 1948, BuAer thrashed out the requirement for a sea-based fighter; the resulting outline specifications called for a two-seat aircraft with an MTOW of 30,000 pounds that was equal in performance to contemporary carrier aircraft.[28]

Convair and the navy realized that the unconventional nature of the Skate-type night fighter meant familiar methods of basing and servicing seaplanes would have to be reevaluated. In response to a BuAer request, Convair submitted a summary of its Skate program in December 1948, covering the airplane's hydrodynamics and aerodynamics, and providing a detailed analysis of how the aircraft could be deployed and supported. For the airplane to accomplish its mission, it had to operate away from its main base for extended periods, relying on expeditionary forces at a beachhead, surface craft, submarines, and even other aircraft for logistical support. It was apparent, too, that all docking maneuvers would have to be automatic, because the airplane was limited to a two-man crew.

Temporary facilities provided support for a Skate squadron in forward combat areas, usually on or near a beach in sheltered waters. From floats connected by walkways, crews could rearm and refuel the aircraft, as well as perform minor electronics and instrument repairs. Alternatively, simple rigid floats could be used as cradles attached to both sides of the airplanes with walkways extending to the shoreline, or floating causeways could be used to moor several airplanes at a time. In both instances, heavier equipment and hoists allowed more ambitious repair and maintenance procedures.

Ships and aircraft supported Skate units at sea. Here the major advantage was flexibility, because virtually any type of ship with cranes of sufficient capacity and open deck space could be used, rendezvousing with the Skate unit at a predetermined remote location near the combat area or on the ferry route from permanent bases in the United States. "Most intriguing," according to the Convair study, was the use of submarines in support of the Skate. Converted to provide fuel, armament, and other equipment, the submarine could use its inherent stealth capabilities to maintain the aircraft deep in hostile territory, maximizing its already formidable tactical advantages. Convair built a one-tenth-scale model of a modernized World War II fleet submarine for compatibility tests with the Skate 7 dynamically similar model. The tests showed that special handling equipment allowed the airplane to "dock" with the partially submerged submarine, which then lifted the airplane clear of the water for routine servicing. To release the Skate, the submarine submerged and the airplane taxied clear.

Finally, Convair saw the advantages of using the XP5Y-1 or larger flying boats for replenishing Skates in remote areas. In this case, the speed of the big flying boats meant even more flexibility and a much wider area of combat operations than would be possible with surface ships or submarines. The only specialized equipment carried by the tanker aircraft was a lightweight boom extending to the Skate, allowing personnel access and supporting the refueling lines. Convair was confident that additional studies would confirm the virtually unlimited range of Skate operations and the airplane's potential capabilities.[29]

In response to BuAer's confidential circular letter of 1 October 1948, only two companies—Convair and Curtiss-Wright—submitted proposals for the high-performance seaplane fighter. Convair's, which reached BuAer on 14

January 1949, was for its night fighter, a 42,000-pound, two-seat airplane featuring a blended wing-hull and low-aspect-ratio 40-degree swept wing much like that demonstrated in the Skate 6 and 7 models. The aircraft had a powerful search radar mounted in the nose and four 20-mm guns in the wings. To minimize frontal area and drag, Convair placed the pilot under a conventional fighter-type canopy slightly offset to the left, with the radar operator sitting down and to his right in the fuselage. The design included leading-edge slats in the wing, flaps, and an all-movable horizontal stabilizer mounted high in the tail. Two 7,920-pound-thrust Westinghouse XJ40-WE-10 turbojets with afterburners gave a top speed of 550 knots (Mach .95) at an altitude of 35,000 feet. The service ceiling was 52,500 feet, and the combat range was 400 nautical miles.

Convair anticipated the airplane would be suited to operations in 5-foot waves in mostly sheltered waters. To minimize spray and water ingestion into the engines the design featured retractable spray dams in front of the wing's leading edge and alternate air intake doors on each side of the hull. A split hydroflap in the tail that doubled as a dive brake in the air assisted water handling, and the hull featured a step that retracted as the air intake doors closed. One static test article and two flight test airplanes would be completed within thirty-six months of the start of the program.[30]

In its proposal Convair went beyond the Skate design to incorporate elements of its 1948 servicing and basing study, suggesting how the airplane might be employed and supported in forward areas. A sequence of photographs in a lavishly illustrated booklet showed the Skate 7 dynamic model rendezvousing with the model submarine, which then surfaced with the Skate resting on deck. Drawings illustrated how the airplane could be serviced from a tender or submarine in a remote Arctic location. Conveniently located hatches on top of the Skate fuselage allowed the repair and replacement of major mechanical components, including the engines.[31]

A company whose greatness lay in the past, Curtiss-Wright submitted a design that was almost pathetic in comparison. Powered by a single Westinghouse XJ40-10, the two-seat airplane had an MTOW of 29,000 pounds and a hull with a low l/b ratio, and featured high swept wings and horizontal tail surfaces. It was inferior to Convair's Skate in nearly every regard. For BuAer's evaluation officers, the aircraft was notable for its high wing loading, miserable takeoff time, and poor altitude performance. In contrast, the only glaring fault of the Skate design was the cockpit layout, with the radar operator awkwardly located in the hull and totally lacking forward visibility. Evaluation of the proposals by BuAer's Fighter Design and Aero and Hydro branches determined that Convair was "obviously the winner of this competition."[32]

Though deficient in comparison to Convair's Skate, the Curtiss design included a feature that the navy and NACA for some time had considered attractive for high-speed seaplanes—a centrally located, retractable hydro-ski. Reports that Alaska bush pilots had sometimes used ski-equipped aircraft to land on and take off from lakes intrigued the All-American Engineering Company in Wilmington, Delaware, which received a navy contract to study the concept using skis on a variety of light aircraft. The navy also experimented at Patuxent River with a Grumman twin-engine JRF-5 equipped with hydro-skis designed by the Edo Corporation. At the time it won the Skate contract, Convair had been investigating the hydro-ski on its Cudda dynamic and wind tunnel models.[33]

BuAer met with Convair representatives in April to plan a development program for the airplane. Because FY 1949 funding limitations precluded committing the full $1.2 million Convair wanted for a comprehensive preliminary design program, BuAer decided on, and Convair agreed to, a $250,000 start-up contract, with the expectation that more money would permit a "reasonably timed development" in fiscal years 1950 through 1953. Officers close to the program worried that stretching the project out over five years would render the Skate inferior to carrier aircraft expected to join the fleet after 1953. There was little choice; the alternative was no airplane at all. On 19 May 1949 Convair signed a letter of intent to proceed with a cost-plus-fixed-fee contract for the first phase of the Skate program. Initially, Convair would evaluate the applicability of hydro-skis to the fighter before moving on to high-speed and low-speed wind tunnel experiments and testing of a dynamically similar model close to the final Skate configuration.[34]

Convair's first Skate progress report in October 1949 was an exercise in optimism; if anything, the airplane would be even better than what the company had proposed in winning the development contract, easily matching or exceeding the performance of its land-based or carrier counterparts. The most obvious change was in the cockpit arrangement, with the radar operator moved out of the fuselage to sit beside and slightly behind the pilot under a larger canopy. MTOW was now up to 44,500 pounds, necessitating widening the hull to increase its volume and maintain the same hydrodynamic and buoyancy characteristics of the original design. Top speed and range remained the same. Convair emphasized the ease of removing the engines, weapons, electronic gear, and other components while the airplane was on the water and stressed the need for integrating the airplane into a comprehensive servicing and handling system.[35]

Theoretically offering greatly improved rough-water performance, the hydro-ski with shock-absorbing struts and a mechanism allowing it to be retracted into the hull also enhanced high-speed aerodynamics. Additionally, the hydro-ski allowed engineers to optimize the attitude of the airplane for takeoff and landing at greater weights than were possible with a conventional, planing-type hull, and it had the potential for operations from snow-covered fields. For a time, the hydrofoil also looked promising to the navy, which along with NACA's Langley lab had examined its potential application to aircraft. Similar to a wing, the hydrofoil generated lift as it passed through the water, reducing hydrodynamic drag and enhancing stability at high speeds. But additional research revealed higher drag and other problems that led the navy to deemphasize hydrofoil work after World War II.[36]

Coming as it did when the Skate project seemed near the design and development phase, the hydro-ski sent Convair's advanced seaplane work in two seemingly contradictory directions. On one hand, tests of Skates 6 and 7 with NACA-type hydro-skis demonstrated that takeoff times and distances, which should have been improved over the conventional Skate, were about the same, while rough-water takeoffs and landings were better. As mandated by BuAer, Convair studied single and dual hydro-ski installations on the Skate, concluding that the weight and complexity of the hydro-ski installation negated any performance gains. BuAer reluctantly acceded to the company's recommendation to continue the Skate program without hydro-skis.[37]

On the other hand, Convair aggressively pursued the hydro-ski on models of the Betta and Cudda. A BuAer officer mused in September 1949 that it would be interesting to see how the company justified rejecting the hydro-ski on one airplane while embracing it on another. Part of the answer lay in Convair's desire to offer a complete range of aircraft, each suited to specific missions and not all benefiting from the supposed advantages of the hydro-ski. Moreover, because the Skate was for all intents and purposes a fixed design by the summer of 1949, modifying it to take best advantage of the hydro-ski would have involved substantial structural changes and unacceptable delays in the program. In contrast, the Betta and Cudda were still in the early stages, and their designs could be changed to optimize the hydro-ski installation. The Skate program, in the meantime, continued into early 1950 minus the hydro-ski. Tests of two one-fifteenth-scale dynamically similar models of the Skate (now designated Y2-1) underscored the results of earlier wind tunnel experiments and provided additional information on stability, spray, and other hydrodynamic characteristics.[38]

By 1950 the triangular, or delta, wing brought the seaplane fighter and the hydro-ski together. Convair had begun studies of delta wings in 1945, based in part on German developments during World War II that showed tail-less configurations with wings swept back at 60 degrees had excellent drag, stability, and control characteristics at speeds up to and exceeding Mach 1. In 1948 Convair's XF-92A, an air force fighter, flew for the first time, verifying the basic configuration, even though it was not able to achieve supersonic speeds until its fuselage was redesigned to incorporate the "area rule" principle, which greatly reduced drag at transonic and supersonic speeds.

Convair found that the delta wing achieved maximum lift on takeoff and landing at high angles of attack, not easily achieved with the blended hull-wing configuration, which of necessity sat low in the water. Hydro-skis, though, raised the entire airplane clear of the surface and optimized the delta wing's angle of attack. Based on the expected performance gains of the delta configuration, Convair engineers made a convincing case to BuAer to modify the 1948 contract to include tests of dynamically similar models of tailless, delta-winged versions of the Betta and Cudda. By mid-July 1949 Convair had redesigned the Cudda to include the hydro-ski in addition to the delta wing and had begun to think about the design as a possible alternative to the Skate blended wing-hull configuration. Wind-tunnel and towing-tank tests of the hydro-ski also looked promising in the Betta.[39]

While still pursuing the Skate, Betta, and Cudda projects, Convair moved ahead in May 1950 with a 16,000-pound, delta-wing research airplane, designated Y2-2, incorporating the latest aerodynamics and hydrodynamics in an aircraft with supersonic performance. Convair began with two one-tenth-scale dynamically similar models of the Y2-2 to explore the airplane's aerodynamic and hydrodynamic characteristics. Three configurations received attention: a small single ski combined with a retractable step; broad twin retractable skis that allowed low-speed takeoffs at high angles of attack; and narrow, flexible "Lambda" skis hinged near the nose of the aircraft suitable for high-speed, high-angle takeoffs. Convair found that all the hydro-skis tested had good spray characteristics and that despite high water resistance the "completely revolutionary" Lambda skis worked best, especially in rough water when the fronts of the skis were extended a short distance from the hull and the rears supported by shock absorbers. Tests also showed that the Lambda skis needed to be more rigid to accommodate the weight of the airplane and that resistance could be reduced if they were only partially extended from the hull during the early stages of takeoff. A ventral fin under the tail of the aircraft provided lateral stability in the water, and the broad delta wing acting as a float balanced the airplane at rest and during low-speed water maneuvers.[40]

In October the company delivered detail specifications for the Y2-2 to the navy. Liking the Convair design and optimistic that it might lead in reasonably short order to an operational fighter, the navy issued a letter of intent for a $4.8 million, cost-plus-fixed-fee contract on 19 January 1951 for two Y2-2s. With an MTOW of 16,300 pounds—less than half that of the Skate— the single-seat airplane had two 6,100-pound-thrust Westinghouse XJ46-WE 2 afterburning engines, giving it an estimated top speed of 943 knots (Mach 1.64) at 35,000 feet. The airplane's ceiling was 53,700 feet, and range was about 500 nautical miles. The design incorporated a 60-degree delta wing similar to that of the XF-92A with engine air inlet ducts located above and slightly behind the junction between the leading edge of the wing and the hull to protect them from spray. Twin retractable Lambda hydro-skis supported the aircraft in the water during high-speed taxiing and takeoff. Thinking that Convair's substantial experience with high-performance waterborne aircraft would accelerate the program, Convair and the navy agreed to an ambitious schedule. By using interim 3,400-pound-thrust Westinghouse J34-WE-32 engines while the J46s were being developed, Convair said it could have the airplane ready for test flights in April 1952.[41]

As it had with the high l/b ratio studies, the XP5Y-1, and the Skate, Convair tested the design using dynamically similar models, including free-flying, rocket-powered models and a one-sixth-scale radio-control model powered by two 30-pound-thrust jet engines. Wind tunnel experiments at the Convair low-speed tunnel and at the company-run Ordnance Aerophysics Laboratory supersonic facility outside Daingerfield, Texas, led to changes in the vertical stabilizer and modifications to the wing planform and the size of the horizontal control surfaces (elevons). Even with its employees working ten-hour shifts, Convair soon found that it could not meet the April 1952 deadline, so the company requested and received permission to put the first flight back to June.[42]

Meanwhile, in April 1951 Convair wound up the Skate project. Begun with the promise of creating a new generation of high-performance seaplanes, Skate fell victim to advancing technology and the navy's need to set priorities and reduce costs. Convair's initial program showed that Skate would meet original estimated performance criteria but could not match that of airplanes expected to come into future service. Because BuAer was determined to move ahead with water-based aircraft equal to those currently on the drawing boards and there was insufficient funding for two seaplane fighters, the obvious choice was a supersonic airplane rather than a subsonic one. Moreover, Convair, reluctant at first about the hydro-ski, had by now been won over to the technology, which with the delta-wing Y2-2 might at last lead to a viable service aircraft. Everything considered, the navy was delighted with the results of the Skate and other advanced seaplane programs. Completely sold on what appeared to be a revolutionary new technology, one officer proclaimed in April 1951 that the aerodynamic drag and structural weight problems of flying boats had been overcome and "that as far as performance is concerned that the undisputed day of the land-plane is past and flying boats of equal performance can now be designed."[43]

A measure of the high hopes the navy and Convair had for the Y2-2 was the decision in August 1951 to redesignate the airplane as the XF2Y-1, an experimental fighter instead of a research airplane. Not everyone concurred with the decision. BuAer's Research Division had understood that the main purpose of the Y2-2 program was to confirm the basic hydrodynamic characteristics of the airplane, after which the program could focus on its aerodynamics and, finally, determine what its operational applications might be. They recommended that Convair think about limiting the airplane to no more than Mach .9 while sorting out what promised to be tricky hydrodynamic problems before moving on to more ambitious goals. The decision to redesignate the airplane indicated to those in the division that the service had ignored their advice and wanted to try to "solve the problems in all three areas at one stroke."[44]

Even though the XF2Y program had fallen behind schedule and the completion of the airplane remained months in the future, the navy invited Convair in October 1951 to present cost proposals for service versions of the aircraft, designated F2Y-1, and on 20 August 1952 amended the original letter of intent to award Convair twelve aircraft valued at $45 million. Subsequently four airplanes were redesignated YF2Y-1s to reflect their preproduction status. Billed as having the "advantage of supersonic combat speed plus the mobility of operation inherent in seaplanes," the F2Y-1 generally adhered to the design of the XF2Y-1, with two Westinghouse J46-WE-2s giving a top speed of 804 knots (Mach 1.4). The MTOW went up to 24,400 pounds. Originally the armament was to consist of forty-four folding-fin rockets, later changed to four 20-mm guns when it became apparent that the rocket installation would be expensive and would involve many more months of development.[45]

Indicative of the navy's enthusiasm for the XF2Y-1 was an address by John F. Floberg, assistant secretary of the navy for air, before the Wings Club in New York on 17 November 1952. Floberg wanted to set the record straight regarding the airplane and Convair's work, which had up to that point been classified and subject to much speculation in the aviation community and the press. He confirmed what most already knew about the XF2Y-1 without elaborating on the details of its design or anticipated performance, stressing that the navy wanted to move beyond models and laboratory work to evaluate the hydro-ski and other advanced features on a combat aircraft. Floberg was confident that the XF2Y-1 "marks the fighter plane's reentry into the water-based field, an area from which it has been absent for some years."

At the same time, he cautioned that Convair's airplane was not a "panacea for anything" and was only part of a wider navy seaplane program. "Even to our most enthusiastic proponents of the hydro-ski—people who have worked for some years on the project—it implies no more than a very worthwhile adjunct to naval aviation," he emphasized. He added that "hydro-ski equipped aircraft are not expected to replace any known type of ship, conventional aircraft or even seaplane aircraft in the Navy." The new technology, did, however, give the navy a new capability to deploy fighter aircraft that combined the advantages of mobility and flexibility with the high performance of their land-based cousins.[46]

Not far into the seaplane fighter program, Convair reported that it could not meet the original delivery schedule and that the last of the F2Y-1s would not leave the plant until May 1955, a year later than planned. The navy considered the revised schedule unacceptable and called Convair officials to Washington in November 1952 to determine what had gone wrong. Convair people explained that the company had not anticipated how its other aircraft projects interfered with the F2Y-1 program, that more engineering and design work had been needed for the operational models than anticipated, and that they had run into labor shortages. Convair assured the skeptical naval officers that it had solved most of the problems by shifting personnel from the B-36 program, using air force facilities as much as possible, and that it would be able to adhere to the revised delivery schedule. The navy recommended the company do more subcontracting and investigate alternative fabrication methods to ensure a "realistic production schedule."[47]

Not until 14 December 1952 was the XF2Y-1 completed and ready for taxi tests in San Diego Bay. Named the Sea Dart and painted dark blue with vivid yellow stripes on the vertical stabilizer, the airplane logged its first flight on 9 April 1953. According to the company's press release, the Sea Dart was the "first known combat-type aircraft to utilize retractable hydro-skis for improved rough water land and takeoff performance," representing "a successful blending of the high speed landbased airplane's performance with the waterbased airplane's inherent versatility and mobility." It was "part of a high performance waterbased 'flying fleet'" being developed by Convair for the navy, which would "expand the air defense perimeter of fleets at sea and installations ashore."[48]

There was ample reason to believe that a seaplane renaissance was imminent. Even if one takes into account what proved to be overoptimistic performance claims early in the program, the Sea Dart with J46 engines compared well to the best air force and navy fighters of the time. For example, the famous North American F-86 Sabre, in its F version of 1952, had an MTOW of 17,900 pounds, a top speed of about 600 miles per hour at 35,000 feet, a ceiling of 50,000 feet, and a maximum range of 1,270 miles. The navy's swept-wing Grumman F9F-8 Cougar of 1953 had an MTOW of 24,763 pounds, a maximum speed of about 600 miles per hour at 35,000 feet, and a service ceiling of 42,000 feet. At 1,200 statute miles, its range well exceeded the Sea Dart's.[49]

Nevertheless, sanguine visions of the seaplane's future began to evaporate even before the XF2Y-1 took to the air. During taxi tests, a severe vibration or "pounding" appeared when the airplane passed 60 miles per hour, threatening its structural integrity and the safety of the pilot. For unexplained reasons, the phenomenon had not revealed itself during tests with models, and everyone agreed that unless it could be solved, the entire program was in jeopardy. Isolating the problem using dynamic models and computer simulations eventually pointed to the blunt shape of the rear part of the hydro-skis as the most likely culprit. Adjustable trailing edge flaps, or "flippers," on the skis damped out most, but not all, of the vibrations at low speeds, but had little effect at high speeds. Nagging doubts remained that the problem was related to the elasticity of the airframe, the hydro-skis, or both, which meant drastic and expensive steps would have to be taken to arrive at a "fix." Even worse, no one knew whether tests of the second airplane, equipped with more powerful J46s, might solve the problem or exacerbate it.[50]

More trouble for Convair's advanced seaplane program came on 15 July 1953. During a high-speed dive, the XP5Y-1 suddenly experienced severe flutter in the horizontal stabilizer, followed by loss of longitudinal control when one of the elevator trim tabs broke away. Don P. Germeraad, Convair's engineering test pilot, alerted sea rescue units and tried to wrestle the aircraft back under control as it roller-coastered through the sky for nearly a half-hour. When it became obvious that he would not be able to land the airplane, he ordered the crew to bail out; all nine got out safely, including Germeraad, and they were quickly picked up in the sea off Point Loma. Charles Richbourg, preparing for a test flight of the Sea Dart, heard that the XP5Y-1 was in trouble and quickly took off to see if there was anything he could do to help. Keeping a safe distance from the stricken airplane, he saw it lurch into a shallow dive, watched the crew parachute out, and followed its descent into the water.[51]

The loss meant Convair could not continue the XP5Y-1 program as planned, because the second airplane had been put in long-term storage and was not in flying condition. Convair reviewed the situation and recommended using the second airplane for tests of beaching gear and portable docking equipment and transferring the remaining funds to the Sea Dart program, which continued to suffer from cost overruns and delays that threatened to hold up completion and testing of the second J46-powered airplane and raised the specter of setting back flight tests considered crucial for the F2Y-1 program. BuAer could not see how the money could be transferred legally under the terms of the XP5Y-1 and XF2Y-1 contracts.[52]

In a confusing financial shell game that would have impressed Wall Street wizards, the navy and Convair decided to amend the production contract in September 1953, canceling the second XF2Y-1, moving it to the production contract, and including it among four F2Y-1 preproduction models, now redesignated YF2Y-1s, to be built on the tooling used for the XF2Y-1. The move left thirteen production models, which were to be procured under a separate contract, and "saved" $1.1 million from the original XF2Y-1 contract to pay for continued flight testing.[53]

NACA engineers worked on the vibration problem at the Langley towing tank in the fall of 1953, finding it even at low speeds in smooth water and confirming what Convair had discovered about the potential dangers of the vibrations at high speeds. In an effort to work around the vibration problem, Convair decided to try a single hydro-ski on the XF2Y-1 in early 1954. BuAer's

Research Division "heartily recommend[ed] proceeding" with the single-ski arrangement and reminded Convair that as early as 1951 it had tried in vain to interest the company in the advantages of the single ski over the twin-ski configuration.[54]

Delays in the Sea Dart program threatened Convair's and the navy's hopes of using the airplane for early demonstrations of mobile basing concepts. In the fall of 1952 Convair had received approval to test the Sea Dart using a navy-designed stern ramp on an escort carrier, permitting the airplane to be recovered at sea while the ship was under way. The navy worried that putting the F2Y-1 program back would jeopardize evaluation of the airplane's suitability for operations with the fleet. Convair was less concerned, estimating that the ramp design was adequate for the XF2Y-1 and would work even better with the F2Y-1, and looking forward to open-sea tests with the service aircraft at the earliest possible time. In 1954 plans included fitting a 60-foot ramp to the stern of a landing ship dock (LSD) to evaluate its suitability before removing it and trying it out on the carrier.[55]

High-speed aerodynamic problems added to the growing litany of disappointment with the Sea Dart. Tests of a solid-rocket-propelled, one-tenth-scale model of the XF2Y-1 at NACA Langley's Pilotless Aircraft Research Division in 1953 revealed that the airplane had severe lateral instability at high altitudes. More disconcerting was the projection that even with the more powerful Westinghouse engines, the airplane would have only marginal supersonic performance. In April 1953 company engineers met with BuAer people to discuss ways of reducing the drag of the airplane and increasing its top speed.[56]

At the top of the list was application of the "area rule" concept. The result of a brilliant insight by Richard T. Whitcomb of NACA's Langley lab, the area rule employed the entire wing-fuselage-tail cross-sectional area in computing total drag, leading Whitcomb to suggest pinching the fuselage at the wing roots to obtain an overall reduction in drag. Convair's YF-102A interceptor, derived from the XF-92A, was the first beneficiary of the principle, its "wasp waist" or Coke bottle–shaped fuselage transforming the airplane into a genuine Mach 1 fighter. Using area rule and changes to the Sea Dart's wings to reduce trim drag at high speeds promised to bring the F2Y-1's speed up to that anticipated when Convair won the contract for the Y2-2 and ultimately to match that of its land-based and carrier-based contemporaries.[57]

Area rule was easier said than done. In a report issued on 15 June 1955, Convair summarized the advantages and disadvantages of the principle in the

XF2Y-1. Considering area rule to be "an important new tool in the field of high speed aerodynamics" that promised major increases in performance, the Convair engineers cautioned that more research was needed to demonstrate what it meant in the operational version of the Sea Dart. To maximize the effects of area rule, the report suggested, the fuselage would have to be lengthened, giving an l/b ratio of 10:1, good for hydrodynamics but bad for the balance of the airplane. Furthermore, reduction in the diameter of the fuselage dictated by the area rule principle would "adversely compromise" the airplane's hydrodynamics. Nevertheless, Convair engineers were confident that relocating the engines forward would restore the airplane's balance, and that select reductions in fuselage width above the hydrodynamic portion of the hull would bring enough of the area rule into play to effect significant drag reductions.[58]

The first YF2Y-1, with J46 engines, was ready for flight testing in mid-1954, picking up where the XF2Y-1 had left off with an ambitious series of open-sea tests that Convair and the navy hoped would demonstrate the viability of the airplane and the concept of an integrated sea-based striking force.[59] Despite the setbacks, no one at Convair or in the navy was prepared to give up on the XP5Y-1 and Sea Dart, even though it was evident that the high-performance seaplane was a tougher technological problem than anyone had thought when research began after World War II. In the face of mounting technical and funding difficulties, Convair and the navy forged ahead, confident the problems would be solved and the two airplanes would live up to the high expectations everyone had for them as possible components of a mobile, sea-based striking force.

# Five

# Designs

In March 1949 a team working under Vice Adm. Robert Carney, DCNO (Logistics), developed a proposal for using long-range flying boats in conjunction with surface ships and submarines to supplement aircraft carriers in nuclear strike and other missions. A tough, practical surface officer who had served as Adm. William F. Halsey's chief of staff in the latter stages of the Pacific war, Carney was no starry-eyed dreamer nostalgically longing for the "good old days" of the flying boat. Carney's office made the salient point that a seaplane unit could offer formidable striking power at less cost than a carrier task force, which had to devote a disproportionate amount of its strength to self-defense. In the fall of 1949, as the navy presented its case for a strategic role before Vinson's unification and strategy committee, Carney repeated his ideas, adding that maintaining and deploying strategic bombers on the scale envisaged by the air force was prohibitively expensive and logistically unwise.[1]

The Operations Evaluation Group in the office of the CNO came to much the same conclusions in a February 1950 study of the economic advantages of the high-performance seaplane in the strike role. Based on a June 1949 report, the group found that a detachment consisting of 100 seaplanes, refueled by tanker submarines, could attack targets 2,000 nautical miles distant for about the same cost as a carrier task force. Both the seaplane unit and the carrier force were "substantially" more economical than large bombers based in the United States, which might cost twice as much to deliver the same amount of ordnance. Not only could the attack seaplane perform the same mission as the aircraft carrier or the land-based bomber, but it could also serve in the strategic reconnaissance role. Both the carrier and the seaplane offered the advantage of mobility, compelling the enemy to distribute its air defenses over a wider area and increasing the effectiveness of the strike aircraft. Most important, the attack seaplane provided "insurance against presently unforeseeable circumstances under which land-based or carrier-based aircraft might be unable to operate."[2]

In the same vein, in February 1949 the navy's Research and Development Board had surveyed various programs and identified the attack seaplane as a priority equal to carrier-based attack aircraft. Emphasizing that carrier aircraft were often limited in the strike role by poor meteorological conditions, the board specified that the seaplane could achieve all-weather capability by having autonomous systems for fire control, bomb delivery, navigation, electronic countermeasures (ECM), communications, and photography. A BuAer report of 19 May 1950, examining German experiences in the 1940 campaign in Norway, showed that the flying boat might be essential in the event that land bases became inoperable or otherwise unavailable in a future conflict.[3]

A major consideration in the postwar years was the navy's mining mission. Not glamorous, but useful, the air-dropped mine had demonstrated its utility at the end of World War II when the army air forces carried out a highly successful mining campaign against Japan. In the immediate postwar years, Lockheed's Operational Research Group studied the problem of minelaying, finding that to be effective, it demanded a large number of mines, accurately positioned. To accomplish this, an airplane had to be capable of making a high-speed approach at minimum altitude and could expect to encounter heavy antiaircraft fire. Survival depended on surprise.[4]

What airplane was best suited for such a demanding and dangerous mission? In June 1949 the Aviation Plans Division in OPNAV reviewed the problem. During the first year of a general war, the navy could be expected to drop seventy thousand 1,000-pound and 2,000-pound mines, using aircraft from the existing eight carriers and twenty-seven patrol squadrons. Considering availability and replenishment capabilities, six thousand mines would be dropped during the first three months of the campaign, using aircraft from two carriers and six patrol squadrons—sufficient, planners thought, to block the main points of exit for Soviet submarines and "greatly reduce" the task of open-ocean ASW forces. For the present, land-based Convair PB4Y-2 Liberators, supplemented by new Martin P4M-1 Mercator land-based patrol planes, from three patrol squadrons, had responsibility for mining. No one was under any illusions about the difficulty of the mission, least of all Vice Adm. Calvin T. Durgin, the DCNO (Air). Durgin concluded in August 1949 that "the problems associated with aerial mining are many and complex" and recommended that "sound planning" was essential to solve them.[5]

Whatever "sound planning" was done over the next two years did little to solve the dilemma of finding a suitable aircraft for the mining job. As the PB4Y slid into obsolescence, the mission increasingly fell to the P4M and the P2V. In June 1951 BuAer's Patrol Design Branch determined to cut through what it considered the "confusion" that had engulfed mining aircraft. The branch found the P2V and the P4M to be solid, versatile airplanes, but both had shortcomings as minelayers. To make either or both satisfactory as interim minelaying aircraft meant equipping them with turboprop engines and carrying out extensive modifications to enhance their payload, speed, and range. Although it might make sense to award Martin a contract for a turboprop version of the P4M, expensive new tooling would be needed. Better, the branch concluded, to use the P4M exclusively for ASW and modify Convair's new XP5Y as a minelayer.[6] Even so, the XP5Y had experienced its own development problems, and a minelaying variant would have to wait until at least mid-1953 before joining the fleet. It was unlikely to be a substitute for an entirely new high-performance flying boat dedicated to minelaying and other strike missions.

BuAer's concept of the attack seaplane evolved over the next year. One of the most significant changes in the bureau's thinking was having the airplane drop down from its cruising altitude for a high-speed dash to the target at sea level. This modification reflected the growing belief that high-flying aircraft were increasingly vulnerable to Soviet warning radars and antiaircraft defenses. It also meant that the airplane would need a stronger structure to cope with the aerodynamic stresses imposed by low-level flight at speeds approaching that of sound, and plenty of reserve power to make a rapid climb out from the target after delivering its weapons.[7]

Those familiar with ideas for new seaplanes were certain that advanced technologies would overcome the past shortcomings of the flying boat, suiting it for the most demanding future missions. Aerodynamic and hydrodynamic improvements, new wind tunnels and testing methodologies, and the promise of virtually limitless power from turbojet engines underlay even the most conservative visions of waterborne aircraft that compared well with, and even exceeded, the performance of their land-based counterparts. Convair had long been the leader, working with the navy, NACA's Langley lab, and the Stevens Institute of Technology on designs for new flying boats with l/b ratios of 10:1 or more. Not to be left out, the Glenn L. Martin Company experimented with an 8.5:1 ratio hull on its XP5M-1, a heavily modified PBM-5, in 1948. Subsequently rebuilt as the Model 270 with a 15:1 ratio hull in the spring of 1952, the airplane confirmed hydrodynamic and aerodynamic model tests in the late 1940s showing that high l/b ratios brought dramatic increases in seaplane performance, especially when coupled with turbojet engines and swept wings.[8]

Since the crisis of 1949, the political atmosphere obligated the navy to concentrate on long-range maritime missions rather than deep nuclear strikes. There was general agreement that mining Soviet harbors and passages to the open sea and bombing enemy submarine bases and support facilities was critical to the success of any future allied antisubmarine campaigns. Existing landplanes, flying boats, and carrier aircraft were not up to the task. The right airplane would need to have several important features: long range; a large bomb bay suitable for a wide variety of heavy weapons (including nuclear); a high cruising speed and fuel efficiency; superior ECM equipment; good high-speed, low-altitude flying characteristics; and an advanced electronic aiming system to ensure the accurate placement of mines and the delivery of nuclear weapons against such "hardened" targets as submarine pens. In a typical mining mission the airplane would take off from an advanced base near the target but out of range of land-based interceptors, cruise to the vicinity of the objective at more than 45,000 feet and 600 knots, descend to wave-top altitude where it was invisible to enemy search radars and difficult for fighters to intercept, streak to the target at high subsonic speeds and most likely in low visibility, execute defensive maneuvers dictated by the tactical situation, release its ordnance, then rapidly exit the target area at low altitude, climb, and return home at high altitude. Some missions would require the airplane to be refueled from a submarine at a preselected meeting point either before or after the operation, or on both legs of the sortie if necessary. To say the least, it was a challenging proposition, and nearly everyone agreed that a flying boat embodying "state of the art" weapons and electronic systems and powered by turbojet engines was the only way to accomplish the goal.

In 1946 the navy contracted with NACA's Langley lab to explore the possibilities of a high-speed minelayer (HSML) airplane. Favorable results from NACA wind tunnel and towing tank experiments led BuAer's Research Division, in conjunction with the Patrol Design Branch of the bureau's Aircraft Division, to begin preliminary engineering analyses of attack seaplanes with MTOWs of approximately 130,000 pounds. NACA tested models of one design, the DR-56, in 1948. Further refinement and experimentation resulted in the DR-77 in March 1949, which evolved into the DR-77A. By early 1951 the Research Division and the Patrol Design Branch concurred that the DR-77A was to be an airplane powered by turbojet engines, with an MTOW of 160,000 pounds, a 30,000-pound payload of bombs or mines, and a combat range of 1,200 nautical miles. The airplane had a gullwing design similar to that of the Martin P5M, which the two BuAer groups believed crucial to raise the engines clear of the water and allow a relatively shallow-depth (and lighter) hull. The general mission profile was similar to that outlined in 1949: the airplane and its crew of three (pilot, copilot, and radar operator/navigator) would fly to the target at an altitude in excess of 40,000 feet; make a high-speed, low-altitude run-in to the objective; deliver the weapons; rapidly leave the target area at low altitude; and return to the advanced base at a high cruising speed at 40,000 feet.[9]

The airplane was also to have the ability to make rough-water takeoffs and landings, negotiating waves 6–8 feet high. Here, BuAer's Research Division had wagered on the eventual success of the hydro-ski, which it had been working on in collaboration with NACA and Convair. Convair had incorporated the concept in studies of its Betta and Cudda attack aircraft and had fitted the Sea Dart interceptor with hydro-skis. In the meantime, models of the DR-77A equipped with hydro-skis underwent extensive testing at the Langley lab's testing tank, with promising results.[10]

Conferences at BuAer, followed on 25 April 1951 by a formal operational requirement from the CNO, culminated in outline specifications for the airplane, issued in May. Among other changes, the specifications increased the number of crew members from three to five because of the complexity of the mission and the variety of weapons. The bureau also stipulated that the airplane had to be able to warm up quickly and take off after a 45-second run. Considered vital to safeguard the airplane from being surprised on the water, the requirement was difficult to meet due to the characteristics of high-performance aircraft, which usually had high wing loadings and required long takeoff runs. The requirement also clashed with one of the pronounced characteristics of the turbojet engine, which needed time to "spool up" to its maximum power. In most other respects, the outline specifications closely adhered to BuAer's preliminary studies.[11]

Ivan H. Driggs, director of BuAer's Research Division, was one of those who scrutinized the outline specifications. On 16 July Driggs asked for clarification of the desired water loads on the hull so that a contractor might be able to employ hydro-skis for high-speed landings and takeoffs, requested more details on the design of the tender to service the airplane, and called for the specification to include means of ensuring that the bomb bay was watertight and that it could be loaded while the airplane was in the water. Of primary consideration was whether the intended 900-nautical-mile range would mean an "excessively large aircraft" with an MTOW of about 200,000 pounds, "which may seriously impair its utility." Far better was a compromise that cut the range to 750 nautical miles, allowing the airplane to be brought down to the original 160,000-pound weight.[12]

BuAer sent out detail specifications to twelve aircraft manufacturers on 30 July 1951 with a deadline of 1 February 1952 to submit design and cost proposals for two prototype aircraft and one static test vehicle. The designs were to be completed by May 1952, the prototypes ready for flight testing by February 1953, and the airplanes ready for Board of Inspection and Survey (BIS) evaluation and acceptance by August 1954. It may have been an ominous sign, but only three aircraft companies responded: Convair, Martin, and the Boeing Company of Seattle. Boeing had an excellent reputation for its large jet bombers and for its prewar and wartime flying boats, but the company subsequently informed BuAer that it would not submit a proposal.[13]

BuAer invited Martin and Convair to send representatives to Washington to discuss their proposals so as to get a "feel" for what the manufacturers planned to do. Martin's people were first, meeting at the bureau on 15 August. Attending were Lt. Cdr. Clarence T. Froscher, who chaired the meeting, five other officers and nine civilians from BuAer, and three Martin representatives. The exercise was an opportunity to debate the merits of the airplane, while revealing the divergent thinking about its mission and capabilities. On one hand, everyone knew that Martin had proposed a potentially versatile airplane that could carry out many different functions, and they wanted to get the most out of it. On the other hand, there was the danger of compromising the airplane's primary minelaying mission and its secondary nuclear strike capability by trying to make it do too much.[14]

Range and payload questions dominated much of the conference with Martin. Martin's representatives wanted to know why the airplane's range had been cut to 750 miles. Cdr. Frederick W. Brown explained that the range had been reduced once BuAer realized a 900-nautical-mile range would demand an airplane of "tremendous size." The present airplane could still reach 900 miles on a reconnaissance mission by carrying no ordnance and employing auxiliary fuel tanks. BuAer thought that it was possible to achieve a modest increase in the airplane's range over the original outline specification, but wanted to wait until it had more information from engine companies about the capabilities of the turbojets then under consideration. There was also the possibility of using JATO to allow the airplane to take off in an overloaded condition, although Martin engineers were not enthusiastic about the logistical problems of getting JATO units to seaplanes at forward bases.[15]

Much debate focused on the airplane's armament—in particular, how the bomb bay was to be configured for present and future nuclear weapons and whether or not some of the stores could be mounted on wing pylons. There was a good deal of discussion about the number and types of mines and at what speeds and altitudes they could be delivered. Some of the civilians from BuAer saw possibilities in using the seaplane as a carrier for the planned Kingfisher guided missile, which weighed nearly 2 tons and had wings that would not fit in the bomb bay. Others insisted that rockets might be mounted on pylons on the top of the wing to be used as part of the airplane's defensive armament. Robert L. Cox Jr. of Martin warned that putting anything on the wings of a high-performance, swept-wing airplane would be detrimental to its performance; trying to rein in some of the more enthusiastic navy representatives, he wisely cautioned that "an airplane can't be all things to all people."[16]

Quick to see that BuAer's requirements complemented its work with high-performance seaplanes—in particular the large Betta attack aircraft—Convair's engineers enthusiastically tackled the HSML challenge. On 3 October, partway through the design process, Convair conferred with BuAer about the outline specifications and possible modifications to the airplane, before committing to its final design. The requirements pointed to an airplane with low drag, high wing loading, and high landing speeds, probably equipped with hydro-skis, which the company's engineers hoped would solve some of the problems of rough-water takeoffs and landings. Convair could not conceive of a way to work retractable hydro-skis into the minelayer design without interfering with the location of bomb bays and related aircraft structure. BuAer's target weight of 160,000 pounds also seemed unrealistic to Convair's engineers, who envisioned an airplane on the order of 190,000 pounds to meet the navy's range and payload requirements. Setting the hydro-ski aside, Convair next turned to the Skate-type blended-wing hull, ingeniously combining the retractable step with the bomb-bay door, only to discover that the airplane would have a much higher center of gravity than the Skate, upsetting its waterborne stability and requiring drag-inducing wing-tip floats.[17]

Apparently caught between the need for high speed and rough-water operations, Convair saw only two alternatives. One was an aircraft with a planing-tail hull, and the other had a long afterbody and a faired step; both had high l/b ratios and promised reasonable takeoff and landing characteristics and good high-speed aerodynamics. As with most aircraft designs, Convair sought a compromise. Company engineers risked a slight degradation of aerodynamics and opted for a carefully shaped planing-tail hull and a moderate faired step. Skate-type retractable spray dams prevented water ingestion into the engines or interference with the aerodynamic control surfaces even when the airplane was overloaded to 225,000 pounds. A ventral fin helped with directional stability in the water. Towing tests with a one-twentieth-scale, dynamically similar model confirmed the validity of the hydrodynamic design. When they finished their preliminary work in January 1952, Convair engineers proudly announced that they had accomplished "what was at first thought impossible" in creating a design that met the navy's difficult requirements.[18]

Conferences in the summer and fall helped clarify BuAer's requirements and provided guidance for the manufacturers. Of the two proposals, Convair's, which reached the bureau on 10 January, was the more conservative—a point in the company's favor, considering the challenging nature of the airplane's mission and the wisdom of taking things one step at a time with such a complex airplane. Convair's proposal called for an airplane with an MTOW of 188,900 pounds—down slightly from the 190,000 pounds its engineers thought was the minimum. The craft would be 130 feet long overall, with a 93.5-foot wing mounted at the top of a hull with an l/b ratio of 10.45:1—high, but only a little more than that of the XP5Y-1. The faired step appears in the drawings; the ventral fin is absent. The wing was swept back 35 degrees and had an area of 1,750 square feet, yielding a wing loading of 108 pounds per square foot. Mines were arranged vertically on each side of two bomb bays, one in front of and the other behind the wing, the weapons released through outward-opening doors on the bottom of the hull. Hatches on the top of the hull allowed loading while the airplane was on the water. A radar-directed, twin-gun turret located in the tail well above the waterline provided defense.

Power came from four 15,400-pound-thrust Wright J67 afterburning engines, paired one above the other in nacelles under the wing roots immediately adjacent to the fuselage and accessible from within the airplane. Only days before submitting its design, Convair learned that BuAer did not consider the J67 an acceptable power plant; this caused a last-minute scramble to rework the proposal around the Westinghouse J40-10, a less powerful and heavier engine. Fortunately, the revision did not affect the airplane's estimated performance. In nearly all respects, though, the proposed airplane did not meet the navy's requirements. With the requisite 30,000-pound payload, the airplane had a combat range of 665 nautical miles, a ceiling of 36,300 feet, a cruising altitude of only 27,500 feet at the start of the mission, a cruising speed of 430 knots, and top speeds of 540 knots at sea level and 480 knots at 35,000 feet. Takeoff time was estimated at 55 seconds. Convair set the cost of Phase I (testing and preliminary engineering) of the project at $1.7 million, Phase II (two prototypes and one static test article) at $27.8 million, and Phase III at $1.5 million. The airplane would be ready for its first flight by May 1955.[19]

Martin submitted its proposal on 1 February. More innovative than Convair's design, and also more risky in some respects, Martin's airplane, known as the Model 275 "SeaMaster," had an MTOW of 154,000 pounds, was 135 feet long, and had a wingspan of nearly 103 feet. Martin's design sharply contrasted with that of Convair in having a stepless, full-length, planing-tail hull of much smaller cross section (9 feet) and significantly less depth. The l/b ratio of 13.7:1 was higher than that of the Convair entry and promised greater aerodynamic efficiency, even though it was well under some of the more radical l/b ratios the two companies had experimented with. A high T-tail was another distinctive characteristic, aesthetically pleasing in addition to being a practical solution to the problem of getting the empennage clear of the water. The horizontal tail surfaces were all-moving, with small, mechanically linked elevators. The Martin's wing sweep was 45 degrees, 10 degrees more than that of the Convair, and with an area of 1,900 square feet, its wing loading of 81 pounds per square foot was lower than the Convair's. To aid directional control on the water, the Martin, like the Convair, employed hydroflaps extending from the hull near the tail. As did their counterparts at Convair, Martin engineers found that the hydro-ski involved mechanical complications and weight penalties that they could ill afford in an airplane already pushing the limits of the weight envelope.

A mine bay with a rotary door in the bottom of the hull was one of the airplane's most innovative features. Demonstrated for the first time in the company's XB-51 medium bomber, the door served a dual function, sealing the bottom of the hull and providing mounting points for the weapons stores.

As the hydraulically activated door rotated through 180 degrees, the ordnance swung with it and was released from a position clear of the bottom of the airplane. The entire door could be removed for loading and unloading while the airplane was ashore on its beaching gear. On the water, ordnance was loaded through side hatches or a hatch on the top of the fuselage, then transferred to the weapons bay by an overhead monorail. Martin promised a high degree of bombing accuracy using a precision automatic minelaying and navigation system incorporating the latest advances in electronics. Like the Convair, the Martin had a radar-directed, twin-gun turret in the tail for defense.

Powering the Model 275 were four Westinghouse 9,350-pound-thrust, J40-18 turbojets—with afterburners bringing them to 11,700 pounds thrust—paired in nacelles on top of the wing just outboard of the fuselage. Carrying a 30,000-pound payload, the Martin had a range of only 560 nautical miles, although it outperformed the Convair with a top speed of 554 knots at sea level and 530 knots at 35,000 feet, a cruising speed of 460 knots at 36,300 feet at the start of the mission, and a ceiling of 43,300 feet. The Model 275's takeoff time exceeded 60 seconds. Martin estimated the cost of Phase I of the program to be $2.5 million, with Phase II to cost $23.9 million, and Phase III $1.6 million. The first airplane would be ready to fly by September 1954.[20]

With the proposals in hand, BuAer began the arduous task of evaluation. Commander Brown of BuAer's Patrol Design Branch examined the proposals and some of the preliminary comments on them from the bureau's technical divisions. To Brown, both designs had their merits; Martin's rotating mine door and Convair's engine installation, which allowed access to the power plants from inside the hull, were the most attractive features of each. Between the two, the Patrol Design Branch preferred the Martin design, chiefly because of its anticipated ability to perform nuclear strike, photographic reconnaissance, and tanker missions. The branch also liked the Martin's superior hydrodynamics and spray suppression, especially in rough water, as well as its novel self-beaching gear and "T-tail" configuration, but it did not want to cut off any avenues that might prove fruitful in the future. Brown pointed out that weight control was likely to be a problem and that it was "anybody's guess" what the production models would weigh; in addition, the bureau would need to evaluate many of the unusual features of the aircraft and the necessity of maintaining an industrial base to support an emergency production effort. For these reasons, Brown argued for letting contracts for building two prototypes and critically evaluating them in a "flyoff."[21]

Ivan Driggs entered the debate on 12 February with a memo explaining why neither design met the outline specifications. From his perspective both companies had deviated too far from BuAer's DR-77A design, particularly in abandoning the gullwing configuration and the hydro-ski. Without the gull-wing, Convair's proposal had a deep hull, which degraded the airplane's aero-dynamic performance, while Martin's concept was likely to have a wet wing that would have to be reinforced to handle high hydrodynamic loads. In both instances, the airplanes were heavier than necessary. Driggs was most puzzled by the absence of the hydro-ski, which had shown so much promise with Con-vair's Betta and was soon to make its appearance in the Sea Dart jet fighter. He recommended letting a contract for one of the two design proposals with the proviso that the specifications include the hydro-ski.[22]

A serious rift developed within BuAer over the merits of the HSML con-cept and the viability of the SSF. After sifting through the Martin and Con-vair proposals and the comments from Brown and Driggs, the Evaluation Division submitted a draft memo to Rear Adm. Thomas S. Combs, BuAer chief, on 29 February, rejecting both designs because they did not meet the necessary performance criteria and specifically criticizing Martin's design for being overweight. Only by increasing the airplane's fuel load by 5,000 pounds and increasing its MTOW could it meet the specifications; if the company were kept to its original MTOW, the airplane would not be able to meet the range requirement with a 30,000-pound payload. A month passed while addi-tional voices were heard on both sides of the dispute, and eventually the Eval-uation Division backed off on its initial negative appraisal, calling for relaxing some of the requirements. But in a revised memo to Combs on 25 March, the division still wanted a fresh competition.[23]

Having had more time to study the competing proposals and sensing the urgency of getting the program under way, Brown reconsidered his earlier conclusions about the expense and delay of evaluating two prototypes. On 28 March he sent a long message to the director of BuAer's Aircraft Division out-lining the justification for the attack seaplane and providing additional specifics on why it made sense to proceed with the Martin proposal. Nothing had happened to change the situation since October 1949, when the CNO had stipulated that priority be given to high-performance seaplane develop-ment. If anything, there was more need for such aircraft considering the "sky-rocketing cost of obtaining, developing and defending the ever increasing real estate requirements of land based aviation." Recent efforts by the air force to gain bases in North Africa had been a "debacle," underscoring the need to move aggressively to solve the problems associated with high-performance seaplanes. "There is nothing so impotent and unmaneuverable as an air force without a base," Brown concluded. Then, invoking a power greater even than the air force, he wrote that "with the God given fact that three-fourths of the earth's surface is water, and the man developed hydro-aero-dynamic technology now available, the Navy is in a position to deliver truly mobile, high performance air power." It was imperative to move ahead quickly with the development of new sea-based aircraft.[24]

That said, Martin and its design proposal looked best. The hydro-ski, which had so much appeal to Driggs and the Research Division, was "very attractive," and although it showed much promise in small, light aircraft, it was not necessarily adaptable to heavier seaplane designs, which featured significant improvements in hull design and construction with corresponding reductions in hydrodynamic drag, thanks to recent engineering advances. Brown also said that the aircraft companies had thoroughly examined the problems associated with meeting the BuAer requirements and had submitted their designs after six months of study. Perhaps it was time for the bureau, which had not been actively involved in a large seaplane design project since 1945 and was unfamiliar with much of the "state of the art," to accept the results, even though they appeared on paper not to meet the original outline specifications. Disputing claims to the contrary, Brown was confident that with the J40 engine the Martin would meet the required time for takeoff and achieve the desired range with a 30,000-pound payload. Moreover, wing designs for transonic aircraft, engine nacelle locations, and other factors were significant variables that did not always accord with BuAer preconceptions and mathematical evaluation techniques.

Brown saw Martin's "startling" rotary bomb bay design, which had generated much commentary, as one of the strong points of the proposal—an "outstanding answer" to a difficult engineering problem and one that enhanced the versatility of the airplane. Martin's experience with the rotary design in the XB-51 had shown that many types of ordnance could be released under a variety of flight conditions. Everyone had expected, however, that the Martin bomb bay would be prone to water sealing problems, only to discover that the ingenious rotary design greatly simplified the situation by removing all of the sealing surfaces from areas of high hydrodynamic pressure and reducing the total length of seal from 117 feet in the Convair design to only 73 feet. Treating the mine door itself as a module and making it removable brought additional benefits, not the least of which was that "prepackaged" stores could be swapped out quickly and that nuclear weapons and guided missiles could be easily fitted. Martin's method of rearming the airplane while it was on the water, using an internal monorail, was also appealing, for it allowed a more rapid transfer of ordnance from small rearming boats or tenders than was possible if the weapons were loaded directly into the bomb bay through an overhead hatch.[25]

Rear Adm. Lucien M. Grant, BuAer's assistant chief for research and development, commented on the proposals in April. He found the wide variation in the weights of the two airplanes "disturbing" and concluded that Martin was overly optimistic about bringing the airplane in at the 154,000-pound estimate, while Convair was probably too pessimistic about its 189,000-pound design. Grant thought it more realistic to add 6,500 pounds to the Martin and subtract 5,800 pounds from the Convair, bringing each of them closer to BuAer's specified 160,000 pounds. Yet Convair insisted that their weight was correct, meaning that the best way to compare the two was to leave both airplanes at their estimated MTOWs but "penalize" the Martin by adding 5,000 pounds to its fuel load. A big problem was that the combat range of both airplanes was "well below" the mission requirement of 750 nautical miles, although the Convair came closer to meeting it than did the Martin. Neither airplane had good takeoff times to begin with, so overloading them to achieve a greater range seemed not to be a viable alternative. The only solution was to cut the desired payload capacity from 30,000 pounds to 16,000 pounds. Convair's mine bay design was unacceptable because it did not permit the release of ordnance at high speeds; Martin's innovative design did, but it was also likely to suffer from sealing problems.

Grant concluded that "fairly extensive" modifications would be needed to both designs to make them acceptable. Martin needed to raise the wing and tail turret to clear the spray; rework the internal compartmentalization, crew access, and flight deck configuration; fit more powerful J40-10 engines; increase the MTOW; and improve the range. Convair had to revise its hull and mine bay arrangement to allow high-speed release, bring the weight down, and decrease the wing loading to cut high takeoff speeds. Martin's proposal was less expensive, but was still likely to run to more than $35 million when government-furnished equipment was added. Grant concluded that neither proposal was good enough to justify a full development contract, but that

Martin's was promising to the extent of awarding a Phase I contract to allow it to conduct more tests and to rethink its design.[26]

Comments on Grant's appraisal underscored how deep the disagreement in BuAer was over the proposals. In route slip comments on Grant's memo, Brown "wholeheartedly" concurred with the decision to award only Martin a Phase I contract. He thought the company's design included "highly desirable, forward looking features which are an ideal nucleus for further development in this field" and pointed out that the "severe delineations" placed on naval aviation by budget and political decisions made it "of utmost importance" for the navy to seek and obtain the best waterborne aircraft possible. Adm. Theodore C. Lonnquest, assistant chief of BuAer, was not so sure. Because both proposals had strayed so far from the outline specifications, and given the uncertainties of such high-performance airplanes, he concluded that it was best to allow both companies more time to refine and resubmit their proposals. He was particularly worried that shutting out Convair would mean not being able to "capitalize" on the advanced hydrodynamics the bureau had been working on with the company "over a long period of years."[27]

Finally, Admiral Combs had had enough. He brought the principals together in his office on 22 April to work out a compromise. Although W. Z. Frisbie, a civilian in BuAer's Evaluation Division, said he was willing to go along with Grant and Brown on awarding Martin a limited Phase I contract, Lonnquest was unbending in his support of Convair, largely because of BuAer's long-time investment in the company's Skate program. He was dismayed by the failure of both companies to meet the outline specifications and was concerned that Martin might fall even further behind if they had to bring the weight of their airplane up. Brown strenuously objected, arguing that the bureau had been too pessimistic in its assessment of Martin's performance estimates. Neither he nor Grant won their case, though, for the final determination was to let both companies revise and resubmit their proposals.[28]

Although Martin appeared to have the edge in the competition, the advantages of its design were not so clear-cut that the bureau could easily eliminate Convair, particularly in light of the partnership that had evolved over the last decade between the company and the navy on advanced seaplane projects. It was also obvious that both companies were likely to have trouble meeting even the relaxed specifications and that the new airplane would push the state of the art in many technical areas. Finally, it seems in retrospect that BuAer wanted to take more time to ensure that the design was fully compatible with any new weapons likely to be developed. In the spring of 1952 the

United States was close to detonating its first thermonuclear device and within a few years could be expected to have operational H-bombs, the first models of which were even larger and heavier than early atomic weapons.[29]

Meetings between BuAer officers and representatives from Martin and Convair helped clear the air and sharpen the focus of the program in preparation for the resubmission of the companies' proposals. On 30 April Admiral Grant and George M. Bunker, Martin's president, met to explain BuAer's decision to extend limited Phase I contracts to both firms and to go over the major weaknesses of the Martin proposal. The next day, Grant met with Ralph Bayless, a Convair engineer, to offer suggestions for improvements to his company's design. Made plain to each of the competitors was the stipulation that the airplane had to meet the minimum 750-nautical-mile range with a 30,000-pound payload, although the bureau eased off on its insistence on top speed by consenting to 550 knots at sea level if a higher speed would mean a loss of maneuverability or an increase in MTOW. It was also willing to compromise on the 30,000-pound payload. On 18 June the two companies received $200,000 each for preliminary engineering studies, which were to be completed by 4 August.[30]

Convair submitted its revised proposal to BuAer on 1 August. The design reflected a thorough reappraisal of the project and an intensive effort by the company's engineering teams to meet the navy's objections to its first design. The MTOW of the airplane was reduced to 173,750 pounds, the length was trimmed to 127 feet overall, and the width of the hull cut by more than a foot to 10 feet, 5 inches. The l/b ratio went up to nearly 11:1. Convair was confident that hydrodynamic stability and spray characteristics would not be impaired by the changes in the hull design, even at high overloads. Convair planned to use 13,500-pound-thrust, nonafterburning Wright J67s, located side by side in nacelles tucked under the wings close to the fuselage. Most significant in terms of reducing takeoff time, which had been one of the objections to the original proposal, the wingspan went up to 105 feet and the area to 2,205 feet, resulting in a decreased loading of 79 pounds per square foot.

The airplane's estimated 990-nautical-mile range with 20,000 pounds of mines or bombs was well within the bureau's revised specifications, and Convair was confident the airplane could reach out 820 miles with 30,000 pounds of ordnance. With a top speed at sea level of 572 knots, the airplane was close to the original outline specification and a little above the bureau's reduced requirement. Cruising speed was up to 460 knots. Moreover, the new scheme estimated the airplane's ceiling to be nearly 46,800 feet, considerably higher than the first proposal.[31]

Convair hoped to meet one of BuAer's major objections to its first design by totally reconfiguring the weapons installation. Instead of the compartments fore and aft of the wing, there now was a single large bay, with the stores mounted on racks fixed to clamshell-type doors. When the doors opened, the weapons moved with them to the exterior of the airplane and on release cleared the airplane at even the highest velocity. An air seal behind the doors blocked off the mine bay and effectively reduced turbulence from the high-speed airstream. Detail changes improved the loading of ordnance from the top of the airplane while it was on the water and from underneath when it was on its beaching gear.[32]

In comparison to Convair's proposal, Martin's, hand-carried to the bureau from Baltimore on 4 August, was substantially unchanged. Responding to skepticism about weight, Martin brought the airplane's MTOW up to 160,000 pounds, providing wider payload and fuel margins than the previous design and allowing an increase in range to 940 nautical miles with 20,000 pounds of mines or bombs and a range with 30,000 pounds that still exceeded the bureau's minimum. Overall length was cut to 132.5 feet, but width stayed the same, and the l/b ratio dropped slightly to about 13.5:1. The wingspan and area remained the same, bringing the loading up to 84 pounds per square foot. Martin reduced the wing sweep from 45 degrees in the original design to 40 degrees in the revised version. Performance was generally better than before: 580 knots at sea level was an improvement over the earlier proposal, 528 knots at 35,000 feet a little worse, and 468 knots cruising speed at 39,100 feet at the start of the mission was up from the estimates for the previous airplane. The ceiling also went up about 5,000 feet to 48,200 feet. Takeoff time was cut significantly, from more than a minute to 49 seconds, only marginally longer than the Convair. Power came from the same nonafterburning Wright J67s as used on Convair's entry.[33]

A comparison of the Martin airplane and the Boeing B-47B medium bomber then in service with the air force is instructive. Both were large, high-wing monoplanes; the most obvious difference was that the Martin used four engines, while the older Boeing needed six, less powerful engines. The Martin's MTOW was about 20,000 pounds less than that of the Boeing, but its 30,000-pound payload far exceeded the Boeing's 18,000 pounds. Where the Martin fell short was in range: its range of 940 nautical miles (1,081 statute miles) was 30 percent less than the 1,600-mile range of the B-47. At altitude the Martin was marginally slower than the Boeing at 528 knots versus 535 knots; at sea level, though, the Martin could make 585 knots, while the Boeing because of structural limitations could achieve only 425 knots.[34]

Knowing that it had an advantage over Convair with its weapons installation, Martin was now in a position to take a more conservative approach. Its engineers made few changes other than to offer different size mine bay doors to accommodate a wider variety of ordnance and to allow greater range on secondary missions. Martin simplified the arrangement of the fuel tanks, which with their attendant piping had been criticized as overly complex in the original design. The company also slightly increased the height of the wings above the water to lessen their "wetness" and to provide better protection of the engines from water ingestion. Finally, there were minor changes to the layout of the flight deck and crew positions to allow easier movement within the airplane and safer exits in emergencies. Like Convair, Martin adhered to its original cost estimates and delivery deadlines.[35]

Grant scrutinized the two proposals. On technical merit, Convair's proposal was the better of the two, superior to that of Martin's in hydrodynamics, fuel management, power plant installation, electronics, interior arrangement, and maintenance. The Martin looked better in aerodynamics, speed, armament, and potential ease of production. It was not easy to choose between the two. In the end, the decision, like many technological choices, was based on factors other than engineering and design. BuAer wanted to keep both companies competitive in the high-speed seaplane field to ensure sources for future procurement. Because Convair had its plate full with the XP5Y-1 and XF2Y-1, and Martin had only the P5M contract, Grant recommended that the contract go to Martin, which, based on studies by BuAer's Industrial Planning Division, was thought to have more engineering and production capacity and had "a greater need for the work" than did Convair.[36]

Brown agreed with Grant's assessment, adding that "if Martin is allowed to fall behind in highspeed seaplane development, there appears to be a strong possibility that ConVair will become our only source of supply with all of the inherent evils of monopoly." Others concluded that the new airplane, regardless of which manufacturer was selected, was destined to become a "powerful complement to the navy's carrier aviation." In the first week of September Grant recommended, and BuAer Chief Combs concurred, that Martin be sent a letter of intent as soon as possible.[37]

Martin received the letter of intent on 30 September 1952, followed by the formal cost-plus-fixed-fee contract on 7 October. Following its original estimates, the company was to provide two airplanes for flight testing and one airframe for static testing, at a cost of $30,861,000, rising to approximately $35 million with the addition of such government-furnished equipment as engines and electronic systems. The program broke down into three phases: the first was developmental, involving additional wind tunnel and towing tank tests; the second centered on the construction of the two prototypes and the static test article; and the third consisted of flight testing and preparation of the airplanes for inspection and acceptance by BuAer. Before the end of the month, BuAer notified the company that the airplane had received the designation XP6M-1.[38] By that time, Martin engineers and shop workers had the project well under way and were confidently looking forward to their new creation becoming the centerpiece of the navy's SSF.

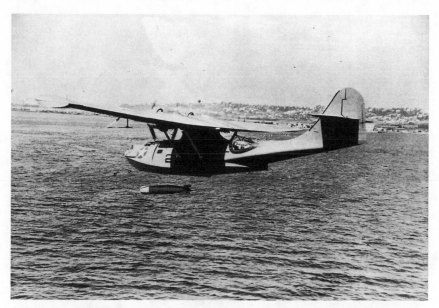

The Convair PBY Catalina seemed in the 1930s to be the navy's aircraft of choice in the long-range attack role. Here a PBY-5A is shown releasing a torpedo during tests in 1942–43. *Naval Historical Center (NH-94118)*

To be effective against enemy fleets, seaplanes needed to have the capability of delivering torpedoes. Hall-Aluminum Aircraft Corporation's XPTBH-2 was an unsuccessful attempt at a dedicated seaplane torpedo bomber. Here the airplane is shown in flight during tests at Anacostia in early 1937. *National Archives (80-G-464943)*

Although obsolescent, PBYs saw action during World War II as strike aircraft. Here a crew arms a PBY-5A with MK 37 depth bombs in the Aleutians. *Naval Historical Center (NH-92483)*

In an effort to gain a nuclear delivery capability in the years after World War II, the navy first used modified Lockheed P2V-3C Neptune patrol bombers. Here a Neptune takes off from the *Midway*-class carrier *Franklin D. Roosevelt* on 26 September 1949. *National Archives (80-G-407511)*

Despite considerable effort, the navy's carrier-based nuclear delivery capability never became fully viable in the 1950s. Designed from the start as a carrier-based heavy attack aircraft, the North American AJ-1 Savage encountered numerous reliability problems in service. Here an AJ-1 is shown aboard the *Essex*-class carrier *Wasp* on 29 February 1952. *National Archives (80-G-442109)*

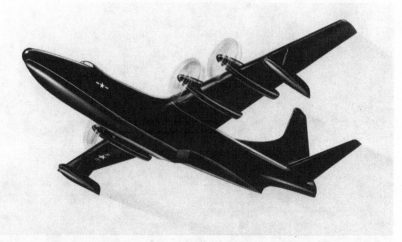

Aerodynamic developments in Germany before and during World War II indicated that flying boats could achieve performance equal or superior to their land-based counterparts. Convair incorporated the most recent advances in its design for the XP5Y-1 long-range flying boat intended for antisubmarine and antishipping missions. In this artist's conception of the aircraft, note the long and narrow (high l/b ratio) hull, which was a key to its superior performance. *National Archives (80-G-706233)*

Again borrowing from the Germans, Convair employed dynamically similar models in testing their postwar seaplane designs. Here is a one-tenth scale model of the XP5Y-1 used for tests in San Diego in 1948. *National Archives (80-G-706673)*

Convair's XP5Y-1 during its initial test flight at San Diego on 18 April 1950. Although a generally successful design, the airplane suffered from deficiencies of its Allison turboprop engines. *National Archives (80-G-413610)*

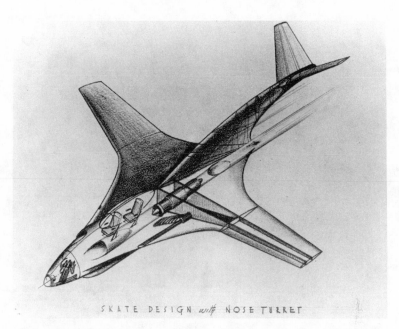

SKATE DESIGN with NOSE TURRET

In 1946 Convair began Project Skate, a program to develop a high-performance turbojet-powered seaplane. Here is an artist's rendering of an early version of the Skate twin-seat jet seaplane interceptor, intended to augment the navy's carrier-borne fighters. *Richard C. Knott*

As part of the Skate program, Convair explored the idea of servicing the fighter from submarines and surface ships as part of a forward-based Seaplane Striking Force. This photo shows tests with a one-tenth scale model fleet submarine and the Skate 7 dynamically similar model in the late 1940s. *Richard C. Knott*

Although Convair ended the Skate program in 1951 without building any aircraft, the idea of a high-performance seaplane fighter augmenting carrier aircraft and supporting a Seaplane Striking Force remained. Convair began work on the Y2-2 single-seat, twin-engine, supersonic delta-wing seaplane fighter in 1950, seen here in an artist's view. *National Archives (80-G-417752)*

The Convair Y2-2 matured into the XF2Y-1 Sea Dart, which used hydro-skis for take-off and landing, as shown here in October 1954. Despite extensive testing, the airplane never reached operational status. *National Archives (80-G-646843)*

From the start, the centerpiece of the navy's postwar Seaplane Striking Force was a large, high-performance attack aircraft. Following a spirited design competition with Convair, the Glenn L. Martin Company won a contract in October 1952 for the XP6M-1 SeaMaster four-engine seaplane, intended for minelaying and other missions. Here the airplane is shown at its rollout on 21 December 1954. *National Archives (80-G-709340)*

Another view of the Martin XP6M-1 SeaMaster at its December 1954 rollout. *National Archives (80-G-653042)*

The Martin SeaMaster on its first test flight, 14 July 1955. The aircraft crashed on 7 December 1955, resulting in the deaths of all four crew members and casting a pall over the entire program. *National Archives (80-G-680767)*

The second XP6M-1 taxis for takeoff during tests in 1956. This aircraft also was lost in an in-flight accident, although all of its flight crew survived the crash, which occurred on 9 November 1956. *National Archives (80-G-679543)*

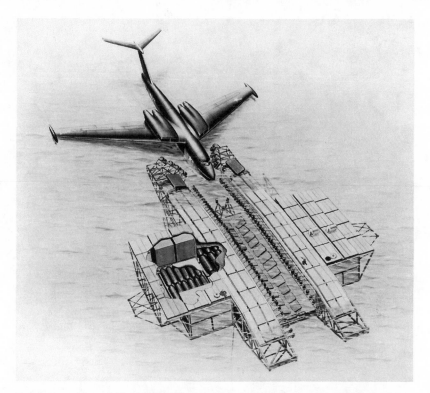

Enhancing the mobility and flexibility of the SeaMaster and the SSF were converted surface ships, submarines, and innovative techniques for servicing and replenishment in forward areas. Both Convair and Martin developed such plans during the 1950s. Included in the Martin 1953 study was this modular, air-transportable floating dry dock for servicing the P6M at a remote site. *Richard C. Knott*

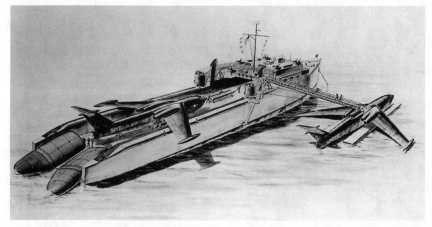

Both Convair and Martin foresaw the use of converted LSDs (landing ship dock) as part of their basing plans for the SSF. This artist's rendering shows an LSD equipped with an inflatable stern ramp and boom for servicing and repairing the P6M. *Richard C. Knott*

Another view of an LSD fitted out for servicing and repairing the SeaMaster and other aircraft at a forward base. *Glenn L. Martin Maryland Aviation Museum (8P-59910)*

*Ashland* (LSD-1) proved the concept of working with large seaplanes during tests with a Martin P5M-2 in the summer of 1957. *Glenn L. Martin Maryland Aviation Museum (P-58112)*

Although the SSF concept stressed the use of small and relatively inexpensive vessels, it was obvious that some larger ships would also be necessary. This is an early proposal for converting a seaplane tender (AV) for servicing and repairing the P6M. Note the long ramp extending from the stern of the ship. *Richard C. Knott*

Beginning in February 1956, the seaplane tender *Albemarle* (AV-5) underwent a conversion that included the telescoping stern ramp to handle the SeaMaster. *National Archives (80-G-1049636)*

Persisting from the start of the SSF concept was the use of submarines in support of attack seaplanes and other elements of the force. *Guavina* (SS-362), converted as a tanker, exercised with P5Ms in 1956 to prove the concept. *National Archives (80-G-679544)*

In keeping with the "New Look" policy of the 1950s, the SeaMaster acquired nuclear delivery capability. Here MK 91 gun-type nuclear weapon practice shapes are fitted to the P6M's rotating mine bay door. *Glenn L. Martin Maryland Aviation Museum (B-20109)*

The SeaMaster program and the Seaplane Striking Force continued despite the loss of the two prototype aircraft, in part because the CNO, Adm. Arleigh A. Burke, was a staunch supporter. *Naval Historical Center (NH-86100)*

What the SSF might have looked like: This is a publicity photo of all six of Martin's YP6M-1 seaplanes arrayed on the ramp at Martin's Middle River plant in October 1958. *Glenn L. Martin Maryland Aviation Museum (P-YP6M-1 6AC)*

A tantalizing glimpse of the future of the SSF with three of the Martin YP6M-1s in formation flight in 1958. *Glenn L. Martin Maryland Aviation Museum (P-61102)*

The P6M-2 was the operational version of the Martin SeaMaster. The original order for twenty-four aircraft underwent a series of cuts until the total procurement was only eight, organized into a single squadron. *Glenn L. Martin Maryland Aviation Museum (P-62241)*

In 1959 Flight Refueling, Ltd. developed a tanker package for the P6M that gave it air refueling capability, extending its range and enhancing its flexibility. *Glenn L. Martin Maryland Aviation Museum (P-21614)*

Vice Adm. Robert B. Pirie, DCNO (Air), made the tough decision in August 1959 to cancel the P6M program, in effect ending the Seaplane Striking Force concept. *National Archives (80-G-626803)*

# Six

# SeaMaster

On a tight schedule and a strict budget, and embarking on a journey that was likely to lead to false leads and dead ends, Martin's engineers wasted little time moving ahead with the XP6M-1 program in the fall of 1952. As company president George Bunker wrote in 1954, it was vital to the success of the program that Martin ensure that every part of the airplane was thoroughly proved. He did not want the SeaMaster to get bogged down as a testbed for engines or other major systems. BuAer agreed; like Martin, the navy desired an operational weapon system as soon as possible and urged the company to use components that had been subjected to extensive development and flight testing before going into the airplane.[1]

BuAer and the navy had a big stake in the program. More funds were available for aircraft procurement in FY 1952—largely as a result of the war in Korea—but the navy still had problems keeping procurement ahead of obsolescence, and faced limits on how much money was available for research and development, and new aircraft designs. Moreover, advocates of the SSF viewed the program in part as an alternative to the big aircraft carrier, which had recently been resurrected with the authorization of CVA 59. Finally, there had been delays in the development of follow-on carrier attack aircraft, opening a window of opportunity for the attack seaplane and adding to the urgency of the P6M-1 program. In short, delays, technical problems, or cost overruns of any major proportion would jeopardize the Martin project and possibly even the entire concept. As a result, Martin instituted comprehensive cost-control measures, allocating money to each of the divisions responsible for the airplane in accordance with an agreed-upon schedule. Meanwhile, in BuAer and the office of the CNO, officers monitored the program with inputs from the bureau's representative in Baltimore.[2]

Success or failure of the XP6M-1 program lay mostly in the hands of one of Martin's vice presidents, George S. Trimble Jr. A native Philadelphian, thirty-seven-year-old Trimble had received his bachelor's degree in aeronautical engineering from MIT in 1936. A year later he started with Martin as a draftsman, working his way up and through a series of managerial positions in aerodynamics before taking over responsibility for the company's advanced designs.[3]

About fifty engineers and shop workers in Baltimore who had been involved in the second round of the design competition formed the nucleus of a much larger group that took on the XP6M-1 engineering program in the fall of 1952. A principal consideration was continuing aerodynamic and hydrodynamic testing. During the design competition, Martin got a head start with aerodynamic tests at CalTech's Cooperative Wind Tunnel and towing tests on a one-thirtieth scale model at the Stevens Institute of Technology, but there was general agreement that more extensive wind-tunnel and towing-tank tests were called for. Representatives from Martin and BuAer met with engineers at NACA's Langley lab on 10 October to discuss the status of the testing program and map out further investigations. More tests were needed on a larger, 14-percent scale model to verify some of the findings of earlier studies. Because there was only limited time available on Langley's 19-foot tunnel, some of the tests were shifted to the Wright Air Development Center in Dayton and to CalTech's Guggenheim Aeronautical Laboratory. Meanwhile, Langley carried out tests at high subsonic speeds in its 16-foot transonic tunnel and did hydrodynamic tests of a powered model built by the navy's David Taylor Model Basin.[4]

Tests continued through 1953 and into 1954, making the XP6M-1 one of the most thoroughly studied airplanes to that time. Though expensive and time consuming, the investigations were crucial to finding a balance between the high-speed aerodynamic performance of the airplane and its hydrodynamic characteristics. Data from the wind-tunnel tests indicated that the area of the horizontal tail surfaces had to be increased to provide greater control at transonic speeds, and engineers used the results of the tests to refine the layout of the engine nacelle inlets. The towing-tank tests revealed that the hydroflaps used for maneuvering in the water needed to be increased in size and moved closer to the front of the airplane; they also uncovered instabilities at certain speeds that necessitated changes in the hull form.[5]

In other areas, dynamic and static load testing enhanced the design of the hull and the wing structures. The wing skin covers, made up of three separate aluminum pieces tapering from one-half-inch thick to one-quarter-inch thick, presented difficult problems in rolling to the required tolerances. Parts of the airplane were made of specially developed bonded honeycomb sheet, and the airplane incorporated unprecedented quantities of titanium, a lightweight metal with excellent heat-resistant qualities but notoriously difficult to fabricate. Changes were made to the construction of the hull in an effort to simplify fabrication and reduce manufacturing costs, and modifications were made to increase the airplane's weapons capacity. Because one of the most innovative features of the airplane was the rotary mine bay door, Martin prepared a mockup of the door during the design competition, and had it ready for inspection after the first week of September.[6]

It did not take long for the project to run into problems with engines, which should have come as no surprise to those familiar with the difficulties of the navy's turbojet programs in the early 1950s. After much deliberation, the choice had narrowed to the J67, an 11,500-pound-thrust engine from the Wright Aeronautical Division of the Curtiss-Wright Corporation that seemed promising mostly because it produced close to the needed power without the complication of fuel-hungry afterburners. BuAer's optimism about the J67 proved short-lived, however, as the company soon fell so far behind in its development of the engine that it was obvious the J67 would not be ready in time for the XP6M-1's first scheduled flight. The Westinghouse J40, which Martin had picked for its first proposal, still looked attractive, and with afterburners it had more than the requisite power. But the J40 was also afflicted with technical problems that pushed deliveries back and eventually led to the cancellation of the program in 1953. In December 1952 BuAer informed Martin that it would not supply the engines for the XP6M-1 as government-furnished equipment, leaving the company to decide what alternative power plants were best for the airplane.[7]

Initially, Martin thought that the Bristol Olympus engine, on which the Wright J67 was based, was the best alternative. Further investigation led to the conclusion that Bristol could not deliver the engines promptly and that they would cost too much. Left with little choice, the company turned to Allison, whose 9,500-pound-thrust J71 was slated for use in the air force

Douglas RB-66 bomber, a derivative of the navy's A3D heavy attack airplane. Allison promised to modify the engine to meet Martin's needs by fitting it with a short afterburner to increase thrust to 13,000 pounds for takeoff. Although the Allison meant the XP6M-1 would have a slightly lower top speed and would have to carry an additional 3,000 pounds of fuel to attain the desired combat range, Martin decided to buy sixteen J71-A4s, plus two ground test articles and associated spare parts, at a cost of $4.3 million.[8] Everyone associated with the XP6M-1 program looked at the Allison as an interim engine pending the introduction of reliable higher capacity turbojets.

Because of the sophistication of the minelaying-navigation system and other electronic equipment in the airplane, BuAer officers in November visited the Collins Radio Corporation in Iowa and the Douglas, North American, Lockheed, and Ryan companies in California. The focus of attention during each of the stops was on how centralized electric power supplies and modular components could reduce weight, ease maintenance, and increase the reliability of the XP6M-1's electronic systems. While they were on the West Coast, the BuAer people discussed the minelaying-navigation system with aviation officers in the Pacific Fleet. They learned that the fleet had recently completed a mine warfare study, the findings of which meshed closely with the expected range and payload capacity of the Martin seaplane, although there was skepticism about the electronic mining system and whether or not mines could be accurately placed at speeds approaching 600 knots.[9]

Early in the new year, workers in Baltimore finished a mockup of the airplane for inspection by representatives of BuAer and other organizations. There were three separate reviews. During the first, beginning on 4 March 1953, officers spent three days critiquing the cockpit layout. A second panel met on 5 March to study the mockup's suitability for nuclear weapons. The formal mockup board, chaired by Commander Brown from BuAer's Aircraft Division, convened at Martin on 9 March 1953 and continued its work over the next four days. The exhaustive appraisal found little to criticize. In their report, Brown's group emphasized that the airplane was intended to "provide the United States with a weapon capable of delivering a large payload, long distances in the face of maximum enemy resistance." Not "just another general purpose patrol plane," the XP6M-1 represented a leap forward in aircraft design where the final determinant was overall weapon system performance and not simply how well a single component worked. Under that criterion, the mockup board weighed the anticipated performance of the Martin against theoretical studies of the minelaying mission based on mathematical projections and operational research.[10]

For the most part, the review board was impressed, finding few deficiencies or areas requiring urgent attention. One of the most pressing difficulties was the Aero X23B tail turret and the twin 20-mm gun installation, an automatic, radar-directed unit supplied by Westinghouse. From the outset, BuAer had not liked how low the turret was to the waterline, expecting problems with sealing and possibly wave and spray damage. A special committee undertook further review of the installation, concluding that despite its shortcomings, the tail turret was the only feasible means of defending the aircraft from attack. The rotary mine bay door received a good deal of attention, too. At one point Martin demonstrated how the door, loaded with 28,000 pounds of mines, could be lowered from the airplane, raised back into position, and rotated to release the weapons. In May the navy approved the mockup with recommended changes, clearing the way for Martin to go ahead with construction of the prototype aircraft.[11]

Through the rest of 1953 and into 1954, Martin increased its work force at its Middle River plant and forged ahead with the first example of the aircraft. Generally things went smoothly, although Martin ran into trouble with the rotary mine bay door seals, which required a redesign and additional tests before they worked satisfactorily. More worrisome were weight increases. It was not uncommon for airplanes to gain pounds as they went from paper to metal, and the SeaMaster was no exception. Not far into the program the weight empty grew from the original specification of 81,400 pounds to 86,000 pounds, leading BuAer to warn the company to institute a draconian weight control program or risk the airplane failing to meet its performance criteria. Martin quickly responded, beefing up its engineering staff in the fall of 1953 and holding weekly weight-reduction contests. By the summer of 1954 the company had the problem solved, reporting the weight empty of the airplane as 82,000 pounds, within range of specifications.[12]

The airplane's reinforced plastic wingtip floats also proved troublesome. Encouraged by BuAer to employ the new material as a means of demonstrating the cost, weight, corrosion, and fabrication advantages of fiberglass in large aircraft components, Martin subcontracted to Lunn Laminates, Inc., of Huntington Station, Long Island, for the floats. The results were discouraging. By mid-June 1955, it became apparent that the floats were overweight, over-budget, and could not pass any static tests. To make matters worse, Lunn teetered on the precipice of bankruptcy. Under pressure to cut weight and costs, Martin wanted out of the contract and wanted to abandon the plastic floats for conventional metal ones, which would have been lighter and cheaper. BuAer, still hoping to stimulate a new technology, and not wishing to lose Lunn as a supplier of other defense products, jawboned Martin into staying with Lunn and keeping the plastic floats on the XP6M-1.[13]

Model tests revealed other problems early in the development program. Hydrodynamic experiments showed that, while the airplane would be able to operate from calm water, it was likely to have difficulties in rough seas. Hull resistance was higher than expected, as was spray; in waves over 4 feet it was likely that the engines would ingest unacceptable amounts of water. Martin anticipated the problem by fitting auxiliary air doors on the outboard engine nacelles to mitigate spray ingestion and lessen the chances of engine flame-out. As for the craft's aerodynamics, they looked good except for a period of mild buffeting at about Mach .85 (560 knots). Opinions differed as to whether the buffeting would restrict the speed of the airplane or limit its ability to carry out its mission.[14]

Committed to the airplane and the SSF concept, the navy was caught in a vicious time-money cycle with the XP6M-1. The service devoted one-third of its precious aircraft development funds to the XP6M-1 in FY 1954 and 1955. In July 1953 the navy had to cancel the construction of the static test airframe in its continuing effort to impose cost restraints. At the same time Martin wanted more money for additional testing and development facilities in Baltimore to ensure completion of the program. There was little the navy could do but accede to the request if it hoped to realize a return on its investment and avoid even more costly delays. Eventually the program reached a total of $46.8 million, far in excess of original estimates, despite what the navy considered the best efforts by Martin to achieve the "utmost economy."[15]

In the spring of 1954, well before the first of the big flying boats took to the air, the SeaMaster program reached a turning point. Sensing the navy's urgency in getting an operational aircraft at the earliest possible time and confident that the SeaMaster was in good shape, Bunker wrote to BuAer in late April 1954 summarizing the status of the program to date and emphasizing that from its inception it had been meant as a fully functioning weapon system. Bunker was satisfied that the company had curbed the airplane's weight gains, that the engines would pass their qualification tests and be ready for installation on time, and that the nagging mine door seal problem had been solved. "The next logical step," he said, was to procure enough additional examples to allow evaluation of the airplane and its equipment under more rigorous fleet conditions. "There is no known way to evaluate the systems of the over-all weapon other than to actually use them under tactical conditions, find the bugs and eliminate them." He went on to request nine more airplanes plus a static test article to replace the one deleted from the XP6M-1 program, to carry out and complete a ten-month evaluation process looking toward delivering thirty SeaMasters to the fleet by mid-1958.[16]

Much as it had with Convair's Sea Dart program, the navy decided to go ahead with a preproduction contract for the SeaMaster. The navy was eager to accelerate the program and confident that Martin was proceeding well with the XP6M prototypes. BuAer's representative in Baltimore endorsed Martin's idea, concluding that "such a phase would be of immeasurable assistance in eventually supplying a proven aircraft to the fleet" and that the time had come for "full-scale operations" to see what the airplane could and could not do.[17]

Rear Adm. Apollo Soucek, BuAer chief, agreed that the program had reached the stage where a decision had to be made about concurrent development and the acquisition of additional airplanes in order to achieve operational status without unacceptable delays. In a letter to the CNO in June 1954 Soucek reported that hydrodynamic and aerodynamic testing would probably not be completed until early 1957. If the navy waited until then to make a decision about additional airplanes, deliveries to the fleet would not take place until early 1960, ensuring "that the design would approach obsolescence after a relatively short service life." Better, he wrote, to proceed with "Y"-version preproduction aircraft as soon as possible, which would allow the airplane to join the fleet as early as 1957. Soucek recommended that the navy procure an additional nine aircraft, plus one airframe for static test purposes to replace that dropped from the XP6M-1 program. The airplanes would go to the Naval Air Test Center at Patuxent River and to a squadron created specifically for additional testing and evaluation. Estimated costs were $85.4 million, of which $34 million included tooling for manufacturing 200 P6Ms at a rate of two per month.[18]

Following extensive negotiations, during which the price of the airplane escalated dramatically, the navy cut the order from nine to six, keeping a seventh for static tests. Martin received a cost-plus-fixed-fee contract for the aircraft, designated YP6M-1, on 28 January 1955. The total cost was $180.2 million, nearly $100 million more than estimated only six months before.

Hoping to keep the program from falling further behind schedule, Martin began almost immediately to install tooling and equipment at Middle River for the limited production run.[19]

Originally scheduled for completion in September 1954, the first airplane was not ready to be rolled out of the hangar until 21 December. What the sparse group of Martin employees and a selection of navy brass saw that winter day in Baltimore was impressive. The SeaMaster, painted a dark blue with white lettering, was a rakish, even menacing-looking craft unlike any seaplane they had ever seen. Few present doubted that they were witnessing the dawn of a new era of naval aviation heralded by an airplane with unprecedented capabilities for power projection. The *Washington Post* concluded that the Sea-Master, as an "important auxiliary to the carrier striking arm," could be used to fight limited conventional wars or to deliver nuclear weapons independently of air force strategic bombers.[20]

Before it could fly, the XP6M-1 underwent an exhaustive series of static and systems tests. These uncovered a nettlesome problem with the two inboard Allison engines, whose afterburners generated vibrations and excessive heat in the adjacent fuselage sufficient to cause Martin's engineers to worry about metal fatigue and failure. Strategically placed titanium panels and additional reinforcing of the hull framework and skin helped some, but did not solve the problem. In the end, Martin decided that the only solution was to reconfigure the engine nacelles so that the exhausts angled away from the fuselage. Because doing so required a major redesign, which at such a late stage of prototype construction was prohibitively expensive and would delay the program, the decision was made to implement the changes on the Y-models and for the time being use only the outboard engines' afterburners, which provided enough power to meet the navy's requirements for takeoffs at maximum weight.[21]

Static hull loading tests revealed other, more worrisome deficiencies. In February and March 1955 load tests on the rear of the airplane revealed buckling of the skin on the underside of the hull around the mine door opening, the wrinkles eventually migrating upward and aft toward the tail section. At close to the designed load limit, failures occurred in parts of the mine bay door actuating mechanism, and the horizontal stabilizers and elevators showed signs of deterioration of the honeycomb structure, which the testers concluded came from inadequate bonding of the materials. Spot welds on the leading edge of the vertical fin also failed, necessitating further delays while the company repaired the damage and beefed up the parts of the airplane that had failed or might fail below the estimated structural limits.[22]

Martin and the navy had high expectations for the aircraft's Aero X-23A minelaying-navigation system, the electronic heart of the airplane and rightly considered crucial for the success of the entire SSF concept. Supplied by General Precision Labs in New York, the system used a Doppler radar, long-range and short-range computers, and a gyroscopically stabilized inertial platform to provide navigation during the cruise to the vicinity of the objective, the high-speed run-in to the target, weapons release according to a preset sequence, and the return flight to base—all without input from the crew. Not surprisingly, given the ambitious nature of the task, there were problems and delays. The system was not ready for flight testing in the second XP6M-1, nor was it completed in time for the first flights of the YP6M-1 three years later.[23]

Not as critical as the minelaying-navigation system, the Aero X-23B tail turret also caused more than its share of headaches for the Martin team. From the start, no one had been happy with the installation, yet no one could think of any alternatives. In July 1955 the BuAer representative in Baltimore reported that the project was over budget and behind schedule. The low temperatures and high vibrations expected in the tail of the airplane degraded the performance of the unit, Westinghouse had not been able to design an adequate watertight seal, and the hydraulic system needed to be upgraded. Another $300,000 would be needed to correct the deficiencies and get the project back on track. BuAer concurred with the recommendation that installation of the turret in the XP6M-1 would be "unsatisfactory and costly" and that it was better to delete the turret from the XP6M-1 and reevaluate its necessity for the YP6M-1.[24]

In the meantime, the SeaMaster project moved toward the first test flights. In addition to the usual sensors and gauges, engineers fitted the first airplane with a special instrumentation panel at the minelaying-navigation station in the airplane, to be monitored by a flight test engineer. Taxi tests, which began on 23 June, showed up problems in the J71 engines, a portent of things to come but not considered insurmountable at the time. Finally, on 14 July 1955 came the long-awaited day when the airplane taxied down the ramp at Middle River and out into Chesapeake Bay for its first flight. Lasting more than an hour and a half, the flight was "uneventful," according to George A. Rodney, one of Martin's most experienced test pilots, who had the controls most of the time. Yet he spoke too soon, for the airplane exhibited a mild aerodynamic buffeting (described also as a "shake" or "buzz") at certain speeds. Anticipated by the tests at Langley, the idiosyncrasy, while not considered serious at the time, raised questions about the soundness of the basic design and would need resolution before the airplane went into service.[25]

Through the rest of the summer and into the fall, the XP6M-1 was in the air on a regular basis, as the company explored the airplane's characteristics and sought solutions to nagging problems. Aerodynamically, the airplane looked good, with few vices other than the vibration phenomenon; hydrodynamic performance was about as expected, with good stability up to and through the critical hump speed. The Allison J71s, however, gave no end of problems, suffering from persistent weld and fatigue cracking and compressor blade failures. Rotations of the mine door in flight caused only minor buffeting. In Martin's upbeat press release on the XP6M-1, issued on 27 September, Bunker emphasized that the flight test program was "well ahead of the most optimistic predictions," and the navy described the new airplane as "unusually promising."[26]

On some early flights the airplane reached a speed of Mach .90 in a shallow glide, so fast that the North American FJ-2 chase plane had a hard time keeping up. The airframe vibration remained, but it seemed to diminish at higher speeds and did not in any way affect the overall stability of the airplane, which according to all indications was excellent. Hydrodynamics, always a major consideration in high-performance seaplanes, were also good, and a spray problem that cropped up in early taxi tests had been eliminated. Nor did the airplane exhibit any porpoising or skipping. The hydroflaps worked well, after changes were made to the actuating mechanism in response to failures during taxi tests. On one flight the mine bay door seal failed, partially flooding the compartment and causing the airplane to rest lower in the water, but otherwise it handled normally.[27]

Hardly an operational aircraft yet, the SeaMaster nevertheless caught the attention of the air force brass in October. In a speech in Miami on 8 October, Gen. Thomas D. White, the air force vice chief of staff, commented that new engines and other technical developments "may enable the water-based bomber to take its place alongside other Air Force airplanes and missiles" in the strategic role. White suggested, too, that the P6M or a successor could fit into his service's aircraft nuclear propulsion (ANP) program. Although the idea now seems ludicrous, if only because of the dangers of an accident on the ground or in the air, nuclear power for airplanes attracted much attention at the time, offering a seemingly irresistible combination of high speed and virtually unlimited range compared to conventionally powered aircraft. Convair even got so far as converting one of its gigantic B-36 intercontinental bombers in 1955 to carry a small nuclear reactor to test shielding and the radiation resistance of aircraft components. White sent a strong message to the navy: "It is conceivable that a nuclear-powered water-based aircraft may become an effective bomber suitable for the Air Force's wartime strategic bombing mission."[28]

Secretary of the Navy Charles S. Thomas was quick to respond to what he and others saw as an air force challenge to the navy's traditional roles and missions. The P6M "promises to be a potent supplement to the new Navy," he said. Nuclear-powered or otherwise, "to achieve its fullest potential, the modern seaplane must be supported and assisted by other ships and integrated with the other offensive team members of the new Navy." In other words, the SeaMaster was a navy project, and the navy could best determine how it would be employed.[29]

At the same time, the navy maintained that another service could not have proprietary or exclusive ownership of a weapon it needed for its own missions. Rather than risk compromising a position that gave the navy a moral claim to nuclear weapons or have the P6M become the focus of an interservice feud such as the one that had embroiled the supercarrier, Thomas S. Combs, now a vice admiral and DCNO (Air), circulated a conciliatory memorandum reminding the air force of the navy's long experience in the "seaplane business" and offering to help with any air force missions that might require a weapon with the P6M's capabilities.[30]

A highlight of the initial testing program was a visit to the factory on the morning of 2 November by Adm. Arleigh Burke, who had become CNO two and a half months earlier. Joining him were Lord Louis Mountbatten of the Royal Navy, BuAer Chief Rear Adm. James S. Russell, and a huge retinue from the press. On the tour the VIPs had a close-up look at the second XP6M-1, which had only recently been completed, and took choice spots on the company's yacht to observe high-speed taxi runs out in the Chesapeake and a dramatic low-altitude flyover. Russell recalled that "the aircraft was beautiful, graceful in lines" and that "our distinguished guests were favorably impressed and made many enthusiastic and laudatory comments."[31] It seemed to everyone that the SeaMaster program had the worst of its problems behind it and that the SSF would soon become part of the navy's and the nation's strategic arsenal.

# Seven

# New Look,
# New Missions

By 1953 only the most skeptical critics of naval aviation could dispute that Convair's and Martin's advanced seaplane projects offered a way for the navy to maintain and even expand its striking power in the event of general war. Operating from advanced bases, the SSF provided the navy with the capability of containing and destroying the Soviet Union's submarine fleet, while at the same time bringing naval air power to bear against the enemy's land-based forces. Carrier aviation had once more demonstrated its worth in the Korean War, and with money flowing freely again, the navy could look forward to more of its coveted large-deck carriers. *Forrestal* (CVA-59) and follow-on sister ships, operating long-range jet attack aircraft—some armed with nuclear weapons—gave the navy additional strategic punch. For the first time since the crisis of 1949–50, the navy seemed to have regained its sea legs and its reason for being.

All that changed with the new administration of President Dwight D. Eisenhower, who came into office determined to end the Korean War and impose fiscal discipline in Washington. No friend of the navy, he regarded its big ships as useless in a general war. Eisenhower charged his advisers with finding means of maintaining the nation's security on a minimum budget. Not surprisingly, the president's mandate earned him the enmity of the Joint Chiefs of Staff, who resisted all efforts at retrenchment and reform. Moreover, the president's own policy makers found the task of ensuring a maximum defense with a minimum of money to be impossible, with the result that the administration's defense statements had a confusing duality to them that did nothing to simplify the navy's job of defining its mission.[1]

Out of these circumstances came NSC 162/2, which set the tone for the administration's military policy through the remainder of the decade. Endorsed by the National Security Council on 30 October 1953, the document emphasized that the nation's military strength lay in the "capability of inflicting massive retaliatory damage by offensive striking power." It did not take much reading between the lines to understand that the emphasis of what came to be called the "New Look" would be on deterrence, and that the threat of nuclear weapons delivered against the Soviet Union by the long-range bombers of the air force Strategic Air Command would be enough to prevent the outbreak of wars big and small. The expectation was that the new policy would allow significant personnel and budget reductions while ensuring the nation's security.[2]

Under the "New Look," cost considerations assumed precedence in all military programs, forcing the navy once again to reappraise its budgets and priorities. BuAer's funding for new aircraft fell by $35 million in FY 1953, from $640 million in 1952, resulting in a decrease in aircraft procurement from 3,797 to 2,649. In successive reductions in late 1952 and early 1953, the navy's original FY 1954 aircraft procurement wound up being cut by 1,200 aircraft. For 1955 the number of aircraft to be acquired dipped to 1,368. Although the procurement total rose to 1,613 for the next fiscal year, it was less than half the peak of 1952.[3]

Facing cuts for the first time since 1950, navy leaders scrambled to find a role that would salvage as much of the fleet and its personnel as possible. Admiral Carney, who had become CNO not long after Eisenhower took office, addressed the dilemma by first securing agreement among the members of the JCS in 1954 that aircraft carriers needed to be included as part of the nation's strategic capability. He also created OP-93, the Long-Range Objectives Group, to survey the geopolitical scene and suggest avenues the navy could follow to enhance its technological and operational capabilities.[4]

Carney confronted a difficult task in getting the navy to fit the mold of the "New Look," which demanded a shift in the navy's strategic thinking. From a broad maritime strategy that required a balanced "mix" of forward-based forces to bring sea power to bear against a continental nation, the navy had to adopt one that emphasized more dispersed units capable of surviving nuclear attack and threatening the enemy's war-making capability. Directly or indirectly, naval forces had to support the nation's strategic deterrent while simultaneously fulfilling their other responsibilities for conducting antisubmarine warfare, defending sea lines of communications, fighting small "brushfire" wars, and "showing the flag" in peacetime.[5]

Within that context, weapons demonstrating both flexibility and low cost had an advantage over those intended for a narrower range of missions. As a result, the thinking about the SSF focused on its assets of mobility, range, and stealth. Martin had conceived of the SeaMaster almost from the start as a component of the integrated attack force, capable of fulfilling its original preemptive offensive role of defeating Soviet submarines before they could threaten the nation's sea lines of communication and delivering conventional ordnance against a variety of land targets, as well as contributing to the new deterrent strategy through its nuclear delivery capability. Martin saw its airplane as an element in a larger system, supported by small, less costly ships with more modest logistical requirements than a large carrier battle group.

Full exploitation of the SeaMaster's capabilities depended to a large extent on the development of an integrated basing and maintenance system for the SSF. BuAer's Brown understood this from the outset, writing in July 1952 that the "new generation" of attack seaplanes would spend a large proportion of their operational lives on the water and would not, like their forebears, be hoisted aboard tenders for routine maintenance. "Thus the requirement exists," he went on, "for improved waterborne maintenance methods," including floating service docks and transportable marine railways on seaplane tenders to allow the aircraft to be taken out of the water for more extensive work. All vessels supporting the new flying boats needed to have spaces and equipment for repairing and maintaining the complex electronic suites on the aircraft in addition to a wide variety of mines, bombs (nuclear and conventional), guided missiles, torpedoes, and depth charges. It made no sense, Brown pointed out, to have a 600-knot seaplane on the water for hours while it was being rearmed and refueled, and its crew transferred to the airplane when it was finally ready for the mission. Only if these "lost time items" were eliminated could the attack seaplane achieve a "bright and useful future in Naval Warfare."[6]

In October 1952, shortly after Martin received the SeaMaster contract, BuAer contracted with the company to explore ideas about providing support for the P6M and other elements of the SSF. In July 1953 Martin completed the preliminary study, emphasizing that the SSF gave the navy "a new offensive potential of tremendous power and flexibility at moderate cost." As conceived, the force was to have three major components: striking, service, and defensive units. The striking unit consisted of from four to eight P6Ms, supported by the service unit, which was made up of modified LSDs, oilers, ammunition ships, and submarines modified as tankers. At the heart of the defensive unit was Convair's Sea Dart, still awaiting its first test flight in San Diego but generally thought to be on the way to becoming a potent fighter-interceptor. Long-range flying boats—modified Martin P5Ms and a follow-on open-ocean seaplane—functioned in the ASW role. The plan foresaw a staged array of bases stretching from existing facilities in the United States to advanced mobile bases close to the theater. Across the globe were innumerable bays, inlets, fjords, lagoons, and river deltas that afforded protection for the force as it deployed in preparation for the attack. Open ocean operations were also feasible. Mobility meant that aircraft could fly from one base and return to another, if need be, reducing the vulnerability of the forward bases and complicating the enemy's problems of detection and defense.[7]

Among the features of the Martin study was the use of refueling submarines. The idea of submarines—relatively inexpensive and stealthy—was not new, originating before World War II and reemerging in Convair's 1948 operations study and Carney's 1949 logistics report. A modified tanker submarine surfaced at a rendezvous point, where the aircraft taxied into position astern and engaged a towing bridle. Replenishment took place under way, after which the submarine submerged, heading for another rendezvous, while the seaplane took off to complete its mission. The procedure expanded the versatility of attack aircraft by permitting them to trade off range, fuel, and payload capacities depending on the mission, weapons, and targets while minimizing the need for fixed bases in proximity to the enemy.

To realize the full potential of the system, the Martin study stressed novel means of maximizing aircraft availability by minimizing turnaround times and streamlining servicing, maintenance, and repair. Submerged rubber fuel caches and buoys allowed refueling several aircraft simultaneously at the advanced base, while doing away with the usual lighters and their crews. A submersible dry dock, consisting of individual transportable aluminum sections, accommodated fully loaded seaplanes offshore and obviated the need for beaching the aircraft except for the most extensive repairs. For routine servicing, a smaller floating platform, using interchangeable dry dock sections, could be attached to the airplane while it sat in the water. More out of the ordinary was Martin's proposal for an air-portable dock, developed by Britain's Saunders-Roe company, that consisted of inflatable rubber sections arranged in varying configurations for emergency repairs or maintenance.

Initially, Martin saw no need for a new, large tender to support the Sea-Master and other aircraft of the striking force. Instead, the company proposed the modification of an LSD to carry supplies and spares, and to provide space for heavy maintenance. Because of the size of the new aircraft, it was not feasible, even with the largest ships and equipment, to hoist the heavy aircraft clear of the water, as was done with conventional seaplane tenders. Martin proposed instead that the well deck of an LSD be fitted with flexible ramps contoured to the shape of the seaplanes' hulls. The well deck flooded when the stern of the ship was submerged, allowing the aircraft to float in and out, guided by cars running along the top of the deck. When the ship's stern was raised, the aircraft was lifted clear of the water and secured, the ramps providing unobstructed space underneath for routine maintenance and repairs, and reloading of the SeaMaster's mine bay door. If the airplane did not need to be taken aboard ship, a ramp or stabilized walkway with a power-driven conveyor could be extended from the ship to allow loading ordnance or other stores. A year later the navy gave Martin a contract to construct prototypes of the beaching vehicle and the dry dock, and provided funding for more detailed studies of the floating service platform and armament equipment.[8]

In 1953 the Office of Naval Research awarded Martin a contract to prepare a study of basing concepts for high-performance seaplanes. Completed in October 1954, Martin's analysis began with the premise that the "New Look" had forced a reevaluation of the forward deployment of strategic weapon systems needed for the nuclear retaliatory mission. Martin examined all the variables affecting the employment of water-based aircraft, including their anticipated roles, operational and economic factors, handling and maneuvering problems, specific aircraft designs, and the relative merits of land-basing versus sea-basing. Four categories of aircraft received attention: heavy attack, light attack, fighter, and transport. Martin people visited army and navy bases, examined intelligence information, and interviewed military personnel. The Scandinavian peninsula served as a model because of the complexity of its topography and its nearness to the Soviet Union. Not surprisingly, the study concluded that water-basing provided a nearly ideal combination of reduced cost and increased flexibility, both considered essential to maximizing the nation's strategic power. The study also recommended the development of a large seaplane transport to haul equipment and troops to forward areas. A result of the Martin study was a proposal for the Model 307 SeaMistress, a 500,000-pound, eight-engine flying boat specifically intended for heavy logistical support.[9]

In November 1954 BuAer completed a revealing study comparing the SSF to the carrier task force. It found that twenty P6Ms and five tanker submarines could deliver about the same weight of bombs as twenty-four A3D twin-engine jet bombers operating from two *Midway*-class carriers. More specifically, the analysis determined that each carrier could launch three strikes, delivering 612,000 pounds of ordnance at ranges up to 1,100 nautical miles from the ship before having to retire for more fuel and stores. In contrast, twenty P6Ms could haul 600,000 pounds of bombs on three strikes out to 1,600 nautical miles using tanker submarines before needing replenishment. More than 13,500 men were needed to man the two carrier task forces, compared to a mere 510 for the attack seaplane force. On cost alone, the SSF made sense. The study estimated that it cost $683 million for the two carrier task forces versus only $165 million for the twenty flying boats and their supporting equipment. A dispersed SSF also had tactical advantages that the tightly knit carrier task force did not. Whereas the carrier force could hit only a small area of the shoreline at extreme range, the SSF's tankers could be arrayed over a wider expanse closer to the objectives, allowing simultaneous attacks over much more enemy territory.[10]

Parallel to BuAer's work was a long-range study of shipbuilding programs by an ad hoc committee chaired by Admiral Combs, the DCNO (Air). Formed in April 1954 to project the service's ship and aircraft requirements through the 1960s, the committee completed its study on 20 December 1954. The committee estimated that carrier aircraft would be supplanted in the strategic role by long-range, surface-to-surface missile systems and by attack seaplanes capable of delivering nuclear weapons. More to the point, the study concluded that "a D-Day force of approximately 72 high performance attack seaplanes will be required in FY 1962–70 for the functions of reconnaissance, mining, and of providing a dispersed, long-range nuclear delivery system for deterring or waging nuclear war."

Completely self-supporting, the SSF would operate from remote, "moderately defended" mobile bases, the aircraft refueled and serviced from surface ships and submarines. The force would be organized into basic task units consisting of twelve attack seaplanes each, supported by one large attack seaplane tender (AVA), one light tender (AVL), one submarine tanker (AOSS), and one small refueler (AVO) located in the forward area. Large cargo seaplanes would provide logistic support. To back up the force, the navy would need by 1962 four AVAs for major repairs at main bases, four AVLs for support at the advanced or mobile bases, six AVOs, and six submarines for refueling at sea either transiting to the advanced bases or en route to their targets. All of the immediate ship requirements could be met by conversion of existing vessels, although new AVAs were desirable to meet the long-term requirements of the force. The estimated cost through 1970 of all conversions and new ship construction was $180 million.

In contrast to earlier concepts, which stressed the attack seaplane's role in a conventional maritime conflict, Combs's committee saw the SSF as inherent to the national nuclear deterrent—quickly deployable, highly mobile, and dispersed in such a manner as to render it largely invulnerable to concentrated attack. Flying from advanced bases 1,500–3,000 miles from their targets, the aircraft would be refueled 500–1,500 miles out by surface ships or submarines. A minimum of two task units would face the Soviet Union from the eastern Mediterranean, and one would be stationed in the western Pacific; a fourth could provide a peacetime presence in the Indian Ocean, poised to deliver an attack on the "exposed southern flanks" of the Soviet Union if war should break out. Eventually, the ships and aircraft of the SSF would supplant carrier heavy attack aircraft in the long-range nuclear delivery mission, carrier aircraft would become smaller and more versatile, and the carriers themselves would be reduced in size as they were phased out of the strategic role.[11]

At the same time, in December 1954, Admiral Carney examined the P6M program in light of the problems it was having and the budgetary limitations dictated by Eisenhower's "New Look." In 1949, as DCNO (Logistics), Carney had been "profoundly impressed" by the strategic possibilities of a "family" of high-performance seaplanes, particularly in light of their advantages of mobility and reduced logistical requirements. Now, "the fundamental conclusions, arrived at in connection with those earlier studies, still appear to be sound. If anything, the validity is enhanced by international developments that place a premium on flexibility and being independent of permissive arrangements with other countries. Quite obviously, the development of any significant seaplane program must go hand in hand with some modification of strategic thinking, reconsideration of certain aspects of existing plans, and the development of supporting plans of both operational and logistical character." He concluded that the program needed reinforcement and encouragement from above and recommended the appointment of a project manager to oversee and expedite the program.[12]

Another Martin study in the spring of 1955 amplified earlier examinations of the attack seaplane concept. Looking ahead five years and assuming that large (100,000 pounds or more) water-based aircraft could perform a variety of tactical missions as well as or better than their land-based counterparts, Martin stressed that the navy could realize important economies in logistics and personnel costs by expanding its commitment to seaplanes. The mobility of seaplanes in effect gave them greater range than land-based aircraft, while enhancing their defensive capability. Although similar to a carrier battle group in being a "self-contained" unit, the SSF required smaller and less expensive ships, and could rely entirely on air transport in remote areas. If need be, a seaplane fighter-bomber force could be concealed along a river such as the Volga, deep within enemy territory, supplied completely by air, and virtually invulnerable to counterattack. In the event of a nuclear attack, a water-based force was less likely to suffer damage than a land-based one.

A close reading of the Martin study revealed obvious problems. Foremost was Martin's assertion that the hydro-ski would be the key to major improvements in future seaplane performance. Even more problematic was the conclusion that future attack seaplanes would be high-density, nonbuoyant aircraft; after they landed on their skis, they would have to taxi to the ship or onto the beach for recovery. This meant the seaplane force would have to operate near a suitable beach or in calm waters where ships could safely bring the aircraft aboard, thus restricting the mobility Martin considered one of their principal advantages.[13] The reduced cost of the seaplane, attributable mostly to the elimination of the need for fixed runways, evaporated as larger numbers of strike aircraft generated more sorties over an extended period.

Even though it had lost the attack seaplane contract to Martin, Convair, with its XP5Y-1 and Sea Dart, still had a big stake in the SSF concept. On its own initiative, the company went ahead with studies of seaplane basing and mobility that underscored the navy's ideas about a flexible, sea-based striking force. In June 1955 Ernest Stout published an article summarizing the company's ideas about such a force. No one questioned the strategic value of the carrier task force, which during World War II had demonstrated its enormous advantages of mobility and firepower. At the same time, it was apparent that keeping the carriers in close proximity to a beachhead to provide air support during an amphibious landing negated the ships' principal attributes and left them vulnerable to enemy air attack. Would it not be better, Stout argued, to deploy a waterborne air unit using relatively inexpensive support ships and tenders to supply air cover to forces ashore, and liberate the carriers for other offensive operations?

For Stout, the possibilities for such a force were virtually "unlimited." It was easy to concentrate the numbers of aircraft needed to "saturate" the air over the landing force and protect the shore bases as they were built. The landing zone could be spread out over a wider area, complicating the enemy's defense and decreasing the vulnerability of the friendly force to counterattack. Stout observed that in the nuclear age dispersal was even more vital, because a single weapon could easily wipe out the entire force. Aircraft ranges could be enhanced by refueling from a submarine or a surface ship, damaged aircraft could land anywhere off shore, and all-weather operations were easier because precise shipboard landings were not necessary. Echoing Martin's earlier study, Stout forecast that water-based aircraft could provide much of the logistical support for a seaplane attack unit.[14]

Convair had just the airplane to meet the requirement. Despite the loss of the XP5Y-1 in 1953, the navy saw enough promise in the design to go ahead with a transport version of the big Convair flying boat, designated the R3Y-1 and known as the Tradewind. Convair had received a contract for three of the aircraft in August 1950, followed by an agreement for five more in February 1951. Looking much like the XP5Y-1, the Tradewind was more than 12 feet longer, and at 145,000 pounds, it was nearly 22,000 pounds heavier. It also had an upgraded wing, and revised vertical and horizontal tail surfaces. The troublesome Allison turboprops were moved into nacelles above the wing. The capacious hull could accommodate eighty passengers or 24 tons of cargo. The airplane flew for the first time on 25 February 1954. Almost exactly one year later, the fourth aircraft demonstrated its long-range capabilities with a nonstop flight from San Diego 2,400 miles across the country to Patuxent River at an average speed of more than 400 miles per hour. A slightly larger version of the airplane, the R3Y-2, provided additional flexibility with a hinged bow permitting roll-on, roll-off accessibility.[15]

Support ships as well as aircraft would be needed if the SSF was to be transformed from concept into reality. Using the Martin and Convair basing studies as a general outline, the navy in the late summer of 1955 identified vessels suitable to supply and maintain the force. Although Martin had proposed using only an LSD, it was clear that the first priority was a bigger ship. The 8,700-ton seaplane tender *Albemarle* (AV-5), completed in 1939 and a veteran of World War II in the Pacific, had been mothballed since 1950. It was large enough to supply and maintain the P6M and other aircraft and to accommodate aircrew and related personnel. Beginning in the late summer of 1955, Martin people and Bureau of Ships officers collaborated on the conversion, which included a large servicing boom and a stern ramp to allow the SeaMaster to be hauled out of the water. The ramp was a minor engineering challenge in itself. It was retractable and, supported by buoyancy tanks, extended more than 100 feet aft of the ship. Light yet robust enough to carry the 40-ton empty weight of the SeaMaster, the ramp included a rubber-tired beaching vehicle that drew the aircraft up to the ship along tracks. Secure spaces for handling nuclear weapons also had to be built into the vessel. The $14 million conversion started at the Philadelphia Naval Shipyard in February 1956, with a second tender, *Currituck* (AV-7) to follow.[16]

Though smaller than the AV, the LSD had the advantage of its well deck, which in the case of the 4,800-ton World War II–vintage *Ashland*-class ships had ample room to accommodate the Sea Dart and the much larger SeaMaster. In the summer of 1954 Convair carried out successful open-sea tests of one of its YF2Y-1s with the *Ashland*-class LSD *Belle Grove* (LSD-2) and the newer *Catamount* (LSD-17), both of which had been modified with 60-foot stern ramps to allow the aircraft to use its beaching gear. In the summer of 1957 *Ashland* (LSD-1) itself conducted experiments with a P5M-2 to demonstrate the feasibility of using the landing ship as a tender for big flying boats. The demonstration went well enough for the navy in 1958 to authorize conversion of *Ashland* and a sister, *White Marsh* (LSD-8), to handle the P6M. Later plans included fitting a *Commencement Bay*–class escort carrier with a stern ramp similar to *Albemarle*'s and two servicing booms instead of the one in the seaplane tender.[17]

From the beginning of the SSF concept, submarines stood out as potentially ideal platforms to supply seaplanes in forward areas. The World War II *Balao*-class submarine *Guavina* (SS-362), which had already been refitted with tanks to handle bulk cargoes, went to the Philadelphia Naval Shipyard in the first part of 1955 to be converted for refueling seaplanes. The modifications included a large square platform over the stern, soon known as the "flight deck." Back in service as a submarine oiler in January 1956, the vessel trained with a squadron of P5Ms in the Caribbean in the spring of 1956.[18]

While the navy took steps to create a fleet of support vessels for the SSF, Convair and Martin continued their respective aircraft programs. Problems persisted with Convair's Sea Dart. Try as they might, Convair's engineers could not resolve the problems associated with the Sea Dart's hydro-ski at speeds just before takeoff. The first YF2Y-1 (the second Sea Dart after the program had been reconfigured) began flight testing in the spring of 1954. Testing uncovered more vibration, which could only be mitigated and not eliminated. Nevertheless, on one flight in August 1954, the airplane flew faster than Mach 1, becoming the first seaplane to exceed the speed of sound.[19]

By the fall of 1954 Convair and the navy decided that it was time for a dramatic demonstration to highlight their new aircraft and generate public and official interest in the mobile base concept. On 4 November 1954 Convair personnel, high-ranking navy and marine officers, and the press gathered at the Convair plant for the show, which featured the R3Y-1, the YF2Y-1, and one of the most unusual navy aircraft of all time, the turboprop XFY-1, a "tail-sitter" vertical takeoff and landing fighter intended to be used from small ships and open areas ashore. After flights by the R3Y-1 and the XFY-1, the Sea Dart was next, taking off and accelerating rapidly east across the bay before turning back to make a high-speed, low-level run in front of the spectators. Then tragedy struck. The airplane suddenly pitched down and exploded in a ball of flame, falling into the water and killing Convair test pilot Charles Richbourg.[20]

The investigation revealed that the accident had been caused by pilot error. At the start of the high-speed run, Richbourg had ignited the afterburners, causing the airplane to pitch down slightly. Richbourg corrected for the movement, in the process inadvertently starting a longitudinal oscillation that almost instantly created aerodynamic forces that exceeded the airplane's structural limits. The wings sheared off at the roots where they joined the fuselage and the engines broke away from their mounts moments before the airplane caught fire and exploded. Early high-speed aircraft had powered hydraulic controls that could be overridden by the pilot under some circumstances. Unless great care was taken, it was possible to induce extreme control surface movements that could quickly lead to the destruction of the airplane. Neither Convair nor the navy thought the accident was due to anything fundamentally wrong with the airplane, and the Sea Dart program continued as part of the SSF.[21]

On the other side of the country, Martin concentrated on the SeaMaster, which, if it were to be considered an element in the country's deterrent package, had to demonstrate its ability to deliver nuclear weapons. During discussions at BuAer in August 1951 of the outline specifications for the attack seaplane, there were questions regarding the size and configuration of atomic weapons and how the airplane was to carry and deliver them as part of its secondary mission. The flexibility of the SeaMaster's mine bay facilitated fitting and delivering nuclear weapons, too. During the mockup inspection of the airplane in March 1953, a group including representatives from the Naval Air Special Weapons Facility at Kirtland Air Force Base spent a day examining the layout of the mine bay and recommended modifications to suit nuclear weapons. It was clear by the summer of 1954 that the SeaMaster was to deliver a wide range of nuclear weapons, among them the MK 5 and MK 7 implosion bombs, the MK 8 and MK 91 gun-type bombs for use against such "hardened" targets as submarine pens, the MK 90 Alias Betty depth charge, the TX 12 BOAR nuclear standoff missile, and the MK 15 thermonuclear, or hydrogen, bomb. Martin test-fit these weapons in the first XP6M-1 in September 1955 and modified the airplane's design so that they could be loaded through the access door on the top of the hull while the airplane was waterborne. Drawings from 1956 tests show two 7,600-pound MK 15 bombs in cradles attached to the rotary mine bay door.[22]

By the spring of 1956 Martin was well along with a detailed study of the SeaMaster's capabilities to deliver multiple nuclear weapons and requested secret information from the Los Alamos Scientific Laboratory regarding the characteristics of those weapons. Throughout the year Martin, the navy, and the special weapons people at Kirtland cooperated to ensure that the airplane was fully compatible with nuclear weapons. BuAer also thought it worthwhile to equip one of the XP6M-1s with instruments to study the effects of nuclear explosions on the airplane; the bureau hoped to have the aircraft ready by the end of 1957, so that it could participate in Operation Hardtack, a series of nuclear tests at Eniwetok, Bikini, and Johnston islands in the spring and summer of 1958. Nuclear weapons were to be more thoroughly tested in the pre-production YP6M-1s, including the new "lightweight," 1,900-pound MK 28 thermonuclear bomb.[23]

Enthusiasm for the capabilities of the SeaMaster as a nuclear delivery platform and for the SSF as a mobile striking force seemed to have no bounds in the fall of 1955. Officers from the CNO's office, the bureaus, and the fleet held a "seaplane symposium" at the Pentagon on 29 November to talk about the numbers of aircraft and how they might be deployed in a major conflict. Rear Adm. Paul H. Ramsey from the CNO's office praised the P6M as a "great advancement in the seaplane art," as did Cdr. M. E. Haller, who liked the idea of "small, highly mobile groups" that could strike "quickly when needed." The consensus was that in the Atlantic seventy-two P6Ms in six squadrons would be available, along with three AVs, four LSDs, and eight submarine tankers. From a major base in the United States the force would quickly advance to

Iceland, the Shetland Islands, and southern France, where strikes could be launched against the Soviet Union. Operators liked the intrinsic flexibility of the seaplane force, which could also be used for ASW, mining, long-range reconnaissance, and air refueling.[24]

Meanwhile, continued flight testing of the XP6M-1 yielded no answers to the persistent vibration problem without revealing anything so severe as to threaten the program. Through November, the airplane had successfully completed flights in which the fully loaded mine bay door was rotated in flight and dummy weapons released. On other tests, the airplane reached an altitude of 46,000 feet, a speed of Mach .95 in a dive, and Mach .85 in level flight—notable because the airplane still had the lower power interim engines. Despite the vibration problem and persistent afterburner malfunctions, the navy thought by the end of November that the test program had advanced to the point where an evaluation team from the Naval Air Test Center at Patuxent River was detailed to work with Martin test pilots. The group arrived in Baltimore on 5 December and began acquainting themselves with the airplane and the company's procedures.[25]

The following day Martin and navy pilots took the airplane out for the first familiarization flight, only to be disappointed to find that the afterburners would not work properly and that takeoffs in the rough water of Chesapeake Bay were impossible. Weather and water conditions were better the next day. Four were aboard on 7 December: Maurice B. Bernhard, a Martin test pilot, in the right seat; a navy evaluation pilot in the left seat; and a Martin flight test engineer and flight engineer in the two crew positions behind them. The morning flight was uneventful. That afternoon a different navy pilot, Lt. Cdr. Victor Utgoff, took his place in the left seat, and the airplane took off a little after 1500, heading south down the bay toward the mouth of the Potomac River. Less than fifteen minutes later, while descending under full power from 8,700 feet just east of St. George's Island, Maryland, and not far from Patuxent River, the airplane exploded in midair and crashed into the Potomac. When boats arrived at the scene minutes later, they found that all four of the crew had perished.[26]

As soon as he learned of the accident, BuAer Chief James Russell dashed off a message to the bureau representative in Baltimore: "Regret the penalty to seaplane pioneering suffered in the crash of the XP6M. I trust reasons can be found and corrections made. Please extend my deepest sympathy to the families of those who lost their lives." George Rodney, Martin's chief test pilot, flew to Patuxent River to help with the investigation into what had caused the big flying boat to go down. A navy salvage vessel arrived the next day, initiating a recovery operation that lasted through the end of the year. Investigators found that the cockpit voice recorder had failed, that there had been no chase plane in the air, and that there had been no radio contact with the airplane. Nevertheless, after three months of salvage operations, the navy located 90 percent of the wreckage and painstakingly assembled it in one of the hangars at Patuxent River. Helping the process were eyewitnesses on the ground, who gave clear and consistent descriptions of what they had seen, and the film of the instrument panel readings, which had somehow survived the explosion and impact.[27]

At the end of one of the most exhaustive aviation accident investigations in navy history, involving more than 100 people and lasting more than four months, it was clear what had happened to the doomed airplane; it was not so obvious why it had happened. At about 5,000 feet, the airplane suddenly pitched over at a sharp angle—a longitudinal divergence, in engineering parlance—imposing enormous stresses on the airframe that tore the engines loose and caused the wings to fold entirely under the airplane before they broke away. Moments later a fire broke out in the aft part of the airplane, flashing forward and triggering an explosion or explosions that ripped the craft to shreds. Utgoff and Bernhard did not have time to exit the airplane. Both flight engineers did get out, but one was knocked unconscious and drowned in the river, and the other's parachute did not fully deploy. The investigatory panel ruled out engine malfunctions, hydraulic system breakdowns, or major structural failures, and concluded that the fire occurred after the airplane had begun to disintegrate under the fierce aerodynamic loads. Pilot error was a possibility, even though the navy pilot had almost 5,000 hours of experience, much of it in large flying boats. The panel could not, however, determine what had caused the accident, and suggested only that it might have been a result of some failure in the actuating mechanism of the horizontal stabilizer. Alterations the panel recommended for the second prototype and the YP6M-1 included changes to the hydraulic control system, the addition of limiters on the horizontal stabilizer control system, and ejection seats for the entire crew. A telemetry system went into the second XP6M-1 to provide additional data from test flights.[28]

Navy confidence in the SeaMaster program remained high despite the devastating loss of the first airplane. In a press announcement, the navy pledged its support for the SeaMaster and SSF programs, and promised Martin that it would continue with acquisition of the six YP6M-1 preproduction airplanes. The navy comptroller reported on 1 February 1956 that through FY 1956, $160,908,000 had been committed to the XP6M-1 and YP6M-1 programs. The airplane was the "first of a type which should be an extremely good one. The accident has not altered long-range plans." In Congress, Admiral Burke "enthusiastically proclaimed that the navy had entered the Forrestal-Seamaster era," placing the airplane on a par with the first of the navy's supercarriers as a major weapon system.[29]

Evidence of the navy's commitment to the SeaMaster and the SSF is apparent in a detailed study of naval aviation by the office of the DCNO (Air) that appeared on 1 February 1956. The study projected level funding and a decline in the number of aircraft procured over the next several fiscal years, while at the same time the navy needed to keep pace with the latest technology to avoid obsolescence. A major concern was the "slippage" of aircraft development projects, caused by tough, but not unforeseen, engineering and technical obstacles, among them turbojet engine designs. "These difficulties are often not discovered until a few of the new articles are actually and intensively flown," warned the report. The result was that despite the inception of the Fleet Introduction of Replacement Models (FIRM) program after the Korean War, it took an inordinate amount of time to obtain new operational aircraft. The solution was to use proven technology wherever possible, ensure that all aircraft undergo rigorous testing programs, including static test articles, and procure at least fifteen examples of each new airplane for flight testing and evaluation.

Projecting requirements to 1964, the study forecast a "substantial increase" in all-weather fighter requirements and a slight decrease in the number of carrier-based attack aircraft. The "mix" of carrier aircraft would shift toward more light attack airplanes capable of delivering small nuclear weapons, and away from long-range, high-performance heavy attack aircraft. Nevertheless, the Mach 2 North American A3J-1 promised a new dimension in long-range, high-performance aircraft with nuclear capability.

The study touched on what it referred to as the "mobile nuclear seaplane reprisal force." Curiously, the document straddled the fence on the P6M's mission, emphasizing its traditional maritime role as a minelayer. In the coming years, the SeaMaster would be configured for ECM reconnaissance missions and for air refueling as both a tanker and a receiver. Out to 1964, the study forecast that there would be one less P6M squadron devoted to the minelaying mission than previously planned. For the immediate future the study called for a supersonic attack-reconnaissance seaplane as a means of "maximizing the seaplane mobile basing concept." This successor to the SeaMaster would feature an advanced automatic all-weather bombing and navigation system and the same forward area mobile basing capabilities as the P6M, but with a Mach 1.3 dash speed at sea level. Another addition to the SSF was a new, open-ocean ASW seaplane to provide antisubmarine protection for the attack seaplane support vessels. Among the airplane's characteristics were low landing speed, simplicity of maintenance, and a dunking (later referred to as dipping) sonar. Like all other components of the SSF, the ASW aircraft would benefit from the perfection of advanced handling equipment and support ships.[30]

Reassured that the loss of the first XP6M-1 did not spell the end of the program, Martin completed a thorough study of basing and logistics for the SSF in April 1956. Although the plan had not been solicited by the navy, Martin submitted it to BuAer in anticipation that it would "generate further thinking and contribute to the early adoption of a [seaplane] support concept." The Martin study regarded the SeaMaster as a "revolutionary strike weapon," in concept analogous to the modern carrier task force and sharing with it the attributes of mobility and dispersion. Although the plan was similar to earlier proposals, it reflected the political and economic realties of the "New Look" in emphasizing the striking force as a means of ensuring a quick and devastating retaliation at the outset of a nuclear war. At the heart of the Martin scheme was the task of knitting together an echelon of mobile bases, radiating from the interior to far-flung strike zones, each segment of which needed a different level of logistic support. Martin estimated that the complex could support thirty-six aircraft, which could deliver 130 nuclear weapons in less than a week.

Around the Eurasian land mass were more than 250 potential sites for the "frontier bases," not including inland areas that might also be suitable for water-based aircraft. Located within 500 miles of the potential target, the bases were intended primarily for retaliatory missions, servicing up to four attack aircraft, armed with nuclear weapons, which rotated in and out at five-day intervals. At each frontier base were a submarine tanker, two P6Ms with tanker packs, and a Model 307 SeaMistress transport aircraft to provide crew quarters, fuel, and supplies.

The "secondary base," about 1,000 miles from the target, was more elaborate, supporting twelve aircraft for up to twenty days. Extensive maintenance and rearming took place there, in wartime including aircraft cycling back from strike missions mounted from the frontier bases. Martin estimated that twenty sorties could be generated in less than two days from the secondary base. In support there were LSTs with twin service booms to supply the aircraft on the water and carry out minor repairs, in addition to providing crew accommodations. Also at the base was an oiler modified to carry jet fuel and aviation gasoline, assisted by more SeaMistress transports.

Much more elaborate was the "major base," located more than 1,500 miles from the objective and well out of range of enemy tactical aircraft. For up to ninety days these bases could serve twelve aircraft and were complete with the equipment needed to remove them from the water for major maintenance and repair. Typically, each major base would have two seaplane tenders (AVs), three LSDs, four LSTs, and two oilers. Portable rubber service and dry docks would be available, carried by the LSDs. The plan estimated that up to eighty strikes could be mounted from the base over a three-week period.

Last was the "advance support base." Mobile, like all of the base facilities within the striking force, but much closer to home, the advance support base was to carry out major aircraft maintenance and overhaul and supply all of the forward strike bases. Twenty-four aircraft could be accommodated—although half that was the usual number in peacetime—for up to six months. At the advance support base only a command ship was needed for berthing and work spaces, along with eight specially designed rubber U-docks to lift the aircraft out of the water for repairs.

As a peacetime deterrent, Martin foresaw the SSF as consisting of two "strike complexes," each with thirty-six aircraft, assigned to the Pacific and the Atlantic. If and when war broke out, two more complexes could be added to round out the force. It was crucial, in the Martin scheme, to have as many SeaMasters based as far forward as possible: "aircraft held at fixed bases in the Zone of Interior are useless when a political or military situation demands prompt reaction." All support ships were to be conversions, since Martin understood the need to pare the costs of the program and recognized that it made no sense to hold off deployment until new ship designs could be promulgated. Immediate action was preferable, but a realistic timetable might have some of the airplane and support bases in place by 1959, followed the next year by the first complex, and two years later by the second.[31]

In June 1956, as Martin looked at ways of employing the SSF, Capt. Charles S. Minter Jr. became the P6M program manager. Minter's appointment was consistent with BuAer's adoption of the weapon system concept, which sought to modernize and accelerate procurement by restructuring weapon programs under strong administrative control with clearly delineated horizontal and vertical lines of responsibility. Under the new scheme, the program manager typically had subordinates working with him who were responsible for oversight of planning, research and development, acquisition, and production. Prime contractors, in most cases airframe manufacturers with established records for reliability and performance, had increased authority under the new management philosophy. Martin and Convair filled the bill perfectly; as early as 1952 the firms had touted their superior expertise in "weapon systems engineering." Martin almost from the beginning emphasized that the SeaMaster was more of a weapon system than a discrete airplane. As George Bunker stressed in his summary of the program in 1954, the company had agreed to "assume systems responsibility for integrating all phases of the program."[32]

An Annapolis graduate in the class of 1937, Minter had earned his wings at Pensacola in 1940 and had gone on to serve in patrol squadrons during World War II and to command Patrol Squadron 28 during the Korean War. He also had experience flying the navy's newest jets and had served a tour of duty as air officer on a carrier. The assignment came out of the blue while Minter was midway through the program at the National War College. Not wanting to miss a choice academic opportunity, he secured a delay long enough to allow him to complete his coursework and graduate. At the Pentagon, Minter took over as head of the Aviation Ships Branch in the DCNO (Air)'s office, with primary responsibility for monitoring the P6M program. He recalled later that he was "astonished at how much authority I had."[33]

"Concerned about the amorphous state of the program," Minter polled his fellow officers at the Pentagon to see what they thought. He found only lukewarm support from Vice Adm. William V. Davis, the DCNO (Air), who "had a lot of reservations" about the SeaMaster and worried that it would divert money from badly needed carrier aircraft programs. At the outset he warned Minter that he would not have carte blanche spending privileges or as much staff support as he would like. Rear Adm. William L. Rees, on the other hand, was "one of the strongest supporters" of the program in Davis's office, although he did not view it as an alternative to the aircraft carrier. Most important, Burke as CNO was "really convinced that this was going to be a great airplane for the navy," and his enthusiasm tended to suppress opposition to the program within the aviation community.[34]

Minter was incredulous that the program existed "in bits and pieces all around the building" and that "no one . . . had any actual responsibility" over one of the navy's biggest and most expensive aviation projects. With no staff responsible for integrating the disparate elements of the SSF, he quickly discovered that he would have to build an administrative structure virtually from scratch. He recalled later that it was almost "unreal" that so much had been invested in the program without any overall direction. Furthermore, despite at least two detailed studies by Martin, no one had systematically examined how to procure the ships and other facilities needed to support the operational P6M squadrons, or even how to train personnel. Skeptical that the P6M "was more a Martin dream than a solid Navy program," he "had the uncomfortable feeling . . . that we had stormy times ahead."[35]

After looking at Martin's production costs and the estimated expense of fielding twelve squadrons—six on each coast—with support ships and bases, Minter came up with a figure between $1 billion and $1.5 billion. He took his estimates to Rear Adm. Frederick N. ("Nappy") Kivette in OP-05, who was justifiably appalled. "A billion dollars," he exclaimed, "you could stack up $100 bills and it would reach as high as the Washington Monument. That's what a billion dollars is." Minter could only reply, "I'm sorry, it may reach that high but this is what it's going to cost, if we know what we're talking about." Self-deception about the real costs of the SSF, Minter believed, negated any realistic assessment of the program and in the end jeopardized its chances to succeed.[36]

Costs aside, some people, in and out of the service, viewed the SSF as an important element of the nation's arsenal and an ideal alternative to fixed bases that invited a direct nuclear assault on the continental United States. In an article in the U.S. Naval Institute *Proceedings* in December 1956, Edgar A. Parsons, a Civil Defense Administration planner, accepted the concept of massive retaliation implicit in the "New Look" and suggested that something like the SSF had two benefits: it enhanced the security of the country's strategic deterrent by making it mobile rather than fixed; and it transferred the battlefields of the next war from the homeland to the oceans or the north polar regions.

At the heart of this potentially "revolutionary" weapon system was the Sea-Master, an airplane Parsons thought was practically "impossible to destroy," and vastly superior to air force strategic bombers, tied as they were to "huge, complicated, expensive installations" that were difficult and expensive to disperse and impossible to conceal. Parsons thought the nation would be defended most effectively by a "triad" of mobile forces consisting of aircraft carriers, nuclear submarines carrying air-breathing missiles, and attack seaplanes, backed up by surface ships and submarines, roving the world's oceans and vir-tually invulnerable to any present or future defenses. Looking ahead, Parsons envisaged the ultimate in mobility and retaliatory capability with the devel-opment of a huge, 500,000-pound, nuclear-powered seaplane, with virtually unlimited range and capable of operating from bases throughout the world.[37]

Burke, a veteran scarred by the battles with the air force and the "revolt of the admirals," understood, better than anyone else at the time, the neces-sity for the navy to adapt to the realities of the "New Look," and he saw the SSF, despite its tribulations, as a major component of the navy's deterrent capability. In a memorandum on 10 August 1956, Burke reassured Admiral Davis that the program was "extremely sound and far-sighted" and an "invalu-able addition to future naval striking power." He went on to insist that the SeaMaster and other elements of the SSF be "given a very high priority and carried out in a bold, imaginative manner." That meant ensuring that the max-imum number of aircraft and supporting ships be acquired to prove the via-bility of the system and having them operational as soon as possible. "If the Navy does not go all out on this, someone else will," he concluded.[38]

Burke's unequivocal support of the SeaMaster program, coupled with the sense of urgency imparted by the Eisenhower administration's "New Look," was enough for the navy to make an even firmer commitment to the SSF. Long-range objectives promulgated by OPNAV made it clear that in addition to its mission as a minelayer, the P6M "can also perform special weapons strikes" and that "in its attack function the P6M will be complementary to our Carrier Striking Forces." How deeply the navy was involved became apparent in a contract signed with Martin on 31 August 1956 for twenty-four production aircraft, designated as P6M-2s, for delivery starting in March 1958. The total cost of the acquisition was estimated at $137.6 million.[39]

In December an ad hoc committee in the office of Clifford C. Furnas, the assistant secretary of defense for research and development, underscored the navy's decision to expand the SSF program. John Stack chaired the panel, which had begun its work in April. An MIT graduate working at NACA's Lan-gley lab, Stack won the prestigious Collier Trophy in 1947 for his research in transonic and supersonic aerodynamics. For some time he had been intrigued by the possibilities of high-speed seaplanes as offensive weapons. Consistent with earlier studies, the Stack committee determined that water basing was a means of guaranteeing the mobility considered critical in the nuclear era. Assuming that large seaplanes were comparable to landplanes in all perfor-mance categories, the "selection of water-based versus land-based aircraft can be made only after analyzing specific weapon-system requirements." In other words, the mission should dictate whether or not high-performance seaplanes were appropriate. Water handling remained a problem, the Stack committee acknowledged, but they were confident that tenders and support ships and water-based transport aircraft would meet the logistical needs of forward-deployed aircraft.

The Stack committee was optimistic about the potential of medium-range, water-based aircraft as a nuclear retaliatory force dispersed around the periphery of the Soviet Union, which would decrease their vulnerability and make it less likely that a Soviet attack would be directed at the continental United States. More important, the panel forecast that high-performance sea-planes "would complement carrier forces as well as Air Force strategic and tactical forces and could ultimately replace some of them." Recommending that "this concept should be aggressively pursued by the Navy," the Stack committee concluded that a "suitable number of P6M aircraft should be deployed in a realistic operational environment at the earliest practicable time."[40]

The Stack committee report came at another critical juncture in the Sea-Master program, which only a few weeks before had suffered a second potentially crushing reverse. On 9 November the surviving XP6M-1, with two Martin test pilots and two company flight engineers on board, took off to investigate the buffeting problem. That afternoon, while descending from 25,000 feet to 21,000 feet at about Mach .90, the airplane nosed over slightly. The pilot, R. S. Turner, corrected, only to find that the airplane continued to pitch up despite all his efforts to prevent it from doing so. As the airplane climbed into a vertical position and started to come around into a high-G inside loop, it experienced structural failure. All four crew members ejected safely, while the stricken craft fell into a spin, then exploded and burned as its remains tumbled to earth. The wreckage spread out over 15 square miles near Odessa, Delaware, one large section landing on the median strip of a busy four-lane highway.

In what must have seemed like a nightmarish sense of déjà vu, Martin and the navy once more assembled a team to investigate the accident, while putting the entire SeaMaster program on hold. Scores of people from Martin, Allison, BuAer, Civil Aeronautics Board (CAB), NACA Langley, and other government agencies spent countless hours sifting through the evidence. Ninety-five percent of the aircraft was recovered. In contrast to the first accident investigation, the team had access to the surviving crew members, observations from the pilots of the chase planes, and a wealth of telemetry data. They were confident they would discover the cause, and they were not disappointed.

After ruling out pilot error, control system problems, engine malfunctions, or structural failure, the investigators turned their attention to the locked elevator–horizontal stabilizer, a modification Martin had made in an effort to lessen the vibration problem. Before making the change, the company had calculated the hinge moments on the horizontal stabilizer by extrapolating wind-tunnel data and had beefed up the hydraulic actuating mechanism to handle the anticipated loads, particularly in tension, which many suspected might have been related to the "up" movement of the stabilizer and the pitch-down that had led to the loss of the first prototype. When the investigators reviewed the wind-tunnel data, they found, much to their chagrin, that there had been a mistake in the calculations of the hinge moment, especially in compression (with the stabilizer down). The forces were such that they overcame the capacity of the hydraulic actuator at speeds at or above Mach .90. Then, any movement of the controls easily overpowered the system, forcing the stabilizer down just long enough for the airplane to climb, in the process generating G loads beyond its structural capacity or the physiological limits of the crew. Under those circumstances, loss of the aircraft was inevitable.[41]

Following the recommendations of the accident investigation report, which came out in January 1957, Martin strengthened the hydraulic actuators and altered the stabilizer configuration to lessen the hinge moment and structural loads, while continuing to study the reasons for the vibration problem. On the YP6M-1 modifications were made to the elevator locking system to limit the aerodynamic loads on the horizontal stabilizer. The biggest visual change was elimination of the "bullet" fairing on the top of the vertical fin and substitution of a "tear-drop" fairing. Similar changes were also incorporated into the design of the P6M-2.[42]

Everyone associated with the SeaMaster and the SSF breathed a sigh of relief that the program had weathered another storm. Still, the cruel fact remained that no SeaMasters flew while the company and the navy digested the effects of the second accident and tried to ensure that the YP6M-1s did not suffer the same fate as the prototypes. There was no margin for error. Even the slightest technical or management difficulties could further delay the program and make it vulnerable to reduction or cancellation; another accident would surely spell its demise.

# Eight

# Toward an Operational Force

For nearly a year the SeaMaster was grounded, while on the West Coast at Convair the Sea Dart program lurched from one crisis to another. The SSF hung precariously in the balance as the contractors and the navy contemplated their next steps. Service leaders began to question whether the SSF deserved continuation, yet the lure of a sea-based "New Look" deterrent proved so strong that the navy kept it going despite cost increases, continued technical problems, and other indicators that it might never become reality. A lot rode on the YP6M-1 program: it needed to pick up the pieces of the tragically truncated XP6M-1 flight test phase, solve the aerodynamic vibration mystery once and for all, prove the minelaying-navigation system and other subsystems needed to turn the corner toward an operational status, and most important, demonstrate how the airplane fit into the SSF. This was a tall order.

Faced with what appeared to be insurmountable obstacles with the Sea Dart's hydrodynamics, Convair determined that it had made a fundamental mistake in assuming that the twin hydro-ski installation had to be designed around maximum landing loads, which proved to be less important than high-speed taxi and takeoff stresses. More specifically, the excessive vibration was due to the flexibility of the hydro-skis and problems with the attachment of the skis to the aircraft's hull. As a solution, Convair proposed reconfiguring the first XF2Y-1 with a single, rigid hydro-ski mounted to the hull with a large, shock-absorbing strut at the front. BuAer's Research Division enthusiastically endorsed the proposal in February 1954, although it thought the ski was more suited for use on a 160,000-pound airplane like the SeaMaster than a relatively small fighter like the Sea Dart. The ski was not retractable; much chastened by its previous experiences, Convair was interested in proof of the concept and not in the drag reduction needed for a fully operational high-speed fighter. The other major change to the airplane was fitting Westinghouse J46 engines with afterburners.[1]

Flights began in late December 1954 and continued until January 1956. During hundreds of hours of testing, the airplane showed that its crosswind landing and takeoff characteristics—even in heavy swells and waves up to 6 feet—were consistent with the expected operational requirements. In some tests in rough seas and crosswinds, the engines ingested spray, yet they remained undamaged because of a fresh-water injection system that kept the compressor blades free of salt incrustation. Periodically blowing steam and walnut shells through the engines also proved effective. The vibration problem, which had so vexed the first series of tests, seemed finally to have been solved.[2]

Encouraged, Convair took one last stab at the twin-ski configuration with the YF2Y-1. The skis were wider and flatter than those fitted to the first and second airplanes, had afterbodies sculpted to cut through the waves and reduce vibrations, and were fully retractable. The third Sea Dart began flight tests in March 1955. It proved to be more stable on the water than the single-ski version, even though early tests demonstrated poor directional stability in certain crosswind conditions. As with the first two twin-ski aircraft, the YF2Y-1 suffered from severe vibrations in moderate and choppy water, and no amount of tinkering with the skis or shock absorbers could solve the problem, which most still thought was caused by the skis flexing. On that discouraging note, test flights ended on 28 April 1955.[3]

Despite heartening results with the single-ski airplane, it became clear by the end of 1955 that the Sea Dart program was doomed. On 27 December 1955 OPNAV concluded that the recent development of high-performance carrier fighter aircraft had rendered the Sea Dart obsolete as an interceptor. From that point on Convair continued the program for research purposes only. In line with this approach, the first Sea Dart received a single, small, fixed hydro-ski in late 1956. Tests in 1957 demonstrated good stability in the water, but it was impossible to rotate the airplane to the angle of attack needed for takeoff, and the vibration problems remained. No one anticipated that the airplane would ever become an operational part of the fleet, and with the Sea Dart died the concept of the sea-based fighter as a component of the SSF.[4]

Disappointing as it was, the failure of the XF2Y to realize Convair's and the navy's expectations for a sea-based fighter with performance comparable to conventional aircraft did not mean the end of the company's involvement with advanced seaplane projects. As early as the fall of 1953, BuAer began working on an open-ocean ASW seaplane, followed in August 1954 by a meeting with Convair engineers to discuss how the new airplane could employ dipping sonar, the most recent innovation for detecting submarines, while sitting quietly on the surface. BuAer's Research Division completed a preliminary design study in April 1955 for a four-engine seaplane with an MTOW of 75,000 pounds. Short takeoffs and landings (STOL) in all weather and virtually any sea state were possible by rotating the wing and engines 30 degrees upward from the horizontal and by using large propellers to blow air over the wings and flaps to generate more lift through boundary layer control. BuAer considered a hybrid power plant installation, with two turboprop engines for high-altitude cruise to and from the operational area and a pair of piston radial engines "to jump from one combat landing to the next" skimming only a few feet above the wavetops.[5]

In February 1956 a staff study by the office of the DCNO (Air) endorsed the BuAer concept as a potential replacement for the venerable Martin P5M in the ASW mission. The new airplane would use advanced magnetic anomaly detection (MAD) gear, search radar, sonobuoys, dipping sonar, and nuclear depth charges to locate and attack submarines, and it would rely on the supply and maintenance infrastructure of the SSF for support.[6]

BuAer refined the concept of the ASW seaplane to include a secondary search-and-rescue mission and issued a circular letter on 19 March 1956 inviting companies to participate in a design competition. By the end of August, Martin and Convair had submitted designs. Already in the process of improving the P5M's ASW capability and thoroughly familiar with the latest technology, Martin thought it had the inside track with its proposal, the Model 313 (or P7M) SubMaster, which used four piston engines and a small General Electric J85 turbojet engine mounted on top of the hull to blow air over the wings for boundary layer control. Convair's submission, designated the P6Y-1, was a 104,000-pound, parasol-winged flying boat with three Wright R-3350 turbo-compound piston engines and two J85s in the nacelle behind the center engine for boundary layer control. The jet exhaust could be redirected aft as needed to provide thrust for higher speeds. On 1 February 1957 the navy informed Convair that it had won the design competition.[7]

Barely a year later Convair learned that due to budget constraints, the navy had "deferred indefinitely" the P6Y-1. Nevertheless, the company continued its involvement with high-performance seaplanes through the remainder of the decade, completing design studies for the navy of advanced high-performance seaplanes, some with hydro-skis and some without. Among them were a twin-engine, 54,000-pound, delta-wing Mach 3 attack airplane; another was a four-engine, 235,000-pound, Mach 2 bomber whose configuration bore some resemblance to Convair's supersonic B-58 Hustler, which flew for the first time in November 1956.[8] These intellectual exercises did nothing more than keep the high-performance seaplane idea alive in San Diego in the wake of the failure of the Sea Dart and the cancellation of the ASW seaplane; no one seriously believed that Convair or any American firm would follow up with real airplanes anytime soon. On the other hand, the fundamental soundness of the Convair P6Y-1 concept is evidenced by the success of the Japanese Shin Meiwa PS-1 STOL ASW seaplane, which first flew in 1967 and is still in operation as a search-and-rescue aircraft today.

By 1958 the only airplane that meant anything to the SSF was Martin's SeaMaster. Of utmost importance to the company and the navy were the changes needed in the design of the YP6M-1 in the wake of the two XP6M-1 crashes. The alterations to the empennage constituted an expensive and time-consuming redesign of the tail section, including the new fairing on the top of the vertical stabilizer, changes to the horizontal stabilizer and elevator control system, the stabilizer-elevator linkage, which had led to the loss of the second prototype, elimination of the outboard engine auxiliary air intakes, and strengthening of the rear portion of the fuselage. The addition of ejection seats for all crew members involved redesigning the flight deck layout and conducting many hours of testing. In September and October 1957 a series of experiments using a rocket-powered sled at the Naval Ordnance Test Station at China Lake, California, verified the design of the ejection system, hatch jettisoning, and cockpit configuration.[9]

Tests of YP6M-1 models at the NACA Langley lab in July and December 1957 indicated that the rudder and vertical and horizontal tail surfaces had improved flutter characteristics, providing encouragement that the changes Martin had made would at least mitigate the aerodynamic buffeting. Martin engineers worried that because the tests had used models with fixed control surfaces they would not provide conclusive answers to the vibration problem, and they recommended additional instruments on the YP6M-1 to obtain data. BuAer engineers, however, believed that the "shake" had probably not been solved and predicted that the Y-model would perform much like the X-model.[10]

Martin and the navy also negotiated changes in policies that both hoped would prevent any misunderstandings and help ensure early approval of the YP6M-1. They agreed on which tests had to be repeated from the XP6M-1 program, what test equipment would be needed, and which reports would have to be resubmitted for approval. Full demonstration of the General Precision Laboratories' Aero X-23A (now redesignated AN/ASQ-29) minelaying-navigation system was vital, as was evidence of the compatibility of the airplane with tenders and handling systems. The number of full-load, rough-water takeoffs and landings was scaled back, and some of the nuclear weapons to be carried were deleted, reflecting the rapid technological changes that had occurred in the U.S. nuclear arsenal. Because there had been concern that Martin had not followed procedures during some of the XP6M-1 test flights, the two parties were to confer on what flight restrictions were necessary, especially during the navy's evaluation of the YP6M-1.[11]

In OPNAV there was a sense of urgency about the SeaMaster and the SSF. Impatient to see a return on the navy's "investment" by having "maximum fleet utilization" as soon as possible, Rear Adm. David L. McDonald, director of the Air Warfare Division in OP-05, suggested in the spring of 1957 that the six YP6M-1s be organized into a provisional force, preferably early in 1959, with P6M-2 squadrons to follow soon after. At the end of September Admiral Burke sent out a revised plan that included an additional twelve airplanes, bringing the total to thirty-six. Following the CNO's long-range objectives for the SSF, three squadrons—VAH-1, VAH-3, and VAH-13—were to be attached to the Atlantic Fleet, pressing into service an unused auxiliary naval air station at Harvey Point, North Carolina, as the principal operating base, with the Jacksonville Naval Air Station as an alternative. Deployment was to start in June 1959, with all the squadrons at full strength by the end of 1961.[12]

OPNAV's thinking sharply contrasted with the technical, political, and fiscal realities of the program. Well before the middle of the year, there were indications that only limited squadrons would be formed, if any. Charles Minter had doubts almost from the start of his tenure as program manager over whether the SSF would ever be fully funded. He recalled that "there was so much that was required in the way of support that we didn't have or were going to have to have [that] I got discouraged." He recommended that plans for thirty-six aircraft be shelved, and noted that until Harvey Point was ready, the navy's test flight facility at Patuxent River would be sufficient for the program's immediate requirements. Meanwhile, on Capitol Hill skeptics were already being heard. In May Rep. Harry R. Sheppard, a Democrat from California, questioned the navy's plans for the conversion of a second seaplane tender for the SSF, emphasizing that although the P6M program would eventually fulfill its promise, "as yet that time has not come." Citing cost overruns and delays, the navy on 21 June 1957 pared the P6M-2 order from twenty-four to eighteen, only half the number OPNAV thought it would need for a viable force.[13]

That additional aircraft were unlikely to be funded did not diminish the potential operators' confidence in the SSF. Vice Adm. Charles R. ("Cat") Brown, a seasoned aviator and commander of the Sixth Fleet in the Mediterranean, concluded in October 1957 that the SSF "furnishes a favorable occasion for once more reiterating the great importance the Navy attaches to its heavy seaplane program" as a means of freeing the navy from dependence on increasingly vulnerable land bases. Brown was concerned that the focus on the "New Look" had possibly driven the navy too far in the direction of a nuclear retaliatory role and limited its traditional flexibility. Nevertheless, he concluded that the CNO needed to "continue to take all measures practicable to pursue at high priority the development of the heavy attack seaplane . . . as a long-range replacement" for land-based and carrier aircraft in the strategic nuclear role.[14]

When the first YP6M-1 took to the air in early 1958, there was a sense of relief that Martin had overcome the early adversities of the program and a feeling that it stood a good chance of moving on to at least minimal operational status. The initial flight, on 20 January 1958, went well, although the vibration again manifested itself when the pilot unlocked the elevator and allowed it to move relative to the horizontal stabilizer. It was obvious that the problem was in the tail of the aircraft, related to the interaction of the elevator and the horizontal stabilizer, but engineers remained puzzled about how to solve it. Martin's people thought that occasional unpredictable operation of the airplane's wing slats contributed to the problem, although modifications to the slats brought only slight improvements. There was also some mild buffeting when the pilots cut back one of the inboard engines to idling power. Martin had increased the area of the engine inlets on the first YP6M-1 to alleviate water ingestion and prevent flameouts, then found from wind tunnel tests in October 1957 that the larger inlet area exacerbated the buffet phenomenon. The second and follow-on Y-models had smaller inlets.[15]

With BuAer's concurrence, Martin expanded the envelope of aircraft performance on subsequent flights, increasing the speed and altitude while keeping a close eye on the function of the stabilizer-elevator combination and its effects on the longitudinal stability of the airplane. It was important for the operational use of the airplane that on the second flight the crew engaged and disengaged the special beaching apparatus without assistance and taxied the aircraft up and down the seaplane ramp using the airplane's own power. Tests also included use of all four afterburners and observations of their effects on rear fuselage heating.[16]

Flight testing continued into the spring and summer of 1958, with two more of the Y-models joining the program. A good sign was that the reduced engine inlet size on the second airplane had nearly eliminated the buffet. Offsetting that were other problems. Afterburners continued to fail, despite modifications to the Allison engines that were supposed to provide a remedy. Moreover, towing-tank tests had indicated the airplane might suffer from more spray and more pitching than normal at the higher gross weight of 172,000 pounds. Sure enough, the problem cropped up on one of the early test flights with the first YP6M-1, and it occurred at a weight of 160,000 pounds and in only moderate seas, causing an engine flameout and raising concerns about the airplane's hydrodynamic characteristics. Martin attempted a quick "fix" by fairing in the rear turret area, without much success. In the fall of 1958 BuAer stopped Martin's tests of airplanes at heavy gross weights and imposed stringent limitations on weights and takeoffs in high sea states, pending a solution to the problem.[17]

Subsystem development and testing contributed to growing concerns about the status of the program. Aside from the airplane itself, the AN/ASQ-29 minelaying-navigation system was the critical element of the entire weapon system, pushing the state of the art in electronics at the time. In May 1955 Martin had outlined the test and development plans for the AN/ASQ-29, parts of which went into a modified Lockheed P2V-4 for evaluation in the summer of 1956.[18]

When these and other tests showed deficiencies in the AN/ASQ-29, BuAer in March 1958 asked Martin to study changes to the equipment, including a digital short-range computer and an upgraded Doppler radar set, which the navy hoped would increase the reliability and accuracy of the system, not only for minelaying but also for high-altitude bombing. Based on these changes and drops of simulated MK 28 thermonuclear weapons, Martin reported to BuAer in April 1958 that the SeaMaster could deliver its ordnance from nearly 50,000 feet with a high degree of accuracy. Nevertheless, faced with rising costs and the prospect of additional delays in the program, BuAer thought better of having Martin undertake major modifications to the system, which was not fitted to the SeaMaster until the third YP6M-1 that June.[19]

Tests of the AN/ASQ-29 through the rest of 1958 and into 1959 brought failures of the radar navigation set and other components of the system in Ship No. 3, although the system seemed to do better in Ship No. 5. Martin did not attempt to test the short-range computer on simulated minelaying runs. Not satisfied with the results of Martin's evaluation, BuAer decided at the end of 1958 to have Patuxent River carry out a more intensive round of tests with the AN/ASQ-29 in the P2V-4 to determine once and for all if the system was ready for operational use. Beginning in April and continuing through mid-September 1959, the trials revealed shortcomings in nearly every part of the system. The conclusion: "The reliability of the system was grossly unacceptable," and "no further evaluation . . . [should] be conducted."[20] The failure of the AN/ASQ-29 was portentous, placing both the SeaMaster program and the SSF in jeopardy.

Meanwhile, all of the navy's aircraft procurement programs came under intense scrutiny. In April 1958 Rear Adm. Robert E. Dixon, BuAer chief, took a critical look at Martin and the SeaMaster program. Following the loss of the second XP6M-1, navy leaders had discussed fundamental deficiencies in the airplane's design and the wisdom of continuing the program into the production phase. Adm. James Russell, then chief of BuAer, had criticized Martin for violations of procedure in testing the XP6M-1 at speeds beyond what had been approved by the bureau's representative in Baltimore. Furthermore, Russell had charged, Martin went ahead with the flights even though it was aware of a leak in the hydraulic system controlling the outboard wing spoilers. Static tests, which had begun in August 1957, soon revealed basic structural deficiencies in the airplane, to which Martin, instead of addressing the problems forthrightly, replied that BuAer needed to scale back its requirements. Dixon insisted that Martin's engineering needed "tightening up," and that the path to operational status lay not in lessening the specifications for the SeaMaster but in ensuring that Martin met or exceeded them. In July 1958

Charles Minter left the Pentagon as P6M program manager to take command of *Albemarle,* the first of the SSF tenders, leaving no administrative successor and unsure whether or not the airplane and the SSF would survive.[21]

By early August 1958 Martin had delivered the last YP6M-1. With six airplanes, the company for the first time could divide up the work load and accelerate the evaluation process, possibly heading off mounting criticism of the program. In October Martin pointed out that the auxiliary air intakes on the inboard engines of the YP6M-1 were critical for minimizing engine flameouts due to spray ingestion. The company urged the navy to allow the auxiliary air intakes to be added to the outboard engines of the YP6M-1 and incorporated in the P6M-2, which was to operate at heavier weights and likely to suffer even more from excessive spray. Wishing to keep weight and costs down on both airplanes, BuAer rejected Martin's proposal.[22]

The bureau's rejection of the proposal may not have been fast enough; BuAer decided in the late summer of 1958 that it was time for a comprehensive review of the program. The study concentrated on rising costs and delays, emphasizing the need for "corrective action" where indicated. Trying to get a feel for what was possible and what was not, Admiral Dixon wrote to Martin on 3 October that he wanted a "thorough and prompt" appraisal of the program, and asked for cost proposals on three alternative plans. Within BuAer there were strong sentiments that a satisfactory SeaMaster production program was unlikely and that the YP6M-1 and P6M-2 contracts needed to be renegotiated as cost plus an incentive rather than the previous fixed-fee arrangement.[23]

At the low end of the scale, Dixon suggested Martin look at the costs of eliminating all operational aircraft, keeping only the Y-models, and supporting them as a quasi-squadron with the converted *Albemarle* at Patuxent River. The airplanes' mission would be limited to bombing, although there would be testing of inflight refueling and photoreconnaissance, and the program would terminate after the completion of the BIS reports. At the high end was the status quo. Martin would continue the YP6M-1 program and keep eighteen P6M-2s, organized in two squadrons. *Albemarle,* a converted LSD, and two submarine tankers would provide support, first at Patuxent River and later at Harvey Point. In the middle was a compromise, with the six YP6M-1s, and eight P6M-2s organized into one squadron and supported by *Albemarle* and one submarine tanker. As in the low-end alternative, the airplanes would be limited to the bombing mission, and as in the high-end plan, they would eventually be based at Harvey Point.[24]

Support from OPNAV, which up to now had staunchly backed the program, began to fade in the summer of 1958, largely because of the influence of Vice Adm. Robert B. Pirie, DCNO (Air). A second-generation Scot with the bewhiskered countenance of an old sea dog, Pirie was a 1926 Annapolis graduate who had learned to fly at Pensacola in 1928 and had gone on to become a navy test pilot in the early 1930s. Before the war he served in the carriers *Langley, Lexington,* and *Yorktown.* He gained administrative experience on the staff of Vice Adm. John Towers, the commander air force Pacific Fleet at Pearl Harbor, and won a Silver Star for his service on the staff of Third Fleet during the Battle of Leyte Gulf in October 1944. Charles Minter had tremendous respect for Pirie, remembering him as "one of the most dynamic individuals I ever knew" and a first-class intellect who did not shrink from making hard choices even at the risk of his career. Pirie came to the CNO's office in May 1958 with the full support of Admiral Burke to make decisions as he saw fit.[25]

It did not take long for Pirie to comprehend that the budget pinch required a thorough evaluation of the navy's aviation programs. Of utmost importance was keeping the carrier building program on track. After years of relatively generous funding for the big ships, including a nuclear-powered carrier in the FY 1957 budget (completed as CVAN 65 *Enterprise*), the defense budget for FY 1959 deferred a second nuclear carrier while providing funding for long-lead-time items for the ship. There was also some sentiment within the navy for a more austere and less expensive nuclear-powered vessel. Working on the FY 1960 budget in the spring of 1958, Pirie insisted that the next ship had to have the speed, deck space, and aircraft capacity of the nuclear-powered *Enterprise,* even though he had doubts about whether or not nuclear power was economical. The House of Representatives eliminated the carrier, while the Senate included it in its version of the defense budget. In the end, the economy-minded Eisenhower compromised by vetoing the nuclear-powered carrier and substituting a conventionally powered ship. Pirie learned that the political circumstances in late 1958 and early 1959 made the acquisition of any big carriers problematical. If he had to make a decision between a carrier and the SSF, which was experiencing technical difficulties and in his mind "exorbitant" cost overruns, he would always opt for the carrier.[26]

Nevertheless, Pirie hoped that Martin and the navy could keep the Sea-Master program going if the company trimmed costs wherever possible. He made the short trip to Baltimore at the end of August 1958 to talk to Jess W.

Sweetser and other Martin executives about the future of the program. He was not impressed with what he heard and concluded that Martin was not serious about cost reductions. "These proposals for saving were in the spare parts and support equipment and did not show any real effort on the part of the Martin company to cut their costs," he confided to his personal log.[27]

A few days later, on 26 August 1958, Pirie met with Undersecretary of the Navy William B. Franke to talk about cutting the P6M program. Franke considered Pirie's recommendations "refreshing" at a time when original ideas were needed to cope with the navy's fiscal difficulties. Pirie noted that Franke "thought while our decision to cut the program might be a sound one, he questioned the political feasibility; however, he would go along with it." Later Franke telephoned to say that the department would support any reductions Pirie thought were needed. Franke subsequently met with his boss, Secretary of the Navy Thomas S. Gates Jr., who approved a reduction in the P6M program. Following this meeting, Pirie drafted a letter for Burke's signature confirming that the YP6M-1 program be terminated after six airplanes had been delivered.[28]

Under these circumstances, Martin officials could not have been surprised when they received in October Admiral Dixon's request for a review of the SeaMaster program. There had been ample indications of unhappiness in Washington about the program, and in July Martin had unsuccessfully attempted to renegotiate the contract with a large contingency fund to cover additional expenses. Working within what it insisted was a "climate of austerity," the company still hoped to salvage as much of the program as possible and took heart that at minimum the navy would let the YP6M-1 program run to completion. Martin delivered its cost estimates on the three alternatives to BuAer on 1 November and waited for the navy's decision. Burke took the middle ground in recommending to Secretary Gates that the program be limited to eight P6M-2s organized into a single squadron, which he considered sufficient "to develop seaplane tactics and to determine maintenance and operating requirements associated with the mobile operating concept." On 24 November 1958 the axe fell on Martin. Admiral Dixon informed the company that "the operational development of the concept which the aircraft embodies can be adequately prosecuted with the lesser number in light of changing concepts and other developments in naval warfare." Consequently, the SeaMaster development program would be ended with fourteen aircraft— six YP6M-1s for training and a single squadron of eight P6M-2s at Harvey Point, supported by *Albemarle* and a single submarine.[29]

The navy's decision to limit the program was a bitter pill for Martin to swallow, leading directly to the dismissal of 1,500 workers in Baltimore. Nevertheless, the program had not been halted altogether. Almost daily flights by the big seaplanes in the fall and early winter gave the appearance that the SeaMaster was moving toward operational status, even though the YP6M-1s continued to show hydrodynamic and aerodynamic deficiencies that defied solution.[30]

Needing to keep the SeaMaster and the SSF alive in the face of growing costs and opposition, proponents of the program desperately sought to demonstrate the multi-mission capability of the P6M. As early as May 1957 BuAer commissioned a study to show how the P6M-2 could be used as a standoff missile carrier to launch the Mach 2 Chance Vought Regulus II delivering a nuclear warhead at targets up to 700 miles distant. Too big for the SeaMaster's mine bay, the Regulus had to be carried piggy-back on the top of the fuselage, potentially causing stability and control problems and damage to the seaplane's empennage from the missile's exhaust. As an alternative, in February 1958 BuAer examined the potential of the P6M-2 to carry internally a 14,000-pound, 1,000-mile-range, two-stage, hypersonic boost-glide missile. Less than a year later, in March 1958, BuAer directed Martin to undertake a preliminary study of the feasibility of using the P6M-2 to launch the Corvus antiradar missile.[31]

Due to its range, speed, and payload capacity, the SeaMaster from the start had been attractive in the photoreconnaissance role. Two of the YP6M-1s were set up for camera packages, or "pods"—one for day and the other for night photography—which were fitted to the mine-bay door and rotated into position. Linked to the AN/ASQ-29 bomb-navigation system, the cameras functioned automatically; flares could also be released from the mine bay for illumination of the target. Delays by the camera contractor meant that Martin could carry out only limited flight testing of the equipment in the YP6M-1s.[32]

Adding to the SeaMaster's versatility was an air refueling system tailored to fit the airplane's mine bay. Initially, Martin had approached Flight Refueling, Ltd. (FRL), a British firm, to explore how its probe-and-drogue means of aerial replenishment could be adapted to the P6M. Simplicity itself, the FRL system employed a hose extended from the tanker, at the end of which was a basketlike receptacle (drogue) that the receiver aircraft engaged with a probe extended from the fuselage or wing.[33]

In June 1956 Martin completed a proposal for BuAer to fit the P6M with a version of the FRL system. Equipping the big flying boats as both tankers and receivers, Martin believed, would increase their range and payload while enhancing their mobility. For an extended mission, one or more SeaMaster tankers could rendezvous with a submarine or surface ship at an advanced location and refuel the strike force aloft as it passed on its way to the target. Alternatively, P6M tankers could accompany the mission from its home base, refueling the strike aircraft en route in what the navy referred to as the "buddy" technique. As a bonus, the P6M could operate in conjunction with carrier task forces, providing them with independent tanker support for their attack aircraft. A refueling package, consisting of a reel, hose, and drogue from FRL attached to the rear of a Martin-designed and -built 2,700-gallon tank, slipped onto the mine-bay door. Once rotated into position, the hose and drogue extended down and behind the airplane, where the receiver picked it up. Little had to be done to reconfigure the P6M other than making minor modifications to hydraulic, electrical, and fuel systems; only the probe and an external fuel line were needed to convert the airplane into a receiver. Martin went ahead with the project based on a letter of intent from BuAer in March 1957.[34]

Delays in getting the prototype refueling unit constructed and installed in the P6M-2 forced Martin to start tests with one of the YP6M-1s at Patuxent River in September 1958. A variety of attack and fighter aircraft held formation with the P6M in simulated refueling positions, where they found the turbulence from the big flying boat with its mine-bay door open "unacceptable." Martin put a good face on the situation, vowing to modify the equipment so that the hose and drogue "flew" outside the area of turbulence and to test a mockup on the YP6M-1 while waiting for the first P6M-2s to fly.[35]

By the spring of 1959 FRL had begun deliveries of the first hose and reel kits, which Martin incorporated into the tanker package for ground tests in early June. Flight tests began on 12 June with Ship No. 9, the first of the P6M-2s. Subsequent flights later that summer included hookups with high-performance Grumman F11F and Chance Vought F8U fighters. On one flight a YP6M-1 flew into position as a receiver but did not make a connection. Martin concluded in August that the evaluation "demonstrated that the P6M will make a satisfactory tanker."[36]

Martin and the navy had a great deal at stake with the P6M-2 program in 1958 and 1959. As the operational variant of the SeaMaster, the P6M-2 had 15,200-pound-thrust Pratt and Whitney J75 engines instead of the 13,000-pound-thrust, afterburning Allison J71s fitted to the XP6M-1 and YP6M-1. Doing away with afterburners on the J75s simplified the cockpit routine on takeoff, increased the MTOW to 195,000 pounds, and enhanced the SeaMaster's maximum and cruising speeds. Martin engineers also short-ened the engine nacelles, widened the intakes to ensure adequate mass airflow and set them back from the leading edge of the wing on an axis perpendicular to the fuselage, and reduced the angle at which the nacelles were canted out-board from the fuselage. With a higher gross load, the airplane sat lower in the water, causing the wingtip floats to submerge under some circumstances. To correct this, Martin redesigned the wings with a slight positive dihedral com-pared to the 1.5-degree "droop," or negative dihedral, characteristic of the wings on the earlier models. Auxiliary air doors on top of the engine nacelles were considered necessary due to increases in spray from the deeper draft fuse-lage. A large Plexiglas canopy enhanced cockpit visibility, and a receiver probe in the nose of the aircraft provided inflight refueling capability.[37]

Originally, Ship No. 7 was to have been the first P6M-2, a prototype lack-ing most of the equipment planned for later production versions. In view of reductions in the numbers of aircraft and in an effort to meet some of the navy's concerns about the pace of the program, Martin decided during the assembly process that the first of the P6M-2s needed to be built to full pro-duction standards, including the complex AN/ASQ-29 bombing/navigation equipment. Therefore, Ship No. 9, the first fully equipped airplane, received priority over Ship No. 7, which dropped back in the production line. After delays, Ship No. 9 was completed in the middle of November 1958 and immediately began ground tests.[38]

Unforeseen technical problems dashed expectations for early flight test-ing. Engine/nacelle tests before the Ship No. 9 rollout revealed that during certain phases of operation the engine encountered low-speed compressor surging, which had to be corrected by installing a "fence" on the leading edge of the inlet duct. Based on experience with the YP6M-1 and uncertainty about how the change in the wing dihedral and other modifications might affect the new version, Martin set strict limits on sea conditions and weights for the air-plane's first flights and suggested that the performance envelope be explored cautiously, pending more information from ground tests.[39]

Martin hoped to get the first P6M-2 in the air before the end of January—only to encounter more difficulties and delays. The experimental engine inlet "fence" that had performed well in ground tests did not work when fitted to Ship No. 9, causing BuAer to delay releasing the airplane for flight until Mar-tin found a permanent solution to the problem. While the engines were being run up in preparation for taxi tests, one of them ingested a loose piece of fairing, causing serious compressor blade damage and requiring the replacement of the engine and additional design work to prevent a recurrence of the mishap.[40]

Despite bitter weather and ice in Chesapeake Bay, taxi tests began in early February. Based on experience, Martin's engineers were concerned about compressor surge, but only one of the engines misbehaved. Instead, the biggest problem was submergence of the wingtip floats at low speeds—despite the change in the wing dihedral. Veteran Martin test pilot George Rodney was at the controls for the first test flight on 17 February, during which the airplane performed well at speeds and altitudes in excess of those flown by the YP6M-1. To everyone's dismay, compressor stall afflicted the inboard engines when the adjacent outboard engines were shut down in flight.[41]

While engineers experimented with various inlet and nacelle configurations to solve the surge problem and conducted more towing-tank tests to see what could be done to lessen the tendency of the wingtip floats to submerge, test flights of the P6M-2 explored aerodynamic realms hitherto unattainable by seaplanes, or for that matter by any large aircraft. Successive flights took the airplane to Mach .8 and beyond, where it began to encounter aerodynamic and control troubles. One was the buffet or "shake" that had shown up in the YP6M-1; with the P6M-2 the problem became apparent at speeds above Mach .83 and under certain G loads in turns. Directional trim shifts and a tendency for a wing to "drop" or lose lift were other problems, always occurring within the same high-speed ranges regardless of altitude.[42]

It did not take long to find that these difficulties were associated with compressibility. As an airplane approached the speed of sound, shock waves formed in front of and along the fuselage, upsetting the flow of air in the boundary layer near the surface of the wings, drastically altering the wings' lift, and reducing the effectiveness of the control surfaces. Intensive wind-tunnel investigations, combined with test flights of Ship No. 9 and the more heavily instrumented Ship No. 8, led Martin engineers to install vortex generators on the wings outboard of the engine nacelles to correct the airplane's high-speed control problems. An extension of the splitter between the two air intakes in the engine nacelles ended compressor stalls, and a flap on the underside of the wings near the floats prevented their submergence at low speeds.[43]

While Martin grappled with one technical problem after another, the navy's enthusiasm for the program rapidly eroded. In January 1959 BuAer curtailed the normal (and expensive) BIS evaluation of the P6M at Patuxent River. The new plan was to have one of the YP6M-1s "undergo a reduced contractor demonstration and a short BIS trial," at the conclusion of which the aircraft would be returned to Martin and stripped for spares to support the P6M-2. The P6M-2, meanwhile, would go through the complete contractor's and BIS evaluation, entering the fleet in limited numbers and operating for no more than five years. Disappointing as this navy mandate was, the decision in March to cancel the BIS evaluation entirely and cut off all YP6M-1 testing other than that needed to prove elements of the P6M-2 program was even worse, guaranteeing that the YP6M-1 program would not extend beyond the middle of the year.[44]

Countless changes and fruitless attempts to fix the vexatious buffeting problems with the YP6M-1 and P6M-2 reinforced the navy's decision to curtail the SeaMaster program. In March 1959 Martin gave in and told BuAer that "despite the continuing effort, the shake has not been isolated or eliminated." Many airplanes, Martin's technical director pointed out, had such vibrations, and normally they did not cause much concern. The SeaMaster, though, had a long forebody, which amplified the oscillations, described by one pilot as similar to those in a multi-engine propeller airplane with the engines out of synchronization. Ship No. 6, the last of the YP6M-1s, demonstrated more "shake" than any of the others, despite all efforts to eliminate the problem. In sum, the vibration was a "nuisance item" that did not affect the airplane's performance or safety, and everyone was going to have to live with it.[45]

That was just about the last thing BuAer wanted to hear. Coming as it did when the SeaMaster and the entire SSF were under intense scrutiny, Martin's conclusion that the vibration problem was insoluble was not acceptable. One BuAer engineer commented that in early flights of the P6M-2, pilots thought the "shake" was more than a "nuisance," and that while it might be tolerated on the YP6M-1, it had to be corrected on the P6M-2, which was destined for squadron service. The bureau's representative at the Martin factory concurred, viewing the company's "complete reversal in its attitude" as odd considering all the attention paid to the problem in the XP6M-1 and YP6M-1. Unless it were eliminated, there was every reason to believe that the performance of the operational aircraft would be adversely affected.[46]

With the navy's patience wearing thin, the YP6M-1 suffered another setback only a couple of weeks later. On 16 April 1959 the fourth example was flying at 8,000 feet at about 440 knots when the pilot found that he could not place the airplane in a nose-down attitude despite pushing forward as hard as he could on the yoke. The loss of longitudinal control happened again, then the problem went away as mysteriously as it had appeared, and the airplane landed safely. With the loss of the second XP6M-1 in everyone's mind, Martin and the navy agreed to ground all of the YP6M-1s and P6M-2s while they determined what had happened. Investigators went over the airplane's hydraulic system, examined the control cables, and pored over telemetry data. All they could find was some contamination of the hydraulic fluid in the first YP6M-1, which was not unusual. Martin pilots took the fourth airplane up on two flights but could not duplicate the malfunction. Verifying that the horizontal stabilizer hinge moments could not override the control system, as they had on the second XP6M-1, and cautioning that pilots had to be conscious of potential longitudinal control problems on high-performance aircraft, the navy on 7 May cleared the SeaMasters to continue flying. The grounding cast another long shadow on an aircraft program that many in and out of the navy considered troubled, if not fated for cancellation.[47]

# Nine

# End of the Line

Pressure mounted on the SeaMaster and SSF programs during the spring of 1959, as the navy struggled to get funding for another large-deck carrier and saw its budget squeezed by the expenses associated with the burgeoning Polaris fleet ballistic missile program. At the same time, BuAer was reluctant to cancel a program in which it had invested nearly ten years of effort and hundreds of millions of dollars and that still had influential supporters. Adm. James Russell as BuAer chief had wanted to continue the program, although his successor, Rear Adm. Robert Dixon, was less enthusiastic and had ordered a thorough review of the program in the fall of 1958. At the same time, Vice Admiral Pirie, the DCNO (Air), questioned the wisdom of continuing a program that had experienced major cost overruns without reaching operational status.

Technical problems continued to vex the SeaMaster program into 1959. Admiral Dixon wrote to Martin's president in February to question some of the company's estimated costs for the second half of FY 1959. Disappointed with Martin's efforts to correct past deficiencies in the airplane and the program, but not yet ready to pronounce the death penalty, Dixon urged Martin to do all it could to rein in expenses and keep the program within estimates. One of "several expressions, both formal and informal" from the navy to Martin, Dixon's letter stressed that it was imperative for the company to streamline its program management and contain costs if the program had any hope of continuing.[1]

A month later Dixon wrote to Admiral Burke, informing him that even though the program had been cut back to six YP6M-1s and eight P6M-2s, further reductions were needed. Increased production expenditures and the addition of auxiliary air doors and other design changes to the P6M-2, combined with termination charges for the YP6M-1 program, had resulted in an additional $14 million deficit. Dixon saw no alternative other than to "take action to reduce the scope of the existing program." For the present, he could save $4 million by using only four of the YP6M-1s as flight demonstrators in support of the P6M-2 program, followed on 1 July by the cessation of all YP6M-1 test flying. Other actions would be needed, though, to curb costs.[2]

Admiral Pirie tried to keep the big picture in view as he thought about ways of preserving and enhancing naval aviation in light of fiscal realities and Cold War military threats. Not long after taking over as DCNO (Air), he initiated an intensive study of the navy's aviation programs and requirements through the 1970s. After many months the preliminary results were in, and Pirie arranged a presentation in early 1959 by the study group for the top brass in the CNO's office and BuAer. As expected, the investigation focused on the big-deck carrier, highlighting its flexibility in comparison with land-based aircraft. But like the November 1954 BuAer analysis, this one found that an attack seaplane force such as the SSF had advantages over the carrier in survivability, reduced operating and maintenance costs, and ability to deliver strategic blows against the Soviet Union. Two BuAer officers recalled Pirie's reaction to the presentation. Fuming with anger, he informed the panel that while its conclusions about the superiority of the carrier were correct, its findings about the seaplane were not, and said that if their study were widely circulated, it might jeopardize future carrier funding.[3]

Biased against the SSF or not, Pirie realized, after scrutinizing the navy's long-range objectives, that the service would have to set funding priorities and adhere to them. He wrote to Admiral Burke on 11 April 1959: "I have a feeling of growing concern, which I must express to you, regarding the future capabilities of our Navy to carry out its tasks under the varying conditions of Cold, Limited, or General War. As you know, I feel that the power of the Navy, for many years to come, must be constituted around the flexibility of attack carriers. . . . We all agree that there is a very definite trend toward diluting Naval Aviation . . . to a degree that is extremely dangerous." Pirie recommended that Burke consider ways of making "vertical cuts" rather than "horizontal," or across-the-board, reductions that jeopardized the navy's "essential capabilities." Anything that did not enhance the navy's offensive capabilities—

that is, carrier striking forces, amphibious forces, or the Polaris fleet ballistic missile program—had to be "accorded secondary priority in the competition for funds." He promised Burke that he would follow up with specific recommendations "to insure that Naval Aviation obtains the maximum value from every dollar made available to it."[4]

"I share your concern over the downward trend in the strength of naval aviation and the effect that this will have on the Navy's capabilities," Burke replied. But "there are many other Navy programs which also require increased budgetary support. Until such time as a substantial increase can be effected in the amount of funds available to the Navy—or a substantial decrease occurs in the cost of things all Navy programs are apt to suffer." In particular, Burke was thinking about Polaris. He had begun navy involvement in the development of a submarine-based, intermediate-range ballistic missile, and had personally selected Rear Adm. William F. Raborn to head the Special Projects Office with carte blanche to make Polaris happen. Even though there was an understanding that the missile part of the program would be paid for with joint Department of Defense funds, the navy would be responsible for the submarines. Because he did not want to sacrifice missile programs or carriers, something would have to give. "All hands" needed to look at each of the navy's weapon systems, Burke concluded, and be prepared in light of overall national security interests to make hard choices about what stayed and what did not.[5]

Such ominous words emanating from OPNAV did not seem to have much effect in Baltimore, where P6M-2 production and testing continued through the spring and into the summer of 1959. As Martin moved ahead, Dixon questioned the number of man-hours and attendant costs of P6M flight tests, which he estimated "greatly exceed any previous or present Navy experience with other airframe contractors." When Martin's representatives could not provide satisfactory reasons why their costs were so high, Dixon ordered the company to reevaluate its estimates and explain why they were so far out of line with those of other manufacturers.[6]

Martin tried to put the best face on things. Despite the aerodynamic problems of the airplane, the company maintained they had not been unexpected and that its engineers were on track to solve those that still remained. Moreover, the "fixes" had been "simple and inexpensive." The YP6M-1 and P6M-2 were "comparable aerodynamically to the best of any transonic aircraft flying today," with better longitudinal stability than the latest large jet transports and in lateral control superior to "any other comparable airframe." What had once been a major flaw, the "shake" that so bedeviled the airplane, became a minor annoyance, vanishing at Mach .96, according to the reports from the most recent high-speed test flights of the P6M-2. To Martin, the SeaMaster was a "highly satisfactory airplane" in every respect, "an exceedingly good flying machine from a pilot's viewpoint and one that can quite proficiently fulfill the intended, and many other, missions."[7]

In the midst of this uncertainty, flight testing in the spring and summer of 1959 went about as well as anyone could have anticipated. The high-speed buffet and the tendency of one of the wings to drop at certain altitudes and speeds remained, although none of the test pilots thought either of the problems was serious. By the end of June the program had moved ahead to the point where Martin planned to hand over the first airplanes for the Navy Preliminary Evaluation (NPE) trials starting on 19 August. Martin and others projected releasing the aircraft to the fleet by the end of 1960.[8]

By midsummer it was evident to close observers of the P6M program that its cancellation was all but a certainty. Costs spiraling out of control in a program that competed for scarce resources with Polaris, additional carriers (some nuclear powered), expensive new carrier aircraft, and missile-firing surface ships made it difficult, if not impossible, to justify the program's continuation. Already skeptical about the airplane and the SSF concept, Admiral Pirie was fully prepared to take the final step and cancel the program. He conferred with Burke, Franke (who had succeeded Gates as secretary of the navy), Assistant Secretary of the Navy for Material Fred A. Bantz, and BuAer Chief Dixon on 10 August to discuss the fate of the program. The group decided to end the P6M program in its entirety. Pirie met the following afternoon with Franke to confirm the decision and work out the details of notification and contract cancellation.[9]

Admiral Russell, now the vice CNO, assessed the situation in a letter to Franke on 13 August. He explained that the decision to deploy a single squadron meant that the airplane would never have operational capability consonant with the navy's investment. With only limited aircraft procurement funds on the horizon, there was no way to justify continuation of a program that added little to the navy's and the nation's offensive capabilities. Furthermore, the seemingly insoluble aerodynamic problems convinced him that the P6M was "not an acceptable aircraft," and the airplane's long gestation had caused its combat capability to be "superseded by other weapon systems." Therefore, he was "firmly convinced that it is in the best interest of the Navy to cancel this program as soon as possible."[10]

On 19 August Bantz provided Secretary of Defense Neil H. McElroy with a detailed justification of why the program had been terminated and what the consequences were likely to be. Because of "steadily mounting costs coupled with continued technical difficulties and development delays," the program had already been reduced to fourteen aircraft, including eight P6M-2s-not enough in any case to contribute materially to the offensive capabilities of the fleet. Costs were likely to go up at least another $7 million if everything went well, and even more if there were any additional problems. The money saved would be reallocated to other programs. As for the effects on Martin, a major defense contractor, Bantz forecast that employment in Baltimore would drop from 4,000 workers to 1,000. It was a big reduction that would cause immediate hardships, but the company had planned to reduce its work force to that level anyway as it phased out the P6M program by stages into early 1960.[11]

News of the cancellation came to Martin by telegram on the afternoon of 20 August. Beginning the following day, all manufacturing, flight testing, and other work ceased on the P6M project. Remaining in the hangar were four completed P6M-2s awaiting finishing touches and their first flights. The other aircraft joined the YP6M-1s that had already been grounded. George Bunker did his best to bolster morale with a statement in the Martin newsletter a few weeks later. He consoled the company's employees and stockholders by saying that the effect of the termination was "not of great magnitude," because most of the program had been completed, and that only a relatively small amount of additional money would have been forthcoming from the navy in any case. Notwithstanding this hopeful outlook, Martin officials in Baltimore expressed surprise that the cancellation came so quickly on the heels of congressional statements by Dixon and other BuAer officers proclaiming confidence in the airplane and the SSF concept.[12]

As with all contract terminations, there were many loose ends to tie up in the fall of 1959. In addition to reminding Martin that the airplanes could not under any circumstances be flown, BuAer stipulated that the company hand over all reports on the aircraft and its subsystems, and develop plans for disposing of all tooling and airframes, while recovering as much material as possible and retaining all support and logistical equipment that might be useful for other aircraft.[13]

The effects of the cancellation on Martin and its people in Baltimore were severe, although they could have been much worse. The company had already furloughed workers when it lost the ASW seaplane contract to Convair early in 1957, and its failure to gain an air force contract for its twin-engine, Mach 2 XB-68 tactical bomber had meant additional layoffs. Mitigating those reverses was BuAer's decision at the end of 1958 to extend a contract for the modification of additional P5M-2s, which guaranteed continued employment at Baltimore through the next couple of years. Still, the prospect of losing more than 6,000 jobs with the SeaMaster and other cutbacks at the Middle River plant prompted Maryland Republican Sen. J. Glenn Beall to wire Secretary of the Navy Gates in protest. When he learned of the P6M cancellation, Beall joined with Rep. George H. Fallon, a Democrat, in a futile effort to convince the navy to reconsider its decision.[14]

Martin fulfilled the termination agreement over the next year, accounting for all material and settling its obligations with 2,800 subcontractors. Most of the P6M engines were salvaged for use in other aircraft, and many of the instruments and electronic gear were removed. The fourteen YP6M-1s and P6M-2s (one YP6M-1 had been earmarked for static tests in June 1959 when the wing failed on the previous static test vehicle) lingered at the Martin plant for the next year or so before being sold for scrap. The total bill to the government for the program, including the ship conversions, was $445.5 million, of which the government recouped $83.8 million from reclaimed material. In the final settlement, Martin received full compensation for all of the work it had undertaken for the government.[15]

Not surprisingly, in the aftermath of the P6M termination there was outrage in some circles about the waste of nearly a half billion dollars on a program that ended with only sixteen flyable aircraft, two of which had been destroyed in accidents—one of them fatal—and none of which had achieved operational status. Robert S. McNamara, secretary of defense in the new Kennedy administration, zeroed in on the P6M program as a case study of the need to "fly before you buy." In testimony before the Joint Economic Committee on Capitol Hill in March 1963, he pointed out that the airplane had been "advanced into the production phase long before even the basic design problems were solved." Even worse, most of the airplane's technical shortcomings "had still not been solved" when the contract was canceled years after the first production order had been placed.[16]

In March 1964 the General Accounting Office (GAO), which served as the federal watchdog for waste and mismanagement, issued a stinging report to Congress on the P6M program. The GAO argued that the navy could have saved more than $209 million had it not awarded Martin the P6M-2 production order or proceeded with ship conversions when it was known at the time that the aerodynamic and hydrodynamic deficiencies of the YP6M-1 made the airplane unlikely ever to meet its original mission requirements. Failing to see the forest for the trees, the navy, astonishingly, had waited nearly two years after signing the production contract before it undertook a major assessment of the program. Meanwhile, ten years' worth of project reports piled up on BuAer desks. Both the navy and Martin had ignored early warning signs from NACA model tests that predicted the airplane would encounter high-speed buffeting that would preclude meeting original performance criteria. The loss of both XP6M-1 aircraft in crashes was another indication of serious problems that went unheeded. The GAO blamed Martin for, among other things, overlooking the early problem of fuselage heating from inboard engine exhausts, deficient hydraulic control systems, understrength wings and tail surfaces, dangerously ambitious flight test schedules, and cavalier redefinition of design and performance parameters when the aircraft did not meet the expected test results.

In its defense, Martin replied that the P6M represented "cutting-edge" technology and that unforeseen obstacles were to be expected. By the time the navy canceled the contract, most of the problems had been overcome, and the company would have provided "a satisfactory weapon system . . . at a total cost equivalent to, or less than, comparable weapon systems." The navy admitted that in retrospect it should have ended the program sooner, but that it had gone ahead in accordance with its policies and procedures at the time. Martin, which had not been guilty of malfeasance or fraud, should not be held accountable for the additional costs incurred under the terms of the contract. The GAO agreed, adding a recommendation that in the future contractors selected on the basis of their competence and experience needed to be held responsible for poor engineering or basic design shortcomings that led to additional expenses. Moreover, the government needed to reexamine its policy of awarding cost-plus-fixed-fee contracts that left manufacturers immune from the consequences of delays and cost overruns.[17]

Immediately after the GAO report appeared, the Senate joined the debate over waste in defense expenditures. On 25 March Sen. John J. Williams, a Republican from Delaware, singled out the P6M contract as "another typical example of the irresponsible manner in which the [defense department] squanders the taxpayers' money." A few months later Sen. George S. McGovern, a Democrat from South Dakota, commended Secretary McNamara for his diligence in identifying and rooting out waste and imposing stricter management controls on military projects. At the same time, he argued, that did not absolve Congress of its responsibility to curb "unnecessary military spending." Among the many examples identified by McGovern, the P6M stood out as an "unjustified expense" that "failed to produce a single serviceable airplane"; he stated that "the national defense has been weakened by this apparent blundering."[18]

Criticism of the P6M and SSF was narrowly focused on the immediate issues of contracts, cost overruns, and official oversight, which had cursed navy and military aircraft procurement since before World War I. At no time in the aftermath of the cancellation did anyone ask basic questions about how or why the program had failed and what the implications were for the weapon system concept. The GAO report was silent on the issue of concurrency in the weapon system approach, which overlapped research and development, evaluation, and production in an attempt to reduce acquisition time.[19] Nor did the report study how the SeaMaster, Sea Dart, Tradewind, ASW seaplane, or support ships and basing plans were to have been integrated into a comprehensive offensive system. And nowhere was there a comparison with such other highly visible and successful programs as the McDonnell F-4 Phantom and Polaris submarine-launched ballistic missile.

The P6M cancellation signaled the end for the SSF but did not deter the navy from entertaining ideas and proposals for even more advanced seaplane projects. Convair and Martin continued working on concepts for high-performance flying boats through the remainder of the decade. Convair had the most eclectic and ambitious studies, beginning as early as December 1955 with a twin-engine, Mach 3, 800-mile-range attack aircraft with a retracting step and hydro-ski. Convair followed with another design concept for a Mach 2, twin-engine attack seaplane with twice the range of the airplane in the previous study. An unusual feature of the design was that the aircraft's podded engines could be tilted up to clear the water for takeoffs and landings. Most intriguing was a preliminary study in July 1958 for a hydro-ski-equipped, 200,000-pound, Mach 4, delta-wing attack seaplane with a range of 1,675 nautical miles. Power came from three Pratt and Whitney J58 turbojet engines—an early potential application of the same power plants later used in the legendary Mach 3 Lockheed SR-71 reconnaissance aircraft. Convair was not unaware of the many problems associated with near-hypersonic flight. To overcome aerodynamic heating, stainless steel construction would be used;

other problems, such as inlet design and skin friction drag, would require more intensive engineering studies.[20]

Martin began exploring supersonic attack seaplane designs in 1954, followed by a contract from the navy for a preliminary engineering study in March 1956. The result was the Model 329, which went through various iterations over the next two years. Most of the studies centered on an airplane weighing about 250,000 pounds, with a range of 1,500 nautical miles and Mach 2 dash speed. Completed in March 1959, the last of Martin's studies was for a 90,000-pound, Mach 3 aircraft with a range of up to 1,800 nautical miles, using a variety of wing planforms and engine installations, and either hydro-skis or hydrofoils. Martin found that a nonbuoyant, high-density fuselage was necessary to achieve the performance levels desired. The General Electric J93 afterburning engines were located under the wing, which meant that the airplane took off and landed inverted.[21]

Among its many advanced projects in the 1950s, Martin joined the ANP quest, along with Fairchild, Convair, General Electric, Pratt and Whitney, and other companies. The air force had already staked out ANP, but not wanting to be excluded, the navy had initiated its own projects, starting in 1953 with studies of a subsonic nuclear-powered seaplane that could be used for long-range antisubmarine patrols. The February 1956 staff study by the office of the DCNO (Air) extended the ANP concept to the SSF. The study recommended the navy begin with a testbed or proof-of-concept vehicle, possibly based on the P6M. Next would be a 200,000-pound, all-weather attack seaplane similar to the SeaMaster that could cruise for 5,000 nautical miles, then deliver nuclear weapons on its target after a sea-level dash at high-subsonic speeds. Finally, the study envisaged a 300,000-pound aircraft with the same capability, except that it would make its final approach to the objective at a speed of Mach 1.3.[22]

Martin provided several feasibility studies between 1953 and 1956 incorporating nuclear power into sea-based aircraft. The Model 331 went through more than twenty variations, one of which closely adhered to the basic P6M design, incorporating a lightweight GE reactor in a hull lengthened by 10 feet, providing power for two turbojet engines located in nacelles above the wing. Later versions—some supersonic—borrowed nothing from the basic P6M design. As the weight of reactors and related components went up, the navy looked for bigger aircraft. One proposal, first suggested in late 1957, was to convert a 300,000-pound MTOW British Saunders-Roe Princess flying boat to carry a small reactor powering turboprop engines. Contracts went to General Electric, Pratt and Whitney, Convair, and Martin the following year. Opposition to the program came from John Hayward, now a vice admiral and DCNO (Research and Development). More knowledgeable about nuclear power and weapons than anyone else in the service, Hayward testified in April 1959 that the nuclear Princess was "a monument to how not to run a technical program." Secretary of Defense McNamara wisely killed the ANP program in the spring of 1961.[23]

Fascinating as they were, the Convair and Martin advanced seaplane studies were the last gasps of a dying concept and did nothing more than keep the companies' design staffs and model-building shops occupied in between other, more promising and realistic projects. Remnants of the SSF remained with the Convair R3Y, *Albemarle, Guavina,* and other converted vessels, but for all intents and purposes the idea of a mobile sea-based attack system was dead with no hope of resurrection.

It would be easy to dismiss the entire idea as an ill-conceived, ill-defined waste of time, money, and the efforts of thousands of men and women. Yet to do so would be to miss an important element of naval aviation that for the better part of three decades offered the only alternative to the carrier- and land-based aircraft. As a complete weapon system, the SSF fell far short of what its proponents advocated, due in part to technological and managerial shortcomings and in part to strategic, operational, and economic realities. Its advantages of low cost and the promise of more rapid deployment cycles than aircraft carriers evaporated as the numbers and costs of dedicated SSF support vessels escalated.

Much of that was evident only in hindsight. Could anyone blame Admiral King for calling for the employment of advanced seaplanes to augment the limited number of carriers available in the Pacific? Was it apparent going into World War II that the United States would have available to it a network of facilities that brought nearly every corner of the globe into range of land-based aircraft? Was it evident to those in the early 1950s who saw the navy losing its traditional role to the new air force that the submarine-launched ballistic missile would prove to be far better as a strategic force than either the carrier or any version of the SSF? We only know after the fact that these alternatives succeeded and that the attack seaplane was a dead end.

Although the flexibility and low cost promised by the SSF proved in the end illusory, even a small force might have had some operational advantages.

Charles Minter, looking back on his tour as P6M program manager, said: "It's too bad in a way. The damned airplane did have some interesting capabilities and it could operate in much heavier sea states than any of the PBYs or PBMs we had before." He regretted that "we didn't operate about six of those airplanes out of Patuxent River . . . to see just what the capabilities were." James Russell, no friend of the program at the time, wrote many years later that "time ran out" on the SSF before all of the aerodynamic problems with the P6M could be resolved and that the decision to cancel was a "heart breaker."[24]

Consider, too, what might have been had the navy deployed one or two P6M squadrons by the end of 1961. As U.S. involvement in the Vietnam War escalated after 1965, it is conceivable that the unit would have been dispatched to the western Pacific. Forward based, say, on one of the deserted Paracel Islands, about 400 miles southeast of Hanoi, with two converted AVs providing support and maintenance, R3Ys replenishing ordnance and other supplies on a "just in time" basis, and the entire self-contained force protected by ASW seaplanes and possibly a variation of the Sea Dart, the squadron would have provided an additional navy contribution to air operations against North Vietnam. With its all-weather, low-altitude capability, the force might have been at least as effective in the strike role as the carrier-based Grumman A-6, and it could have been effective in mining Haiphong harbor.

Speculation, yes, but historians often begin their analyses with speculation. It remains that the SSF, however intriguing and however promising it appeared, was never to play a role in the navy's offensive mission. For a variety of reasons, the concept and its constituent elements seemed always one or two steps behind events, both before and after World War II. Advocates of the concept did themselves no favors either, by consistently underestimating its costs and the time needed for its development. It should have been obvious, too, that the SSF, while enjoying support at the highest echelons of the navy leadership, could never overcome a fundamental cultural difference within the service. Carrier aviators, who came to dominate nearly all levels of the navy bureaucracy, were unwilling to commit to a weapon that appeared to compete directly with their ships and aircraft, especially in times of defense budget reductions.[25]

It is tempting to argue that the SSF would have succeeded in the 1950s had the navy more quickly identified it as a weapon system and imposed on it a more rigorous program management structure, along the lines of the F-4 or Polaris. Yet historian Glenn Bugos cautions that program management could also lead to even "bigger failures," such as the TFX multi-mission/multi-role/multi-service fighter, and that in the 1970s the trend reversed to focus on smaller, simpler, and more flexible program models. The much-cited example of system management in Polaris, as Harvey Sapolsky has shown, was more an exercise in public relations than a revolution in large-scale organization.[26] One should keep in mind, too, the axiom that failures can often be more revealing and instructive than successes.

Perhaps the most important lesson to be learned from the SSF was that with technology there are almost always alternatives and choices that, taken objectively, are equally viable. Only through a combination of factors—many of them nontechnical—does one technology or another emerge supreme. That the SSF ultimately did not become a reality provides a sobering glimpse of the limitations of technology in complex, rapidly changing strategic, polit-ical, cultural, and economic environments. Planners and strategists would do well to take the lessons of the SSF to heart before forging ahead with costly technologies based on preconceived expectations that they will provide swift and simple solutions to difficult military problems or bring about a revolution in the way wars are fought and won.

# Chronology

| | |
|---|---|
| 1935, 15 March | Consolidated's XP3Y-1 flying boat begins flight tests. |
| 1936, October–November | Four VP squadrons, supported by the tender *Wright* and eight smaller vessels, participate in simulated bombing attacks in the vicinity of Hawaii. |
| 1937, February | Hall-Aluminum Aircraft Corporation delivers the XPTBH-2 torpedo floatplane to the navy for flight tests. |
| 1938 | NACA publication of Walter Sottorf's research on high l/b ratio seaplane hulls stimulates new interest in the flying boat. |
| 1938, March–April | In Fleet Problem XIX, Consolidated PBYs "attack" the carriers *Lexington* and *Saratoga* off the California coast. |
| 1938, July | Convair begins tests of advanced flying boat concepts in San Diego. |
| 1941, August | Cdr. Wilford Jay ("Jasper") Holmes publishes "Rendezvous" in *The Saturday Evening Post,* under the pseudonym Alec Hudson. |
| 1941, 27 December | PBYs flying from the island of Ambon off New Guinea fly 800 miles to bomb the Japanese base of Jolo. |
| 1942, 3–4 March | In the Japanese K Operation, two four-engine Kawanishi H8K "Emily" flying boats fly 1,900 miles from Wotje in the Marshall Islands, refueling from submarines, in an unsuccessful attack on Hawaii. |
| 1942, 11 June | PBYs mount around-the-clock bombing "blitz" against Japanese ships and shore installations on the island of Kiska. |
| 1942–43 | Radar-equipped PBY-5 "Black Cat" squadrons, operating mainly at night, attack Japanese transports and warships during the Guadalcanal campaign. |

| | |
|---|---|
| 1944, 1 September | Convair receives a navy contract for studies of advanced flying boats with high l/b ratios. |
| 1946, 19 June | Convair executes a contract to build two XP5Y-1 heavily armed flying boats for long-range antishipping and ASW missions. |
| 1947, 17 January | The 27A program to upgrade *Essex*-class carriers for heavy, long-range attack aircraft is approved. |
| 1948, 28 April | A modified P2V-2 Neptune takes off from the *Midway*-class carrier *Coral Sea* and flies ashore to the Norfolk Naval Air Station. |
| 1948, 3 July | The North American XAJ-1 carrier attack bomber flies for the first time. |
| 1949, 3 March | A team under Vice Adm. Robert Carney, DCNO (Logistics), presents a proposal for using long-range flying boats in conjunction with surface ships and submarines to supplement aircraft carriers in nuclear strike and other missions. |
| 1949, 23 April | Secretary of Defense Louis A. Johnson cancels construction of the supercarrier *United States*. |
| 1949, 19 May | Convair receives a navy contract for the Skate jet seaplane night fighter. |
| 1949, 27 October | Adm. Louis Denfeld is relieved as CNO in the aftermath of the "revolt of the admirals." |
| 1950, 18 April | The Convair XP5Y-1 flies for the first time. |
| 1951, 19 January | Convair receives a navy contract for two Y2-2 delta-wing jet seaplane fighters (later redesignated XF2Y-1). |
| 1951, 5 February | VAH-1 deploys overseas for the first time. |
| 1951, 30 July | BuAer calls for proposals from the industry for the HSML seaplane. |
| 1952, 10 January | Convair submits its proposal for the HSML. |
| 1952, 1 February | The Glenn L. Martin Company submits its HSML proposal, known as the Model 275 SeaMaster. |
| 1952, 22 April | BuAer asks Convair and Martin to resubmit proposals for the HSML. |
| 1952, 1 August | Convair submits its revised HSML proposal to BuAer. |
| 1952, 4 August | Martin submits its revised HSML proposal to BuAer. |
| 1952, 20 August | Convair receives a navy contract to build twelve F2Y-1 Sea Dart fighter aircraft. |
| 1952, 7 October | Martin receives a navy contract for two Model 275 Sea-Masters, with the designation XP6M-1. |
| 1952, 28 October | The Douglas twin-jet A3D Skywarrior carrier bomber flies for the first time. |
| 1953, 2 March | Martin's XP6M-1 mockup is completed. |
| 1953, 9 April | Convair's XF2Y-1 makes its first flight. |

| | |
|---|---|
| 1953, July | Martin completes a preliminary study of the basing and logistical support requirements for the SSF. |
| 1953, 15 July | The Convair XP5Y-1 crashes during a routine test flight in San Diego. |
| 1953, 30 October | The National Security Council approves NSC 162/2, establishing the Eisenhower administration's "New Look" military policy. |
| 1954, 25 February | Convair's R3Y-1 Tradewind flies for the first time. |
| 1954, 1 October | Martin submits a study incorporating the SSF into the "New Look" policy. |
| 1954, 1 November | BuAer completes a study favorably comparing the SSF to the carrier task force. |
| 1954, 4 November | Convair's YF2Y-1 Sea Dart crashes in San Diego, killing the pilot. |
| 1954, 21 December | Martin rolls out the first XP6M-1 SeaMaster. |
| 1954, 28 December | CNO Adm. Robert Carney concludes that the P6M program adds to the navy's strategic flexibility. |
| 1955, 28 January | Martin receives a contract for six preproduction versions of the SeaMaster, designated YP6M-1. |
| 1955, 14 July | The Martin XP6M-1 SeaMaster makes its first flight. |
| 1955, 2 November | CNO Adm. Arleigh Burke and Lord Louis Mountbatten view XP6M-1 flights at the Martin plant. |
| 1955, 7 December | The first XP6M-1 is lost in a crash that kills all four crew members. |
| 1956, January | The submarine *Guavina* (SS-362) returns to service after conversion as an AOSS to support SSF operations. |
| 1956, February | The seaplane tender *Albemarle* (AV-5) begins conversion to handle the Martin P6M. |
| 1956, 17 April | Martin completes another study of basing and logistics requirements for the SSF. |
| 1956, June | Capt. Charles S. Minter Jr. takes over as the navy's P6M program manager. |
| 1956, 31 August | Martin receives a contract for twenty-four production SeaMasters, designated as P6M-2s. |
| 1956, 9 November | The second XP6M-1 crashes; all four crew members escape. |
| 1957, 1 February | Convair wins a design competition for an open-ocean ASW seaplane, designated P6Y-1. |
| 1957, 21 June | The navy cuts Martin's P6M-2 order from twenty-four to eighteen airplanes. |
| 1958, 20 January | The YP6M-1 makes its initial flight. |
| 1958, 26 May | Vice Adm. Robert B. Pirie becomes DCNO (Air). |
| 1958, 24 November | The navy cuts the P6M-2 program to eight airplanes. |
| 1959, 17 February | The first P6M-2 flies for the first time. |

| | |
|---|---|
| 1959, 12 June | Flight tests begin with the P6M-2 equipped with inflight refueling apparatus. |
| 1959, 20 August | The navy informs the Martin Company of cancellation of the P6M program. |
| 1964, March | GAO issues a report to Congress identifying the P6M program as an example of waste and mismanagement in defense procurement. |

# Notes

## Chapter 1. Naval Aviation in Crisis

1. Alec Hudson, *"Up Periscope!" and Other Stories* (Annapolis, MD: Naval Institute Press, 1992), pp. vi, 1–40 (especially pp. 1–8, 20–24); Edwin T. Layton, with Roger Pineau and John Costello, *"And I Was There": Pearl Harbor and Midway—Breaking the Secrets* (New York: William Morrow, 1985), p. 374.

2. Layton, *"And I Was There,"* pp. 372–74; John Prados, *Combined Fleet Decoded: The Secret History of American Intelligence and the Japanese Navy in World War II* (New York: Random House, 1995), pp. 282–84.

3. David R. Mets, "The Influence of Aviation on the Evolution of American Naval Thought," in Philip S. Meilinger, ed., *The Paths of Heaven: The Evolution of Airpower Theory* (Maxwell Air Force Base, AL: Air University Press, 1997), pp. 131–37; Jeffrey G. Barlow, *Revolt of the Admirals: The Fight for Naval Aviation, 1945–1950* (Washington, DC: Naval Historical Center, 1994), pp. 30–32, 108–14; Fred Kaplan, *The Wizards of Armageddon* (New York: Simon and Schuster, 1983), pp. 232–33.

4. Memo, Adm. Robert B. Carney to Vice Chief of Naval Operations, 28 December 1954, file A1-1, box 1, Double Zero Files, 1954, Operational Archives, Naval Historical Center (hereafter cited as OANHC).

5. Stan Piet and Al Raithel, *Martin P6M SeaMaster* (Bel Air, MD: Martineer Press, 2001), especially p. 23. Piet and Raithel's study is the most detailed history of the airplane. For other components of the system, see B. J. Long, *Convair XF2Y-1 and YF2Y-1 Sea Dart Experimental Supersonic Seaplane Interceptors* (Simi Valley, CA: Steve Ginter, 1992); and Steve Ginter, *Convair XP5Y-1 and R3Y-1/2 Tradewind* (Simi Valley, CA: Steve Ginter, 1996).

6. Edward S. Miller, *War Plan Orange: The U.S. Strategy to Defeat Japan, 1897–1945* (Annapolis, MD: Naval Institute Press, 1991), pp. 178–79.

7. Jerry Miller, *Nuclear Weapons and Aircraft Carriers* (Washington, DC: Smithsonian Institution Press, 2001), p. 238.

148    NOTES TO PAGES 5–12

8. Barlow, *Revolt of the Admirals,* p. 222; Norman Friedman, *U.S. Aircraft Carriers: An Illustrated Design History* (Annapolis, MD: Naval Institute Press, 1983), p. 263.

9. Miller, *Nuclear Weapons and Aircraft Carriers,* pp. 77–109.

10. Kenneth P. Werrell, *The Evolution of the Cruise Missile* (Maxwell Air Force Base, AL: Air University Press, 1985), pp. 114–19.

11. Glenn E. Bugos, *Engineering the F-4 Phantom II: Parts into Systems* (Annapolis, MD: Naval Institute Press, 1996), pp. 3, 7, 19, 56; for a definition of "weapon system," see Lawrence R. Benson, *Acquisition Management in the United States Air Force and Its Predecessors* (Washington, DC: Air Force History and Museums Program, 1997), p. 24.

12. Carl H. Builder, *The Masks of War: American Military Styles in Strategy and Analysis* (Baltimore: Johns Hopkins University Press, 1989), pp. 18, 25; George A. Rodney, "The P6M Seamaster," undated speech, file AM-201680-0, Martin Seamaster Family, NASM Library, Washington, DC; Capt. Robert B. Greenwood to Adm. James S. Russell, 6 January 1986 (courtesy of Vice Adm. Charles S. Minter Jr.).

13. Laurence K. Loftin Jr., *Quest for Performance: The Evolution of Modern Aircraft* (Washington, DC: NASA, 1985), pp. 213–15.

14. For "disruptive technologies," see Clayton M. Christensen, *The Innovator's Dilemma: When New Technologies Cause Great Firms to Fail* (Boston: Harvard Business School Press, 1997), pp. xv–xvii.

## Chapter 2. Seaplanes and Strategy

1. Miller, *War Plan Orange,* pp. 86–143.

2. Ibid., pp. 175–77.

3. Memo for files, Cdr. Richmond Kelly Turner, 16 October 1929, Aer-P-2-EMN VP L8(1) A1-3(30), file VP, box 7; memo, W. D. Clark to Design Section, BuAer, 10 March 1930, Aer-D-14-LH VP, vol. 1, file VP, box 5182; both in Records of Divisions and Offices, Office Services Division/Administrative Services, Secret Correspondence, 1921–38, Records of the Bureau of Aeronautics, Record Group 72, National Archives (hereafter cited as Divisions and Offices, OSD/Admin. Services, BuAer Records, RG 72, NA).

4. F. J. Horne, Commander, Aircraft, Scouting Force, to CNO, 13 April 1931, VP/A4-3(609), file VP-VT, box 264, Formerly Secret Correspondence, 1927–39, Office of the Secretary of the Navy, General Records of the Department of the Navy, 1798–1947, Record Group 80, National Archives (hereafter cited as SecNav, Gen. Records of Dept. of the Navy, 1798–1947, RG 80, NA).

5. Rear Adm. W. A. Moffett to CNO, 7 May 1931, Aer-P-EMN, VP, FF11-1, VPM1/F1-1, file VP-VT; Moffett to Asst. SecNav for Aeronautics, 3 July 1931, Aer-P-EMN, Aero-560-Bu-31, file VV; both in box 264, Formerly Secret Correspondence, 1927–39, SecNav, Gen. Records of Dept. of the Navy, 1798–1947, RG 80, NA. Thomas C. Hone, Norman Friedman, and Mark D. Mandeles, *American and British Aircraft Carrier Development, 1919–1941* (Annapolis, MD: Naval Institute Press, 1999), pp. 59–60; Richard C. Knott, *The American Flying Boat: An Illustrated History* (Annapolis, MD: Naval Institute Press, 1979), pp. 96–100.

6. Friedman, *U.S. Aircraft Carriers,* pp. 79–83.

7. Thomas Wildenberg, *All the Factors of Victory: Adm. Joseph Mason Reeves and the Origins of Carrier Airpower* (Washington, DC: Brassey's, 2003), pp. 240–41; Miller, *War Plan Orange,* p. 178.

8. Roscoe Creed, *PBY: The Catalina Flying Boat* (Annapolis, MD: Naval Institute Press, 1985), pp. 24–28, 306.

9. Ibid., pp. 28–34, 306.

10. Lt. Cdr. D. Royce to Plans Div., 31 October 1933, Aer-D-171-IE F41-9 VP, vol. 3, file VP, box 5182, Divisions and Offices, OSD/Admin. Services, BuAer Records, RG 72, NA; Adm. Harold R. Stark, Chief, BuOrd, to CNO, 23 October 1935, VZ/S1-1(2/150) (Ma11) (G10), file VZ, box 212, Formerly Confidential Correspondence, 1927–39, Secretary of the Navy, General Records of Department of the Navy, 1798–1947, RG 80, NA; Bureau of Aeronautics, Resume of Progress, 1933–36, p. 7 (from BuAer Records, RG 72, NA, courtesy of Thomas Wildenberg).

11. Detail Specification for Model XPTBH-1 Airplane, Twin-Float Monoplane (Class VPTB) Patrol-Torpedo-Bomber, 22 March 1934; Contract, XPTBH-1, Bureau of Supplies and Accounts, 30 June 1934; both in file XPTBH-2, box 158, Aircraft Specification file, Records of the Bureau of Aeronautics, Record Group 72, National Archives (hereafter cited as Aircraft Spec. file, BuAer Records, RG 72, NA).

12. Memo, Ralph Weyerbacher, Material Div., to Chief, BuAer, 22 December 1934, Aer-E-14-EP C-37178, vol. 4, file C-37178, box 681, Contract Correspondence, 1926–39, Records of the Bureau of Aeronautics, Record Group 72, National Archives (hereafter cited as Contract Corresp., 1926–39, BuAer Records, RG 72, NA); King to Inspector of Naval Aircraft, New York, 31 December 1934, Aer-E-14-IE C-37178, file XPTBH-2, box 158, Aircraft Spec. file, BuAer Records, RG 72, NA.

13. Detail Specification for Model XPTBH-2 Airplane, Twin-Float Monoplane (Class VPTB) Patrol-Torpedo-Bomber, 23 January 1935; Report of Mockup Inspection of the Model XPTBH-2 Airplane, Contract 37178, 16 May 1935; both in file XPTBH-2, box 158, Aircraft Spec. file, BuAer Records, RG 72, NA. E. H. Van Patten (Bureau of Supplies and Accounts) to Hall-Aluminum Aircraft Corp., 13 March 1936, Nos-37178, SPD, vol. 1, file 37178, box 680; flight test information, vol. 9, file 37178, box 682; Rear Adm. A. B. Cook to Asst. SecNav, 2 March 1938, Aer-PL-EMN C-37178 QM(58) VP, vol. 10, file 37178, box 683; all in Contract Corresp., 1926–39, BuAer Records, RG 72, NA. *New York Times,* 18 February 1938.

14. "Facilities Afloat and Ashore Required to Operate Enlarged Aviation Program," Chairman General Board to SecNav, 5 September 1934, G.B. No. 404 (Serial No. 1650), Confidential, 404, 1934 file; Chief, BuAer to CNO, 6 March 1934, Aer-P-EMN AV A19(11), enclosure to 1st Indorsement, CNO to SecNav, 17 March 1934, Op-23X-BD, (SC)N1-9; both in box 19, General Board Subject File, General Records of the Department of the Navy, Record Group 80, National Archives (hereafter cited as GB Subject File, GB Records, Gen. Records of Dept. of the Navy, RG 80, NA).

15. "Facilities Afloat and Ashore Required to Operate Enlarged Aviation Program," Chairman General Board to SecNav, 5 September 1934; Notes on discussion re air force appropriate to a Treaty Navy—by Admiral Standley, 31 July 1934, T.S.W.; memo, King to General Board, 31 March 1934, Aer-P-1-EMN A1-3(1) QB/EN15;

all in 404, 1934 file, G.B. No. 404 (Serial No. 1650), box 19, GB Subject File, GB Records, Gen. Records of Dept. of the Navy, RG 80, NA.

16. Hearings before the General Board of the Navy, 1934, vol. 1 (micro roll 10), pp. 68, 72, 82.

17. Notes on discussion re air force appropriate to Treaty Navy—Rear Admiral King, 31 July 1934, R.E.S., 404, 1934 file, G.B. No. 404 (Serial No. 1650), box 19, GB Subject File, GB Records, Gen. Records of Dept. of the Navy, RG 80, NA.

18. Memo, King to General Board, 2 August 1934, Aer-PL-EMN VPB VTB QB/EN15, 404, 1934 file, G.B. No. 404 (Serial No. 1650), box 19, GB Subject File, GB Records, Gen. Records of Dept. of the Navy, RG 80, NA.

19. King to General Board, 9 August 1934, Aer-PL-EMN A1-3(1) A21-1 QB/EN15, 404, 1934 file, G.B. No. 404 (Serial No. 1650), box 19, GB Subject File, GB Records, Gen. Records of Dept. of the Navy, RG 80, NA.

20. Hearings before the General Board of the Navy, 1934, vol. 1 (micro roll 10), pp. 116–20, 125.

21. "Facilities Afloat and Ashore Required to Operate Enlarged Aviation Program," Chairman General Board to SecNav, 5 September 1934, 404, 1934 file, G.B. No. 404 (Serial No. 1650), box 19, GB Subject File, GB Records, Gen. Records of Dept. of the Navy, RG 80, NA.

22. King to CNO, 27 September 1934, Aer-PL-1-EMN A1-3(1) QB/EN 15, 1934 file, G.B. No. 404 (Serial No. 1673), box 19, GB Subject File, GB Records, Gen. Records of Dept. of the Navy, RG 80, NA.

23. Memo, Engineering Div., BuAer, to Plans Div., 12 October 1934, Aer-E-21-EP VP, vol. 3, file VP, box 5182, Divisions and Offices, OSD/Admin. Services, BuAer Records, RG 72, NA; J. S. Woods to CNO, 24 August 1937, Op-12B-CTB (SC)AA/A1-3, box 142, Formerly Confidential Correspondence, 1927–39, SecNav, Gen. Records of Dept. of the Navy, 1798–1947, RG 80, NA (courtesy of Thomas Wildenberg).

24. CNO to CinCUS, undated (probably January 1935), Op-12Y-CTB, file VP-VT, box 264, Formerly Secret Correspondence, 1927–39, SecNav, Gen. Records of Dept. of the Navy, 1798–1947, RG 80, NA.

25. G. J. Meyers to CNO, 11 February 1935, Op-12-CTB, file VP-VT, box 264, Formerly Secret Correspondence, 1927–39, SecNav, Gen. Records of Dept. of the Navy, 1798–1947, RG 80, NA.

26. Memo, King to CNO, 22 March 1935, file VP-VT, box 264, Formerly Secret Correspondence, 1927–39, SecNav, Gen. Records of Dept. of the Navy, 1798–1947, RG 80, NA.

27. CNO to CinCUS and President Naval War College, 1 April 1935, Op-12-CTS (SC)VP, file VP-VT, box 264, Formerly Secret Correspondence, 1927–39, SecNav, Gen. Records of Dept. of the Navy, 1798–1947, RG 80, NA.

28. Memo, G. J. Meyers to CNO, 4 April 1935, Op-12-CTB (D-2388), file VP-VT, box 264, Formerly Secret Correspondence, 1927–39, SecNav, Gen. Records of Dept. of the Navy, 1798–1947, RG 80, NA.

29. Reeves to CNO, 28 June 1935, F1/3069 95-Gn-(0); memo, W. S. Pye to CNO, 23 July 1935, Op-12-CTB (SC)VP (D-3478); both in file VB to VV, box 212, Formerly Confidential Correspondence, 1927–39, SecNav, Gen. Records of Dept. of the Navy, 1798–1947, RG 80, NA.

30. Memo, A. G. Kirk, Director, Ships Movements Div., to Director, War Plans Div., 14 August 1935, Op-38-E-EMR (SC)VP, file VP-VT, box 264, Formerly Secret Correspondence, 1927–39, SecNav, Gen. Records of Dept. of the Navy, 1798–1947, RG 80, NA.

31. King to CinCUS, 23 November 1936, A16-3/A4-3 378; King to CinCUS, 7 December 1936, A16-3 395; King to CinCUS, 8 December 1936, A4-3/A16-3 403; all in file Advanced Base Exercise South of Hawaii, box 107, Warfare Operations, Commander Aircraft, United States Fleet, Scouting Force, General Correspondence, Naval Operating Forces, Record Group 313, National Archives (hereafter cited as U.S. Fleet, Scouting Force, Gen. Corresp., Naval Operating Forces, RG 313, NA).

32. Miller, *War Plan Orange,* pp. 200–201.

33. Clark G. Reynolds, *Admiral John H. Towers: The Struggle for Naval Air Supremacy* (Annapolis, MD: Naval Institute Press, 1991), pp. 276–79.

34. Ibid., p. 241; J. S. Woods to CNO, 24 August 1937, Op-12B-CTB (SC)AA/A1-3, box 142, Formerly Confidential Correspondence, 1927–39, SecNav, Gen. Records of Dept. of the Navy, 1798–1947, RG 80, NA (courtesy of Thomas Wildenberg). Capt. A. C. Read to CNO, 25 June 1937, Aer-E-34-NS SS VP; Adm. J. O. Richardson to Chief of Bureau of Construction and Repair, 30 June 1937, Op-23C-MS (SC)L8-4 Serial 4296; both in SS file, box 7, Divisions and Offices, OSD/Admin. Services, Secret Corresp., 1921–38, BuAer Records, RG 72, NA.

35. A. B. Cook to Commandant Twelfth Naval District, 23 January 1940, A16-3 0132, file A16-3, box 107, Warfare Operations, Commander Aircraft, U.S. Fleet, Scouting Force, Gen. Corresp., Naval Operating Forces, RG 313, NA; Miller, *War Plan Orange,* pp. 243–44.

36. H. R. Stark to Chairman General Board, 21 November 1941, Op-12-CTB (SC)F1-1 D-36418 Serial 0123412, file G. B. 449-1942, box 195, GB Records, Gen. Records of Dept. of the Navy, RG 80, NA.

37. Creed, *PBY,* pp. 86–87, 105–9.

38. Ibid., pp. 128–42.

39. Ibid., pp. 162–77, 263–73; Richard C. Knott, *Black Cat Raiders of World War II* (Annapolis, MD: Nautical and Aviation Publishing Company of America, 1981), pp. 103–84.

## Chapter 3. The Carrier Conundrum

1. Barlow, *Revolt of the Admirals,* pp. 184–91; John L. Sullivan to Louis Johnson, 26 April 1949, file A1, box 9, Double Zero Files, 1951, OANHC.

2. Barlow, *Revolt of the Admirals,* pp. 205–9, 215–33.

3. Ibid., pp. 247–54, 269–77.

4. Ibid., pp. 164–73, 277–81.

5. Ibid., pp. 283–87; memo, Rear Adm. J. H. Cassady, ACNO (Air) to Rear Adm. Ralph Ofstie, 29 April 1949, file A21/1-1/1, box 150, OP-23 files, OANHC (emphasis in document).

6. For Project Jupiter, see Bureau of Aeronautics, Research and Development Master Program, Fiscal Year 1947, BuAer Records, RG 72, NA (courtesy of Bob Hunter, University of Illinois, Chicago).

7. David A. Rosenberg and Floyd D. Kennedy Jr., *History of the Strategic Arms Competition, 1945–1972* and supporting study *US Aircraft Carriers in the Strategic Role, Part I—Naval Strategy in a Period of Change: Interservice Rivalry, Strategic Interaction, and the Development of Nuclear Attack Capability, 1945–1951* (Falls Church, VA: Lulejian and Associates, 1975), p. I-17; Barlow, *Revolt of the Admirals,* pp. 106–7.

8. Barlow, *Revolt of the Admirals,* pp. 115–16; Michael A. Palmer, *Origins of the Maritime Strategy: American Naval Strategy in the First Postwar Decade* (Washington, DC: Naval Historical Center, 1988), pp. 27–28.

9. Rosenberg and Kennedy, *US Aircraft Carriers in the Strategic Role,* pp. I-43 through I-53.

10. "Naval Air Power," pp. 1–5, file A21-1, box 715, Formerly Classified General Correspondence of the Deputy Chief of Naval Operations, 1948–51, Records of the Office of the Chief of Naval Operations, General Records of the Department of the Navy, 1947–, Record Group 428, National Archives (hereafter cited as DCNO Gen. Corresp., CNO Records, Gen. Records of Dept. of the Navy, 1947–, RG 428, NA); Robert S. Jordan, "The Balance of Power and the Anglo-American Maritime Relationship," in John B. Hattendorf and Robert S. Jordan, eds., *Maritime Strategy and the Balance of Power: Britain and America in the Twentieth Century* (New York: St. Martin's Press, 1989), p. 12.

11. Joel J. Sapolsky, *Seapower in the Nuclear Age: The United States Navy and NATO, 1949–80* (Annapolis, MD: Naval Institute Press, 1991), pp. 12–13, 65; Eric Grove and Geoffrey Till, "Anglo-American Maritime Strategy in the Era of Massive Retaliation," in Hattendorf and Jordan, eds., *Maritime Strategy and the Balance of Power,* pp. 280–81.

12. Barlow, *Revolt of the Admirals,* pp. 52–55, 117–23.

13. Ibid., p. 107.

14. Friedman, *U.S. Aircraft Carriers,* pp. 289, 291, 295; L. D. Coates, Deputy Director, Piloted Aircraft Div., BuAer, to CNO, 12 January 1950, Aer-AC-1, file JA, box 718, DCNO Gen. Corresp., CNO Records, Gen. Records of Dept. of the Navy, 1947–, RG 428, NA; Miller, *Nuclear Weapons and Aircraft Carriers,* pp. 186–91.

15. Barlow, *Revolt of the Admirals,* pp. 131–35. For information and data on the MK III and other nuclear weapons, this study uses Chuck Hansen, *U.S. Nuclear Weapons: The Secret History* (Arlington, TX: Aerofax, 1988), pp. 122–54.

16. Friedman, *U.S. Aircraft Carriers,* pp. 242–43, 248–51, 396–97; Barlow, *Revolt of the Admirals,* pp. 139–43.

17. J. H. Doolittle to Carl Hinshaw, vice chairman, Congressional Aviation Policy Board, 14 February 1948, file A21, box 149, OP-23 files, OANHC.

18. Barlow, *Revolt of the Admirals,* pp. 143–45.

19. Budget figures are from a variety of sources, including the following: Barlow, *Revolt of the Admirals,* p. 162; Maurer Maurer, *Aviation in the U.S. Army, 1919–1939* (Washington, DC: Office of Air Force History, 1987), p. 350; U.S. Department of the Navy, *Annual Reports of the Secretary of the Navy, Fiscal Years 1935–1939* (Washington, DC: GPO, 1935–39).

20. Barlow, *Revolt of the Admirals,* pp. 223–24.

21. Chuck Hansen, "Nuclear Neptunes: Early Days of Composite Squadrons 5 and 6," *American Aviation Historical Society Journal* 24 (Fourth Quarter, 1979): 262; Rear Adm. Thomas H. Robbins Jr., memo for Vice Admiral Radford, 6 February 1947, file A21/4 Jet, box 111, OP-23 files, OANHC.

22. Rosenberg and Kennedy, *US Aircraft Carriers in the Strategic Role,* p. I-157; Hansen, "Nuclear Neptunes," pp. 262–65. See also John T. Hayward and C. W. Borklund, *Blue Jacket Admiral: The Navy Career of Chick Hayward* (Annapolis, MD: Naval Institute Press, 2000), pp. 166–70.

23. Roy A. Grossnick, ed., *United States Naval Aviation, 1910–1995* (Washington, DC: Naval Historical Center, 1997), p. 171; Hayward and Borklund, *Blue Jacket Admiral,* pp. 180–81.

24. Memo, Vice Adm. John Dale Price to CNO, 14 September 1948, Op-57-fb (SC)A4-3, VV Serial: 00263P57, file 22, Op-03 (DCNO for Operations), box 3, Double Zero Files, 1948, OANHC.

25. Hansen, "Nuclear Neptunes," pp. 264–65; Hayward and Borklund, *Blue Jacket Admiral,* p. 183.

26. Rosenberg and Kennedy, *US Aircraft Carriers in the Strategic Role,* pp. I-154 through I-155; Hansen, "Nuclear Neptunes," pp. 265–66; T. B. Hill to DCNO (Air), 16 March 1950, Op-362/kg, Serial 00174P36, file A4-3, box 712, DCNO Gen. Corresp., CNO Records, Gen. Records of Dept. of the Navy, 1947–, RG 428, NA.

27. Gordon Swanborough and Peter M. Bowers, *United States Navy Aircraft since 1911,* 3d ed. (Annapolis, MD: Naval Institute Press, 1990), p. 517; Barlow, *Revolt of the Admirals,* pp. 132–34.

28. Rosenberg and Kennedy, *US Aircraft Carriers in the Strategic Role,* pp. I-155 through I-156; CNO to distribution list, 30 March 1950, Op-55106/blq, Serial: 0025P551, file A4-3, box 712, DCNO Gen. Corresp., CNO Records, Gen. Records of Dept. of the Navy, 1947–, RG 428, NA.

29. Miller, *Nuclear Weapons and Aircraft Carriers,* pp. 90–99; L. D. Coates, deputy director, Piloted Aircraft Division, BuAer, to CNO, 12 January 1950, Aer-AC-1, file JA, box 718, DCNO Gen. Corresp., CNO Records, Gen. Records of Dept. of the Navy, 1947–, RG 428, NA; Grossnick, ed., *United States Naval Aviation, 1910–1995,* p. 184; Hayward and Borklund, *Blue Jacket Admiral,* p. 194; unidentified newspaper clippings in file AN 650052-01, Martin SeaMaster Family, National Air and Space Museum (NASM) Library, Washington, DC.

30. HQ Sandia Base, Final Report of Test of Facilities Conducted Aboard USS *Coral Sea,* 25 February–3 March 1950, and Special Sea Trial, 16–18 March 1950, SBOP/2, file S1, box 717; CNO to Chief, BuOrd, 24 February 1950, Op-362/rk A23

Serial 00121P36, file JA, box 718; both in DCNO Gen. Corresp., CNO Records, Gen. Records of Dept. of the Navy, 1947–, RG 428, NA.

31. Rosenberg and Kennedy, *US Aircraft Carriers in the Strategic Role,* pp. I-165 and I-166; Hayward and Borklund, *Blue Jacket Admiral,* p. 171; Miller, *Nuclear Weapons and Aircraft Carriers,* pp. 187–89.

32. Hansen, "Nuclear Neptunes," pp. 266–67; Rosenberg and Kennedy, *US Aircraft Carriers in the Strategic Role,* pp. I-165, I-176; T. B. Hill to DCNO (Air), 16 March 1950, Op-362/kg, Serial 00174P36, file A4-3, box 712, DCNO Gen. Corresp., CNO Records, Gen. Records of Dept. of the Navy, 1947–, RG 428, NA.

33. Rosenberg and Kennedy, *US Aircraft Carriers in the Strategic Role,* p. I-177; Adm. W. M. Fechteler to CinC Pacific Fleet and CinC Atlantic Fleet, 28 May 1952, Op-33191/aj, Ser: 00108P33, file A16-10, box 2, Double Zero Files, 1952, OANHC.

34. L. D. Coates, Deputy Director, Piloted Aircraft Div., BuAer, to CNO—Op-551, 12 January 1950, Aer-AC-1, file JA, box 718, DCNO Gen. Corresp., CNO Records, Gen. Records of Dept. of the Navy, 1947–, RG 428, NA; Annual Report of the Chief of the Bureau of Aeronautics to the Secretary of the Navy, Fiscal Year 1952, 16 December 1952, pp. 18–19, box 2, BuAer Records, RG 72, NA (courtesy of Bob Hunter).

35. L. D. Coates, Deputy Director, Piloted Aircraft Div., BuAer, to CNO—Op-551, 12 January 1950, Aer-AC-1, file JA, box 718, DCNO Gen. Corresp., CNO Records, Gen. Records of Dept. of the Navy, 1947–, RG 428, NA; Swanborough and Bowers, *United States Navy Aircraft since 1911,* pp. 202–5; Miller, *Nuclear Weapons and Aircraft Carriers,* pp. 99–109.

36. Rosenberg and Kennedy, *US Aircraft Carriers in the Strategic Role,* pp. I-167 and I-168.

37. Memo, Rear Adm. J. H. Cassady to Rear Adm. Ralph A. Ofstie, 29 April 1949, file A21/1-1, box 150, OP-23 files, OANHC; memo, Cassady to CNO, 12 May 1950, DCNO (Air) Official Correspondence, January 1950–May 1952, Vice Admiral Cassady, Series I, box 3, nos. 11 and 12, Personal and Official Correspondence, 1943–1962, DCNO (Air) file, Aviation History Branch, Naval Historical Center (hereafter cited as AHNHC).

38. Friedman, *U.S. Aircraft Carriers,* pp. 256–64.

39. Ibid., pp. 256, 342.

40. Grove and Till, "Anglo-American Maritime Strategy," p. 28; OP 03 to OP 09, 11/7/58, file A3(1), Top Secret, Subject Files A3(1) through A4–5, box 4, Double Zero Files, 1958, OANHC; 23 June 1958 entry, Vice Adm. Robert B. Pirie Personal Log, May 1958–September 1960, box 12, nos. 22–27, Personal and Official Correspondence, 1943–62, DCNO (Air) file, AHNHC.

41. Rosenberg and Kennedy, *US Aircraft Carriers in the Strategic Role,* p. I-175.

## Chapter 4. Seaplane Reborn

1. Loftin, *Quest for Performance,* pp. 163–68.

2. Ernest G. Stout, "Development of High-Speed Water-Based Aircraft," *Journal of the Aeronautical Sciences* 17 (August 1950): 469–70.

3. Ibid., pp. 476–77; Ernest G. Stout, "Bases Unlimited," *Aeronautical Engineering Review* 14 (June 1955): 42–43.

4. Stout, "Bases Unlimited," p. 43.

5. DVL Hulls 1, 1a, and 7, Complete Tank Tests, W. Sottorf, Part I, 1935, Report No. ZH-005; Original Report, Complete Tank Tests, DVL Hulls No. 8, 17, 18, 19, Parts II and III, 19 August 1935, Report No. ZH-014; both in Convair Collection (Gillespie Field Annex), Archives, San Diego Aerospace Museum (hereafter cited as SDAM); Stout, "Development of High-Speed Water-Based Aircraft," p. 458.

6. "Ernest G. Stout," undated, GD/Convair, Personnel, Convair Collection, Archives, SDAM; Stout, "Development of High-Speed Water-Based Aircraft," pp. 457–58; Alexander McSurely, "Design for a Supersonic Flying Boat?" *Aviation Week* 55 (23 October 1950): 14; Ernest G. Stout, "Experimental Determination of Hydrodynamic Stability," *Journal of the Aeronautical Sciences* 8 (December 1940): 55–61.

7. BuAer, Preliminary Airplane Design Section, "A Comparative Study of Landplanes and Flying Boats as Long Range Bombers," ADR No. R-17, 23 April 1943, Defense Technical Information Center, Ft. Belvoir, VA (hereafter cited as DTIC), AD896810, pp. 1, 4–9.

8. Richard K. Smith, "The Intercontinental Airliner and the Essence of Airplane Performance, 1929–1939," *Technology and Culture* 24 (July 1983): 428–49; Glenn L. Martin, "The Case for the Flying Boat," *Aero Digest* 46 (1 September 1944): 78–79.

9. Stout, "Development of High-Speed Water-Based Aircraft," pp. 463–65.

10. Ernest G. Stout, "Development of Precision Radio-Controlled Dynamically Similar Flying Models," *Journal of the Aeronautical Sciences* 13 (July 1946): 335–45; Flying Boat Development, Report No. ZH-011, August 1943, p. 11, GD/Convair, Design Proposals/Seaplanes, Convair Collection, Archives, SDAM; Robert E. Bradley, "Convair Post World War II Seaplane Studies, Part One," *Aerospace Projects Review* 2 (July–August 2000): 11.

11. Flying Boat Development, Report No. ZH-011, August 1943, pp. 2–3, 5, 11, 13, 16, GD/Convair, Design Proposals/Seaplanes, Convair Collection, Archives, SDAM.

12. Stout, "Development of High-Speed Water-Based Aircraft," pp. 458, 465–66; memo, Lt. R. H. Lee, 29 August 1944, NOa(s)4472 P/D EN11-22221, vol. 1, box 1394, file NOas 4472, Records of Divisions and Offices, Contract Records, 1940–60, Records of the Bureau of Aeronautics, Record Group 72, National Archives (hereafter cited as Divisions and Offices, Contract Records, 1940–60, BuAer Records, RG 72, NA); Flying Boat Development, Report No. ZH-011, August 1943, p. 4, GD/Convair, Design Proposals/Seaplanes, Convair Collection, Archives, SDAM.

13. Proposal for Hydrodynamic Test Program of CVAC Long Range Flying Boat Development, Report No. ZH-017, 17 July 1944; NACA to Chief, BuAer, 3 August 1944; both in vol. 1, box 1394, file NOas 4472, Divisions and Offices, Contract Records, 1940–60, BuAer Records, RG 72, NA. Resume of Seaplane Development Contracts, file 1.11, XP6M-1, 1952, box 25, Correspondence of the Patrol Design Branch, 1944–53, BuAer Records, RG 72, NA.

14. Walter Diehl to Bureau of Aeronautics Representative (BAR), San Diego, 10 April 1945, Aer-E-23-WSD NOas 4472, vol. 2; H. E. Brooke, Convair, Status Report

on Navy Contract NOa(s)4472, 22 May 1946, vol. 3; Rear Adm. L. C. Stevens (by direction, Chief, BuAer) to Commandant, Naval Training Station, San Diego, 13 June 1946, Aer-AC-54, vol. 3; all in box 1395, file NOas 4472, Divisions and Offices, Contract Records, 1940–60, BuAer Records, RG 72, NA.

15. A Comparison of Performance between the Model 37 and a Flying Boat Version of the Same Airplane, Report ZH-026, 17 August 1945, file ZH-026, GD/Convair, Design Proposals/Seaplanes, Convair Collection, SDAM.

16. T. P. Hall, Convair, to Chief, BuAer, 11 October 1945, vol. 2, box 1395, file NOas 4472; Convair, Proposal for a Preliminary Naval Seaplane Development Program, Report ZH-028, 26 October 1945, vol. 1, box 1856, file NOas 7919; both in Divisions and Offices, Contract Records, 1940–60, BuAer Records, RG 72, NA. Resume of Seaplane Development Contracts, 10 September 1952, file 1.11, XP6M-1, 1952, box 25, Correspondence of the Patrol Design Branch, 1944–53, BuAer Records, RG 72, NA; William Green, *The Warplanes of the Third Reich* (Garden City, NY: Doubleday, 1970), pp. 97–99.

17. *Who's Who in American Aeronautics, 1928* (New York: Aviation Publishing, 1928), p. 32. See, for example, Diehl route slip comments, 2 February 1945, on BAR, San Diego, to Chief, BuAer, 22 January 1945, vol. 2, box 1395, file NOas 4472, Divisions and Offices, Contract Records, 1940–60, BuAer Records, RG 72, NA.

18. Chief, BuAer, to Director, David Taylor Model Basin, 7 April 1948, NOa(s)7919 FF30, vol. 5, box 1856, file NOas 7919, Divisions and Offices, Contract Records, 1940–60, BuAer Records, RG 72, NA; Green, *Warplanes of the Third Reich,* p. 97.

19. XP5Y-1 Contract History and Engineering Data, XP5Y-1 file, Convair Collection, Archives, SDAM; Report, Hydrodynamic Characteristics of XP5Y-1, November 1949, Report No. ZH-117-011, #2175, Convair Collection (Gillespie Field Annex), Archives, SDAM; Stout, "Development of High-Speed Water-Based Aircraft," pp. 458–59, 467, 480.

20. H. E. Brooke, Convair, Status Report on Navy Contract NOa(s)7919, 12 June 1947, vol. 3, box 1856, file NOas 7919, Divisions and Offices, Contract Records, 1940–60, BuAer Records, RG 72, NA; Ginter, *Convair XP5Y-1 and R3Y-1/2 Tradewind,* pp. 1–13; Robert F. Dorr, "Convair R3Y Tradewind," *Wings of Fame* 18 (2000): 6; Stout, "Development of High-Speed Water-Based Aircraft," pp. 458–59; Ernest G. Stout, "A Review of High-Speed Hydrodynamic Development," Hydro Research, Convair, March 1951, file ZH-080, p. 27, Convair Collection, Archives, SDAM.

21. James R. Hansen, *Engineer in Charge: A History of the Langley Aeronautical Laboratory, 1917–1958* (Washington, DC: NASA, 1987), pp. 69–72.

22. Stout, "Development of High-Speed Water-Based Aircraft," pp. 459–61.

23. Hydrodynamic Design of the Consolidated Vultee Seaplane Night Fighter, December 1948, pp. 3, 5–6, 54, 56–57, 72, Report No. ZH-061, GD/Convair, Design Proposals/Fighters, Convair Collection, Archives, SDAM; Ernest G. Stout, "High-Speed Water-Based Aircraft," *Aircraft Engineering* 25 (February 1953): 46–47.

24. W. F. Rodee to Chief, BuAer, 14 May 1947, NOa(s) 7919 Serial 718 T2:fc; Cdr. A. B. Metsger (by direction, Chief, BuAer) to BAR, Convair, 30 July 1947, Aer-

AC-21 NOas 7919; both in vol. 3, box 1856, file NOas 7919, Divisions and Offices, Contract Records, 1940–60, BuAer Records, RG 72, NA.

25. Peter London, *Saunders and Saro Aircraft since 1917* (London: Putnam, 1988), pp. 196–210.

26. Convair, Program for Continued Hydrodynamic Research on High Mach Number Forms, 21 March 1949, Report ZH-064, vol. 3; BuAer, Request for Authority to Contract, 21 April 1948, Air 6718, NOa(s)9722, vol. 1; F. W. Fink, Convair, to Chief, BuAer, 6 October 1949, no. 4781, vol. 4; H. E. Brooke, Status Report of Navy Contract NOa(s)-9722, 26 October 1949, vol. 4; all in box 258, file NOas 9722, acc. no. 6525, Divisions and Offices, Contract Records, 1940–60, BuAer Records, RG 72, NA. Bradley, "Convair Post World War II Seaplane Studies, Part One," pp. 14–18; Robert E. Bradley, "Convair Post World War II Seaplane Studies, Part Two," *Aerospace Projects Review* 2 (September–October 2000): 13–15.

27. Hydrodynamic Design of the Consolidated Vultee Seaplane Night Fighter, December 1948, p. 4, Report No. ZH-061, GD/Convair, Design Proposals/Fighters, Convair Collection, Archives, SDAM; H. E. Brooke, Status Report of Navy Contract NOa(s)-9722, 26 October 1949; H. E. Brooke, Status Report of Navy Contract NOa(s)-9722, 15 November 1949; both in vol. 4, box 258, file NOas 9722, acc. no. 6525, Divisions and Offices, Contract Records, 1940–60, BuAer Records, RG 72, NA.

28. Memo, Lloyd Harrison to Chief, BuAer, 5 April 1949, vol. 1, box 5, file NOas 10507, acc. no. 9833, Divisions and Offices, Contract Records, 1940–60, BuAer Records, RG 72, NA.

29. Hydrodynamic Design of the Consolidated Vultee Seaplane Night Fighter, December 1948, pp. 79–82, 86–91, Report No. ZH-061, GD/Convair, Design Proposals/Fighters, Convair Collection, Archives, SDAM.

30. BuAer, Model Seaplane Night Fighter Request for Proposal, 1 October 1948, Aer-AC-25, vol. 1, box 5; Report No. ZD-012, Outline Specification for Consolidated Vultee "Skate" Airplane, United States Navy Class VF Seaplane Night Fighter, 5 January 1949, box 4; R. L. Mussen, Convair, to Chief, BuAer, 28 January 1949, 11-1-2561, vol. 1, box 5; all in file NOas 10507, acc. no. 9833, Divisions and Offices, Contract Records, 1940–60, BuAer Records, RG 72, NA.

31. Seaplane Night Fighter Design Proposal, Convair Skate, 14 January 1949, box 4, file NOas 10507, acc. no. 9833, Divisions and Offices, Contract Records, 1940–60, BuAer Records, RG 72, NA.

32. Curtiss-Wright Corp., Airplane Division, Analysis of Towing Tank Tests Conducted on a Navy Seaplane Fighter at the Stevens Institute of Technology, 25 March 1949, Report No. P565-Y6, Convair Collection (Gillespie Field Annex), Archives, SDAM; memo, Lloyd Harrison to Chief, BuAer, 5 April 1949, vol. 1, box 5, file NOas 10507, acc. no. 9833, Divisions and Offices, Contract Records, 1940–60, BuAer Records, RG 72, NA.

33. Glenn L. Martin Co., "Water-Based Aircraft: An Analysis of Their Potential," ER 6600, 1 October 1954, DTIC, AD056773, p. 75; Bradley, "Convair Post World War II Seaplane Studies, Part One," pp. 14–15.

34. Memo, Lloyd Harrison to Chief, BuAer, 5 April 1949; Authority to Contract, 19 May 1949; both in vol. 1, box 5, file NOas 10507, acc. no. 9833, Divisions and Offices, Contract Records, 1940–60, BuAer Records, RG 72, NA.

35. Skate Progress Report, 28 October 1949, pp. 19, 61–62, 76, 79, Report No. ZM-2-003, GD/Convair, Design Proposals/Fighters, Convair Collection, Archives, SDAM.

36. H. E. Brooke, Status Report of Navy Contract NOa(s)-9722, 13 May 1949; H. E. Brooke, Status Report of Navy Contract NOa(s)-9722, 15 July 1949; F. A. Louden, (by direction, Chief, BuAer), to BAR, San Diego, 3 April 1950, Aer-DE-31/30 NOa(s)9722; all in vol. 3, box 258, file NOas 9722, acc. no. 6525, Divisions and Offices, Contract Records, 1940–60, BuAer Records, RG 72, NA. Rear Adm. A. M. Pride to Vice Adm. John Dale Price, 7 December 1948, Admiral Price's Semi-Official Correspondence, Series I, box 2, nos. 7–10, Personal and Official Correspondence, 1943–62, DCNO (Air) file, AHNHC.

37. Skate Progress Report, 28 October 1949, pp. 65–67, Report No. ZM-2-003, GD/Convair, Design Proposals/Fighters, Convair Collection, Archives, SDAM; Rear Adm. A. M. Pride to BAR, San Diego, 30 November 1949, Aer-AC-25, NOa(s)10507, vol. 1, box 5, file NOas 10507, acc. no. 9833, Records of Divisions and Offices, Contract Records, 1940–60, BuAer Records, RG 72, NA.

38. Aero and Hydro Branch comments on Convair Skate Airplane Ski Evaluation Report, 21 September 1949, vol. 1, box 5, file NOas 10507, acc. no. 9833, Records of Divisions and Offices, Contract Records, 1940–60, BuAer Records, RG 72, NA; Report on the Testing of Two 1/15 Scale Models of the Y2-1, Report No. ZH-2-002, July 1950, GD/Convair, Design Proposals/Fighters, Convair Collection, Archives, SDAM.

39. Stout, "High Speed Water-Based Aircraft," p. 47; H. E. Brooke, Status Report of Navy Contract NOa(s)-9722, 15 July 1949, vol. 3, box 258, file NOas 9722, acc. no. 6525, Records of Divisions and Offices, Contract Records, 1940–60, BuAer Records, RG 72, NA; Report CVAL 56, Low Speed Wind Tunnel Tests on a .08 Scale Model of the Betta 1, 12 June 1950, Betta 1, CVAL #56, GD/Convair, Design Proposals/Seaplanes, Convair Collection, Archives, SDAM.

40. Interim Progress Report on Y2-2 Hydrodynamic Development, pp. 2–3, 9–10, 14, 16, Report No. ZH-2-003, October 1950, box 4, file NOas 10507, acc. no. 9833, Records of Divisions and Offices, Contract Records, 1940–60, BuAer Records, RG 72, NA; Resume of Seaplane Development Contracts, 10 September 1952, file 1.11, XP6M-1, 1952, box 25, Correspondence of the Patrol Design Branch, 1944–53, BuAer Records, RG 72, NA; Abraham Hyatt (by direction, Director, Research Div., BuAer) to Director, Aircraft Div., BuAer, 5 October 1953, Aer-RS-3, vol. 22, box 20, file NOas 51-527, acc. no. 11920, Records of Divisions and Offices, Contract Records, 1940–60, BuAer Records, RG 72, NA.

41. Y2-2 Supersonic Water Based Aircraft, 1st Progress Report, 30 October 1950, box 4, file NOas 10507, acc. no. 9833; Letter of Intent, contract no. NOas 51-527, 19 January 1951, vol. 1, box 12, file NOas 51-527, acc. no. 62A-2988; both in Records of Divisions and Offices, Contract Records, 1940–60, BuAer Records, RG 72, NA.

42. Y2-2 Supersonic Water Based Aircraft, 2d Progress Report, 11 May 1951; J. M. Tompkins (by direction, Chief, BuAer) to BAR, San Diego, 5 July 1951, Aer-PD-22, 66450; both in box 4, file NOas 10507, acc. no. 9833, Records of Divisions and Offices, Contract Records, 1940–60, BuAer Records, RG 72, NA. Stout, "Bases Unlimited," p. 50.

43. General Plan of Operation—F2Y Water Based Fighter, Contract History, 7 November 1952, YF2Y-1 file, GD/Convair, Programs/F2Y, Convair Collection, Archives, SDAM; BAR, San Diego, CVAC Skate Design Study, 4-12-51, vol. D, box 5, file NOas 10507, acc. no. 9833, Records of Divisions and Offices, Contract Records, 1940–60, BuAer Records, RG 72, NA; unsigned memo, 4 April 1951, file 1.11, General Seaplane Information, 1953, box 25, Correspondence of the Patrol Design Branch, 1944–53, BuAer Records, RG 72, NA.

44. Memo, W. M. Vincent to Director, Aircraft Div., BuAer, 21 September 1951, Aer-12-33, vol. 1, box 46; Abraham Hyatt (by direction, Director, Research Div., BuAer) to Director, Aircraft Div., BuAer, 5 October 1953, Aer-RS-3, vol. 22, box 20; both in file NOas 51-527, acc. no. 11922, Records of Divisions and Offices, Contract Records, 1940–60, BuAer Records, RG 72, NA.

45. G. F. Beardsley, Director, Production Div., BuAer, to Chief, BuAer, 27 July 1953, Aer-PD-2, NOa(s) 52-835, NOa(s)53-882, vol. 8; Mock-Up Board Report for Model F2Y-1 Aircraft, 27 August 1953, Aer-AC-25, NOa(s) 52-835, vol. 10; Dudley H. Digges, Convair, to Chief, BuAer, 27 July 1953, EF:dm, 11-4-5452, vol. 8; all in box 24, file NOas 52-835, acc. no. 15700, Records of Divisions and Offices, Contract Records, 1940–60, BuAer Records, RG 72, NA.

46. Address by Hon. John F. Floberg, assistant secretary of the navy for air, before the Wings Club, New York, 17 November 1952, Water-Based A/C file, GD/Convair, Design Proposals/Seaplanes, Convair Collection, Archives, SDAM.

47. John B. Moss, BuAer, first endorsement on J. V. Naish, Convair, to Chief, BuAer, 26 September 1952, 11-4-3050, vol. 2; memo for the record, F2Y-1 and R3Y-1 programs, 20 November 1952, vol. 2; G. F. Beardsley, Director, Production Div., BuAer, to Chief, BuAer, 27 July 1953, Aer-PD-2, NOa(s) 52-835, NOa(s)53-882, vol. 8; all in box 24, file NOas 52-835, acc. no. 15700, Records of Divisions and Offices, Contract Records, 1940–60, BuAer Records, RG 72, NA.

48. Experimental Flight Test Plan, Model XF2Y-1, Bu. No. 137634, Flight Test No. 1, 4/7/53 #351, Convair Collection (Gillespie Field Annex), Archives, SDAM; C. E. Root, Public Relations Manager, Convair, to Security Review Branch, Office of Information, DoD, 21 April 1953, vol. 3, box 46, file NOas 51-527, acc. no. 11922, Records of Divisions and Offices, Contract Records, 1940–60, BuAer Records, RG 72, NA.

49. Gordon Swanborough and Peter M. Bowers, *United States Military Aircraft since 1909* (Washington, DC: Smithsonian Institution Press, 1989), pp. 483–88; Swanborough and Bowers, *United States Navy Aircraft since 1911*, p. 255.

50. F. H. Sharp, Convair, to Chief, BuAer, 17 August 1953, FHS:REL:mss 6-3712; C. W. Stirling, BAR, San Diego, first endorsement on above letter, 31 August 1953, WCB:glw EN11-23/51-527 Ser 0-1923; both in vol. 22, box 20, file NOas 51-527,

acc. no. 11920, Records of Divisions and Offices, Contract Records, 1940–60, BuAer Records, RG 72, NA.

51. Memo, W. W. Fox, Convair, to Those Concerned, 16 July 1953, #819, Convair Collection (Gillespie Field Annex), Archives, SDAM.

52. J. G. Zevely, Convair, to Chief, BuAer, 10 August 1953, 11-4-5581, vol. 22, box 20, file NOas 51-527, acc. no. 11920, Records of Divisions and Offices, Contract Records, 1940–60, BuAer Records, RG 72, NA.

53. Proposed Flight Test Program and Flight Test Schedule, Contract NOa(s) 51-527, 15 October 1952, box 9, file NOas 51-527, acc. no. 15392; F. E. Bardwell, Director, Aircraft Div., BuAer, to Deputy and Asst. Chief, BuAer, 27 May 1953, Aer-AC-25, vol. 7, box 24, file NOas 52-835, acc. no. 15700; memo, J. W. Murphy to AER, 17 September 1953, Aer-AC-25, vol. 4, box 46, file NOas 51-527, acc. no. 11922; all in Records of Divisions and Offices, Contract Records, 1940–60, BuAer Records, RG 72, NA.

54. F. H. Sharp to Chief, BuAer, 10 November 1953, FHS:mss 6-5544, vol. 23, box 20, file NOas 51-527, acc. no. 11920; Abraham Hyatt, Acting Director, Research Div., BuAer, to Director, Aircraft Div., BuAer, 19 February 1954, Aer-RS-3, vol. 5, box 12, file NOas 51-527, acc. no. 62A-2988; both in Records of Divisions and Offices, Contract Records, 1940–60, BuAer Records, RG 72, NA.

55. F. E. Bardwell (by direction, Chief, BuAer) to CNO, 13 January 1953, Aer-Ac-25, NOa(s) 52-835, 0652, vol. 3, box 24, file NOas 52-835, acc. no. 15700; F. H. Sharp, Convair, to Chief, BuShips, 9 April 1953, vol. 5, box 24, file NOas 52-835, acc. no. 15700; Lt. Col. W. E. Clasen, USMC, comments, 23 February 1954, vol. 5, box 12, file NOas 51-527, acc. no. 62A-2988; all in Records of Divisions and Offices, Contract Records, 1940–60, BuAer Records, RG 72, NA.

56. NACA Research Memorandum, "Results of a Power-on Flight of a 1/10-Scale Rocket-Propelled Model of the Convair XF2Y-1 Airplane," NACA TED No. 365, 28 September 1953, DTIC, AD030940; F. H. Sharp, Convair, to Chief, BuAer, 5 May 1953, FHS:RHS:vmg, 6-1784, vol. 7, box 24, file NOas 52-835, acc. no. 15700, Records of Divisions and Offices, Contract Records, 1940–60, BuAer Records, RG 72, NA.

57. Hansen, *Engineer in Charge,* pp. 334–40.

58. Study of Application of Area Rule Theory to Tactical Versions of F2Y Airplane, Report No. ZP-12-008, 15 June 1955, GD/Convair, Design Proposals/Fighters, Convair Collection, Archives, SDAM.

59. F. W. Fink, Chief Engineer, Convair, to Chief, BuAer, 2 September 1954, FWF:TWS:lm 6-4201, vol. 5, box 32, file NOas 51-527, acc. no. 15757, Records of Divisions and Offices, Contract Records, 1940–60, BuAer Records, RG 72, NA.

## Chapter 5. Designs

1. Memo, Adm. Robert B. Carney to Vice CNO, 28 December 1954, file A1-1, box 1, Double Zero Files, 1954, OANHC; U.S. Cong., House, *Hearings before the Committee on Armed Services: The National Defense Program—Unification and Strategy,* 81st Cong., 1st sess. (Washington, DC: GPO, 1949), pp. 301–4; Operations Evaluation Group, "A Comparison of the Economic Cost and Military Suitability of

the High Performance Seaplane with Other Alternative Aircraft for Bombardment Missions," Study 384, 10 February 1950, DTIC, ADA950177, pp. 1–3.

2. Operations Evaluation Group, "A Comparison of the Economic Cost and Military Suitability of the High Performance Seaplane with Other Alternative Aircraft for Bombardment Missions," Study 384, 10 February 1950, DTIC, ADA950177, pp. 1–3, 7, 11, 14.

3. Research and Development Board, Importance Ratings of Master Plan Technical Objectives, 25 February 1949, file A1/EM-3/11, Research and Development Board—1949, box 136, OP-23 files, OANHC; BuAer report, 19 May 1950, file 1.11, General Seaplane Information, 1953, box 25, Correspondence of the Patrol Design Branch, 1944–53, BuAer Records, RG 72, NA.

4. U.S. Navy XP6M-1 High Speed minelayer Mock-Up Design Review, March 1953, vol. 2, box 22, file NOas 53-455, acc. no. 15491, Records of Divisions and Offices, Contract Records, 1940–60, BuAer Records, RG 72, NA.

5. J. L. Kane (by direction) to OP-55, 17 June 1949, Op-501/scd, Serial: 00123P50 (SC)A16-3, secret; Rear Adm. L. A. Moebus to Op-31, 27 July 1949, Op-502/dd, Serial: 00141P50; Rear Adm. L. A. Moebus to Op-03, 22 August 1949, Op-501/scd, Serial: 00181P50, (SC)VV/A4-3; all in file S75-S90, box 685, DCNO Gen. Corresp., CNO Records, Gen. Records of Dept. of the Navy, 1947–, RG 428, NA.

6. J. J. Munson to Chief, BuAer, 8 June 1951, Aer-AC-54, file 1.10, Seaplane Design Competition, box 25, Correspondence of the Patrol Design Branch, 1944–53, BuAer Records, RG 72, NA.

7. Memo, Abraham Hyatt for Ivan H. Driggs, Director, Research Div., to Director, Piloted Aircraft Div., 3 May 1951, Aer-RS-1, file 1.10, Seaplane Design Competition, box 25, Correspondence of the Patrol Design Branch, 1944–53, BuAer Records, RG 72, NA.

8. Unsigned, undated overview and analysis (probably by Cdr. W. D. King, 4 April 1951), file 1.11, General Seaplane Information, box 25, Correspondence of the Patrol Design Branch, 1944–53, BuAer Records, RG 72, NA; Piet and Raithel, *Martin P6M SeaMaster,* pp. 18, 25–27.

9. Piet and Raithel, *Martin P6M SeaMaster,* pp. 22–23. Memo, W. D. King (AC-53) to AC, 6 February 1951, Aer-AC-53, file 1.10, Seaplane Design Competition; Ivan H. Driggs to Assistant Chief, BuAer for Research and Development, 12 February 1952, Aer-RS-3, file 1.11, XP6M-1, 1952; both in box 25, Correspondence of the Patrol Design Branch, 1944–53, BuAer Records, RG 72, NA.

10. Vice Adm. J. D. Price (DCNO (Air)) to Vannevar Bush, Carnegie Institution, 2 May 1949, Admiral Price's Semi-Official Correspondence, Series I, box 2, nos. 7–10, Personal and Official Correspondence, 1943–62, DCNO (Air) file, AHNHC; Ivan H. Driggs to Assistant Chief, BuAer, for Research and Development, 12 February 1952, Aer-RS-3, file 1.11, XP6M-1, 1952, box 25, Correspondence of the Patrol Design Branch, 1944–53, BuAer Records, RG 72, NA; Long, *Convair Sea Dart,* p. 2.

11. L. M. Grant (asst. chief, BuAer, Research and Development) to Chief, BuAer, 11 April 1952, Aer-EV-1, file 1.11 [list of enclosures provides dates]; Statement of Mining Problem, enclosure in Ivan H. Driggs to Director, Piloted Aircraft Div., 3 May

1951, Aer-RS-1, file 1.10; both in Seaplane Design Competition, box 25, Correspondence of the Patrol Design Branch, 1944–53, BuAer Records, RG 72, NA.

12. Ivan H. Driggs, Research Div. Comments on Outline Specification OS-125, 16 July 1951, file 1.10, Seaplane Design Competition, box 25, Correspondence of the Patrol Design Branch, 1944–53, BuAer Records, RG 72, NA.

13. Paul H. Ramsey (by direction, Chief, BuAer) to manufacturers, 30 July 1951, Aer-AC-56; High Performance Seaplane Minelayer Historical Summary, 9 October 1951; L. M. Grant (asst. chief, BuAer, Research and Development) to Chief, BuAer, 11 April 1952, Aer-EV-1, file 1.11 [list of references and notes]; all in file 1.10, Seaplane Design Competition, box 25, Correspondence of the Patrol Design Branch, 1944–53, BuAer Records, RG 72, NA.

14. Conference on Outline Specification for Class VP High Performance Flying Boat, 15 August 1951, in file 1.10, Seaplane Design Competition, pp. 7, 11, box 25, Correspondence of the Patrol Design Branch, 1944–53, BuAer Records, RG 72, NA.

15. Ibid., pp. 1–2, 30–32, 34–35.

16. Ibid., pp. 6–7, 9–11, 14, 16, 18. For Kingfisher, see Norman Friedman, *U.S. Naval Weapons: Every Gun, Missile, Mine and Torpedo Used by the U.S. Navy from 1883 to the Present Day* (Annapolis, MD: Naval Institute Press, 1982), p. 203.

17. High Performance Seaplane Minelayer Historical Summary, 9 October 1951, file 1.10, Seaplane Design Competition, box 25, Correspondence of the Patrol Design Branch, 1944–53, BuAer Records, RG 72, NA; Hydrodynamic Design of the Convair High Performance Flying Boat, pp. 3–5, 8, Report No. ZH-085, GD/Convair, Design Proposals/Seaplanes, Convair Collection, Archives, SDAM.

18. Hydrodynamic Design of the Convair High Performance Flying Boat, pp. 5–8, 13–15, 57, Report No. ZH-085, GD/Convair, Design Proposals/Seaplanes, Convair Collection, Archives, SDAM.

19. L. M. Grant (asst. chief, BuAer, Research and Development) to Chief, BuAer, 11 April 1952, Aer-EV-1, file 1.11, Seaplane Design Competition, box 25, Correspondence of the Patrol Design Branch, 1944–53, BuAer Records, RG 72, NA [list of enclosures provides dates].

20. Piet and Raithel, *Martin P6M SeaMaster,* pp. 30–33; L. M. Grant (asst. chief, BuAer, Research and Development) to Chief, BuAer, 11 April 1952, Aer-EV-1, file 1.11, Seaplane Design Competition, box 25, Correspondence of the Patrol Design Branch, 1944–53, BuAer Records, RG 72, NA.

21. High Performance Seaplane Minelayer Historical Summary, 10 July 1952; memo, F. W. Brown, Patrol Design Branch, to Aircraft Div., BuAer, 8 February 1952, Aer-AC-56; both in file 1.11, XP6M-1, 1952, box 25, Correspondence of the Patrol Design Branch, 1944–53, BuAer Records, RG 72, NA.

22. Ivan H. Driggs to Asst. Chief, BuAer, for Research and Development, 12 February 1952, Aer-RS-3, file 1.11, XP6M-1, 1952, box 25, Correspondence of the Patrol Design Branch, 1944–53, BuAer Records, RG 72, NA.

23. High Performance Seaplane Minelayer Historical Summary, 10 July 1952, file 1.11, XP6M-1, 1952, box 25, Correspondence of the Patrol Design Branch, 1944–53, BuAer Records, RG 72, NA.

24. "Appraisal of High Performance Seaplane Minelayer," 28 March 1952, Aer-AC-56, enclosure in Brown to Director, Aircraft Div., 31 March 1952, file 1.11, XP6M-1, 1952, box 25, Correspondence of the Patrol Design Branch, 1944–53, BuAer Records, RG 72, NA.

25. Ibid.

26. L. M. Grant (asst. chief, BuAer, Research and Development) to Chief, BuAer, 11 April 1952, Aer-EV-1, file 1.11, Seaplane Design Competition, box 25, Correspondence of the Patrol Design Branch, 1944–53, BuAer Records, RG 72, NA.

27. Brown route slip comments, 7 April 1952, on L. M. Grant to Chief, BuAer, 11 April 1952, Aer-EV-1; memo, Adm. T. C. Lonnquest to Adm. Thomas S. Combs, 14 April 1952; both in file 1.11, Seaplane Design Competition, box 25, Correspondence of the Patrol Design Branch, 1944–53, BuAer Records, RG 72, NA.

28. High Performance Seaplane Minelayer Historical Summary, 10 July 1952, file 1.11, XP6M-1, 1952, box 25, Correspondence of the Patrol Design Branch, 1944–53, BuAer Records, RG 72, NA.

29. Piet and Raithel, *Martin P6M SeaMaster,* p. 35.

30. High Performance Seaplane Minelayer Historical Summary, 10 July 1952; F. E. Bardwell (by direction, Chief, BuAer) to Consolidated Vultee Aircraft Corporation, 23 June 1952, Aer-AC-58, no. 012620; both in file 1.11, XP6M-1, 1952, box 25, Correspondence of the Patrol Design Branch, 1944–1953, BuAer Records, RG 72, NA; High Speed minelayer Design Notes—BuAer Conferences, May 1–5, 2 June 1952, High Performance Flying Boat file, GD/Convair, Design Proposals/Seaplanes, Convair Collection, Archives, SDAM.

31. F. W. Fink (chief engineer, Convair) to Chief, BuAer, 1 August 1952, no. 6-3904, file 1.11, XP6M-1, 1952, box 25, Correspondence of the Patrol Design Branch, 1944–53, BuAer Records, RG 72, NA; Class VP Airplane, High Performance Flying Boat, August 1952, Hydrodynamic Report, No. ZH-089, pp. 5–7, 19–20, 59–60, GD/Convair, Design Proposals/Seaplanes, Convair Collection, Archives, SDAM; memo, L. M. Grant to Chief, BuAer (no date, probably early September 1952), Aer-EV-1, vol. 1, box 51, file NOas 52-1136, acc. no. 15700, Records of Divisions and Offices, Contract Records, 1940–60, BuAer Records, RG 72, NA.

32. F. W. Fink (chief engineer, Convair) to Chief, BuAer, 1 August 1952, no. 6-3904, file 1.11, XP6M-1, 1952, box 25, Correspondence of the Patrol Design Branch, 1944–53, BuAer Records, RG 72, NA; memo, L. M. Grant to Chief, BuAer (no date, probably early September 1952), Aer-EV-1, vol. 1, box 51, file NOas 52-1136, acc. no. 15700, Records of Divisions and Offices, Contract Records, 1940–60, BuAer Records, RG 72, NA.

33. Glenn L. Martin Company to Chief, BuAer, 4 August 1952; memo, L. M. Grant to Chief, BuAer (no date, probably early September 1952), Aer-EV-1; both in vol. 1, box 51, file NOas 52-1136, acc. no. 15700, Records of Divisions and Offices, Contract Records, 1940–60, BuAer Records, RG 72, NA.

34. Performance Comparison of Attack and Mining Aircraft, attachment to Rear Adm. A. Soucek to CNO, 2 June 1954, Aer-AC-5 010778, vol. 14, box 22, file NOas 53-455, acc. no. 15491, Records of Divisions and Offices, Contract Records,

1940–60, BuAer Records, RG 72, NA. Swanborough and Bowers, *United States Military Aircraft since 1909,* pp. 132–35, has statistics for the B-47 E-model.

35. Memo, L. M. Grant to Chief, BuAer (no date, probably early September 1952), Aer-EV-1, vol. 1, box 51, file NOas 52-1136, acc. no. 15700, Records of Divisions and Offices, Contract Records, 1940–60, BuAer Records, RG 72, NA.

36. Ibid.

37. Ibid., with Brown route slip comments, 10 September 1952; remarks on attack seaplane, 9 September 1952, file 1.11, XP6M-1, 1952, box 25, Correspondence of the Patrol Design Branch, 1944–53, BuAer Records, RG 72, NA.

38. George M. Bunker (president, Martin Co.) to Chief, BuAer, 29 April 1954, vol. 14, box 22, file NOas 53-455, acc. no. 15491, Contract Records, 1940–60, Records of Divisions and Offices, BuAer Records, RG 72, NA; Piet and Raithel, *Martin P6M SeaMaster,* p. 37; F. W. Brown (by direction, Chief, BuAer) to Glenn L. Martin Co., 27 October 1952, Aer-AC-56, NOas 43-455, ser: 151963, file 1.11, XP6M-1, 1952, box 25, Correspondence of the Patrol Design Branch, 1944–53, BuAer Records, RG 72, NA.

## Chapter 6. SeaMaster

1. George M. Bunker to Chief, BuAer, 29 April 1954, vol. 14, box 22, file NOas 53-455, acc. no. 15491, Records of Divisions and Offices, Contract Records, 1940–60, BuAer Records, RG 72, NA; Classified Annex to Part IV of the Annual Management Report from the Chief of the Bureau of Aeronautics to the Secretary of the Navy, Fiscal Year 1953, 28 May 1954, p. 18, box 2, BuAer Records, RG 72, NA (courtesy of Bob Hunter).

2. Annual Report of the Chief of the Bureau of Aeronautics to the Secretary of the Navy, Fiscal Year 1952, 16 December 1952, pp. 1–2, 5, 15–16, box 2, BuAer Records, RG 72, NA (courtesy of Bob Hunter).

3. NASA Biographical Data Sheet, "George Simpson Trimble Jr.," n.d., NASA Manned Spacecraft Center, Houston, TX (courtesy of Kristen Starr). George S. Trimble is no relation to the author.

4. Memo for files, F. A. Louden, BuAer, 13 October 1952, file 1.11, XP6M-1, 1952, box 25, Correspondence of the Patrol Design Branch, 1944–53, BuAer Records, RG 72, NA. High Performance Seaplane Minelayer Progress Report, August, September, 1952, ER 5276, 1 October 1952, pp. 3, 6–8; J. N. Murphy (by direction, Chief, BuAer) to NACA, 4 December 1952, Aer-DE-31, 023165; both in vol. 1, box 51, file NOas 52-1136, acc. no. 15700, Records of Divisions and Offices, Contract Records, 1940–60, BuAer Records, RG 72, NA. F. W. Brown (by direction, Chief, BuAer) to BAR, Baltimore, 21 April 1953, Aer-AC-56, 06575, vol. 5, box 22, file NOas 53-455, acc. no. 15491, Records of Divisions and Offices, Contract Records, 1940–60, BuAer Records, RG 72, NA.

5. Piet and Raithel, *Martin P6M SeaMaster,* p. 39. High Performance Seaplane Minelayer Progress Report, August, September, 1952, ER 5276, 1 October 1952, pp.

6–7, vol. 1, box 51, file NOas 52-1136, acc. no. 15700; BAR, Baltimore, Summary of Hydrodynamic Testing on XP6M Model program, 15 March 1954, vol. 14, box 22, file NOas 53-455, acc. no. 15491; both in Records of Divisions and Offices, Contract Records, 1940–60, BuAer Records, RG 72, NA.

6. High Performance Seaplane Minelayer Progress Report, August, September, 1952, ER 5276, 1 October 1952, pp. 6–7, vol. 1, box 51, file NOas 52-1136, acc. no. 15700, Records of Divisions and Offices, Contract Records, 1940–60, BuAer Records, RG 72, NA; Piet and Raithel, *Martin P6M SeaMaster*, p. 47; W. G. Eager Jr., Martin Co., to Robert L. Kemelhor, BuAer, 8 September 1952, file 1.11, XP6M-1, 1952, box 25, Correspondence of the Patrol Design Branch, 1944–53, BuAer Records, RG 72, NA.

7. Piet and Raithel, *Martin P6M SeaMaster*, pp. 39–40; James S. Tassin, BuAer, to Martin Co., 1 December 1952, Aer-PP-212, Ser: 022919, file 1.11, XP6M-1, 1952, box 25, Correspondence of the Patrol Design Branch, 1944–53, BuAer Records, RG 72, NA; memo, J. A. Thomas, Director, Aircraft Div., BuAer, to Director, Production Div., 26 October 1955, Aer-AC-541, vol. 29, box 21, file NOas 53-455, acc. no. 15491, Records of Divisions and Offices, Contract Records, 1940–60, BuAer Records, RG 72, NA. Information on the J67 comes from "The Last Great Act of Defiance: The Memoirs of Ernest C. Simpson, Aero Propulsion Pioneer," Aero Propulsion Laboratory, Air Force Wright Aeronautical Laboratories, Wright-Patterson AFB, Dayton, OH, 1 June 1987, pp. 61, 111 (courtesy of Rick Leyes, NASM). For the J40, see U.S. Cong., House, *Navy Jet Aircraft Procurement Program: Hearings before a Subcommittee of the Committee on Government Operations*, 84th Cong., 1st sess., 24, 25, 27 October 1955 (Washington, DC: GPO, 1956), pp. 18, 27–29, 210–12.

8. W. G. Eager Jr., Martin Co., to Chief, BuAer, 4 February 1953, WGE:140, 275-0039, vol. 1, box 22, file NOas 53-455, acc. no. 15491, Records of Divisions and Offices, Contract Records, 1940–60, BuAer Records, RG 72, NA; Piet and Raithel, *Martin P6M SeaMaster*, pp. 39–40. For information on the J71, see Richard A. Leyes II and William A. Fleming, *The History of North American Small Gas Turbine Aircraft Engines* (Washington, DC: NASM and American Institute of Aeronautics and Astronautics, 1999), p. 533.

9. Report of Field Trip, 17–21 November 1952, 25 November 1952, file 1.11, XP6M-1, 1952, box 25, Correspondence of the Patrol Design Branch, 1944–53, BuAer Records, RG 72, NA.

10. Cdr. F. W. Brown (by direction, Chief, BuAer) to BuAer Gen. Rep., Eastern District, 24 February 1953, Aer-AC-56, box 514, file VP6M-1/F1, "Unclassified" General Correspondence, 1953, BuAer Records, RG 72, NA; U.S. Navy XP6M-1 High Speed Minelayer Mock-Up Design Review, March 1953, vol. 2, box 22, file NOas 53-455, acc. no. 15491, Records of Divisions and Offices, Contract Records, 1940–60, BuAer Records, RG 72, NA.

11. U.S. Navy XP6M-1 High Speed Minelayer Mock-Up Design Review, March 1953, vol. 2, box 22; A. E. Paddock (BAR, Baltimore) to Chief, BuAer, 20 July 1955,

J11/P6M. No. 01873, vol. 26, box 21; both in file NOas 53-455, acc. no. 15491, Records of Divisions and Offices, Contract Records, 1940–60, BuAer Records, RG 72, NA; Piet and Raithel, *Martin P6M SeaMaster,* p. 40.

12. George M. Bunker to Chief, BuAer, 29 April 1954, vol. 14, box 22; C. T. Ray, project engineer, Martin Co., to Chief, BuAer, 13 November 1953, EJW:383, vol. 10, box 22; C. T. Ray, project engineer, Martin Co., to Chief, BuAer, 20 August 1954, BJW: 383, vol. 18, box 21; all in file NOas 53-455, acc. no. 15491, Records of Divisions and Offices, Contract Records, 1940–60, BuAer Records, RG 72, NA.

13. A. L. Varrieur, Martin Co., to BuAer, 17 June 1955, no. 275-1039, vol. 17, box 20; D. M. Wisehaupt, BuAer, to James S. Lunn, 23 June 1955, vol. 15, box 20; both in file NOas 53-455, acc. no. 15491, Records of Divisions and Offices, Contract Records, 1940–60, BuAer Records, RG 72, NA. A. J. Perry, Martin Co., to BuAer, 6 March 1956, vol. 18B, box 46, file NOas 53-455, acc. no. 59-1789, Records of Divisions and Offices, Contract Records, 1940–60, BuAer Records, RG 72, NA.

14. Rear Adm. Apollo Soucek to CNO, 2 June 1954, Aer-AC-5, 010778, vol. 14, box 22, file NOas 53-455, acc. no. 15491, Records of Divisions and Offices, Contract Records, 1940–60, BuAer Records, RG 72, NA.

15. Memo, R. E. Dixon, Director, Aircraft Div., BuAer, to Director, Industrial Planning Div., BuAer, 26 March 1954, Aer-AC-56, vol. 14, box 22, file NOas 53-455, acc. no. 15491, Records of Divisions and Offices, Contract Records, 1940–60, BuAer Records, RG 72, NA; U.S. General Accounting Office, *Report to the Congress of the United States: Additional Costs Incurred in the Procurement of P6M Seaplanes from the Glenn L. Martin Company, Baltimore, Maryland* (Washington, DC: Comptroller General of the United States, 1964), pp. 3, 14 (hereafter cited as GAO, *Report: Additional Costs of P6M Seaplanes*).

16. George M. Bunker, Martin Co., to Chief, BuAer, 29 April 1954, GMB:1 275 0452, vol. 14, box 22, file NOas 53-455, acc. no. 15491, Records of Divisions and Offices, Contract Records, 1940–60, BuAer Records, RG 72, NA.

17. A. E. Paddock (BAR, Baltimore) to Chief, BuAer, 3 May 1954, 1:mlc F8-2/54-4558, vol. 14, box 22, file NOas 53-455, acc. no. 15491, Records of Divisions and Offices, Contract Records, 1940–60, BuAer Records, RG 72, NA.

18. Rear Adm. Apollo Soucek to CNO, 2 June 1954, Aer-AC-5, 010778, vol. 14, box 22, file NOas 53-455, acc. no. 15491, Records of Divisions and Offices, Contract Records, 1940–60, BuAer Records, RG 72, NA.

19. GAO, *Report: Additional Costs of P6M Seaplanes,* pp. 3, 14; Piet and Raithel, *Martin P6M SeaMaster,* p. 50.

20. Piet and Raithel, *Martin P6M SeaMaster,* p. 50; *Washington Post,* 24 January 1955.

21. A. E. Paddock (BAR, Baltimore) to Chief, BuAer, 13 May 1955, 41-hm F1/P6M, no. 01281, vol. 1, box 12, file NOas 55-535, acc. no. 15448, Records of Divisions and Offices, Contract Records, 1940–60, BuAer Records, RG 72, NA.

22. A. E. Paddock (BAR, Baltimore) to Chief, BuAer, 21 March 1955, 41/44-paj F2/53-455S, vol. 21A, box 21, file NOas-455, acc. no 15491, Records of Divisions and Offices, Contract Records, 1940–60, BuAer Records, RG 72, NA.

23. Aero X-23A Navigation-Minelaying for the XP6M-1 Jet Seaplane, enclosure to C. T. Ray, Martin Co. project engineer, to Chief, BuAer, 22 June 1955, 275-1-45 SH:383, vol. 35, box 46, file NOas 53-455, acc. no. 59-1789, Records of Divisions and Offices, Contract Records, 1940–60, BuAer Records, RG 72, NA; Piet and Raithel, *Martin P6M SeaMaster,* pp. 55, 133–35.

24. A. E. Paddock (BAR, Baltimore) to Chief, BuAer, 20 July 1955, J11/P6M, no. 01873, vol. 26, box 21, file NOas 53-455, acc. no. 59-1789, Records of Divisions and Offices, Contract Records, 1940–60, BuAer Records, RG 72, NA.

25. Piet and Raithel, *Martin P6M SeaMaster,* pp. 57–58.

26. News about Martin, 27 September 1955, file AM-201680, Martin XP6M-1 Seamaster (Model 275), NASM Library, Washington, DC; Piet and Raithel, *Martin P6M SeaMaster,* p. 59.

27. Memo, R. E. Dixon, Director, Aircraft Div., BuAer, to Chief, BuAer, 26 July 1955, Aer-AC-51, vol. 26A, box 21, file NOas 53-455, acc. no. 15491, Records of Divisions and Offices, Contract Records, 1940–60, BuAer Records, RG 72, NA.

28. *New York Times,* 9 October 1955.

29. Ibid., 16 October 1955.

30. Piet and Raithel, *Martin P6M SeaMaster,* p. 64.

31. Ibid., p. 62; James S. Russell, "Sea Master—P6M: The Last of the Navy's Flying Boats," 1986, p. 3 (courtesy of Vice Adm. Charles S. Minter Jr.).

## Chapter 7. New Look, New Missions

1. Michael T. Isenberg, *Shield of the Republic: The United States Navy in an Era of Cold War and Violent Peace, 1945–1962* (New York: St. Martin's Press, 1993), pp. 572–75.

2. Ibid., pp. 592–93.

3. Classified Annex to Part IV of the Annual Management Report from the Chief of the Bureau of Aeronautics to the Secretary of the Navy, Fiscal Year 1953, pp. 1, 3–5; Classified Annex to Parts I, II, III of the Annual Report from the Chief of the Bureau of Aeronautics to the Secretary of the Navy, Fiscal Year 1955, pp. 3–4; both in box 2, BuAer Records, RG 72, NA (courtesy of Bob Hunter).

4. Isenberg, *Shield of the Republic,* p. 595.

5. Ibid., p. 597; Palmer, *Origins of the Maritime Strategy,* pp. 80–82; Sapolsky, *Seapower in the Nuclear Age,* pp. 72–73.

6. Memo, F. W. Brown to Capt. A. W. McKechnie, 31 July 1952, Aer-AC-56, file 1.11, General Seaplane Information, 1953, box 25, Correspondence of the Patrol Design Branch, 1944–53, BuAer Records, RG 72, NA.

7. Piet and Raithel, *Martin P6M SeaMaster,* p. 173; F. E. Bardwell (by direction, Chief, BuAer) to Chief, BuShips, 14 November 1952, Aer-AC-56, ser: 022009, file 1.11, XP6M-1, 1952, box 25, Correspondence of the Patrol Design Branch, 1944–53, BuAer Records, RG 72, NA; Glenn L. Martin Company, "A Plan for Seaplane Handling for the United States Navy," ER 5612, July 1953 (courtesy of Stan Piet and Al Raithel).

8. Glenn L. Martin Company, "A Plan for Seaplane Handling for the United States Navy," ER 5612, July 1953 (courtesy of Stan Piet and Al Raithel); Piet and Raithel, *Martin P6M SeaMaster,* p. 173.

9. Chief of Naval Research to CNO, 21 September 1954, ONR:461: KEW:dln, Ser 01653, file A1, box 1, Double Zero Files, 1954, OANHC; Glenn L. Martin Co., "Water-Based Aircraft: An Analysis of Their Potential," ER 6600, 1 October 1954, DTIC, AD056773, pp. xi, 1, 9–52, 117–32; Piet and Raithel, *Martin P6M SeaMaster,* pp. 185–86.

10. BuAer, Research Division, "The Attack Seaplane Task Force vs. the Attack Carrier Task Force, A Preliminary Comparison," Report No. DR-1700, 1 November 1954 (courtesy of Hal Andrews).

11. Report of the Ad Hoc Committee to Study Long-Range Shipbuilding Plans and Programs, 20 December 1955, pp. 13–14, A-15 through A-16, A-24 through A-27, A-80, box 11, Double Zero Files, 1955, OANHC.

12. Memo, Adm. Robert B. Carney to VCNO, 28 December 1954, file A1-1, box 1, Double Zero Files, 1954, OANHC.

13. Glenn L. Martin Co., "Water-Based Aircraft: An Analysis of Their Potential Attack Missions," ER 6602, 30 April 1955, DTIC, AD063941, pp. xi–xii, 1, 10, 13, 25–26, 37, 39–43, 47, 59–66, B2.

14. Stout, "Bases Unlimited," pp. 52–55.

15. Ginter, *Convair XP5Y-1 and R3Y-1/2 Tradewind,* pp. 19–20, 22; Dorr, "Convair R3Y Tradewind," pp. 9–11.

16. *Dictionary of American Naval Fighting Ships,* vol. 1 (Washington, DC: Naval Historical Center, 1991), pp. 140–44. Minutes of Engineering Coordination Meeting, P6M-AV-5 Conversion, 9 September 1955; Minutes of Engineering Coordination Meeting, P6M-AV-5 Conversion, 22 November 1955; both in vol. 1, box 12, file NOas 55-535, acc. no. 15448, Records of Divisions and Offices, Contract Records, 1940–60, BuAer Records, RG 72, NA.

17. Lt. Col. W. E. Clasen, USMC, comments, 23 February 1954, vol. 5, box 12, file NOas 51-527, acc. no. 62A-2988; F. W. Fink, chief engineer, Convair, to Chief, BuAer, 2 September 1954, FWF:TWS:lm 6-4201, vol. 5, box 32, file NOas 51-527, acc. no. 15757; both in Records of Divisions and Offices, Contract Records, 1940–60, BuAer Records, RG 72, NA. Piet and Raithel, *Martin P6M SeaMaster,* p. 165; Friedman, *U.S. Aircraft Carriers,* p. 346.

18. *Dictionary of American Naval Fighting Ships,* vol. 3 (Washington, DC: Naval Historical Center, 1968), pp. 179–80. See also vol. 2, box 261, file QM/Glenn L. Martin Co. July 1956–, "Unclassified" General Correspondence, 1956, BuAer Records, RG 72, NA.

19. John Wegg, *General Dynamics Aircraft and Their Predecessors* (Annapolis, MD: Naval Institute Press, 1990), p. 205.

20. Long, *Convair Sea Dart,* pp. 21–25.

21. Ibid., pp. 25–26.

22. F. W. Brown (by direction, Chief, BuAer) to BuAer General Rep., Eastern District, 24 February 1953, Aer-AC-56, box 514, file VP6M1/F1, "Unclassified" General

Correspondence, 1953, BuAer Records, RG 72, NA. Naval Speed Letter, J. A. Jaap to Chief, BuAer, 6 August 1954, Aer-AR-13, vol. 17, box 21, file NOas 53-455, acc. no. 15491; Joseph Lynn (by direction, Chief, BuAer) to Martin Co., 6 February 1956, NOas 55-535, vol. 2A, box 93, file NOas 55-535, acc. no. 59-1789; both in Records of Divisions and Offices, Contract Records, 1940–60, BuAer Records, RG 72, NA.

23. Naval Speed Letter, G. E. Marcus to BAR, Baltimore, 28 November 1956, DRM:hrg F Ser: 1095, box 442, file VP6M1/F1, "Unclassified" General Correspondence, 1953, BuAer Records, RG 72, NA. V. C. Tompkins Jr. (by direction, Chief, BuAer) to Director, Division of Military Applications, AEC, 25 May 1956, NOas-55-535, 09170, vol. 2A, box 93, file NOas 55-535, acc. no. 59-1789; Joseph Lynn (by direction, Chief, BuAer) to Martin Co., 31 August 1956, NOas 55-535, 015094, vol. 4, box 93, file NOas 55-535, acc. no. 59-1789; YP6M-1 Armament Characteristics Report, May 1958, vol. 56B, box 36, file NOas 55-535, acc. no. 61A-3254; all in Records of Divisions and Offices, Contract Records, 1940–60, BuAer Records, RG 72, NA. Piet and Raithel, *Martin P6M SeaMaster*, pp. 148–49.

24. Rear Adm. David L. McDonald (by direction, CNO) to Distribution List, 9 January 1956, Op-554D2/mb, Ser 004P554 (courtesy of Al Raithel).

25. Flight Test Activities Report No. 14, 29 October 1955 to 4 November 1955 Incl., vol. 30, box 21, file NOas 53-455, acc. no. 15491, Records of Divisions and Offices, Contract Records, 1940–60, BuAer Records, RG 72, NA; Piet and Raithel, *Martin P6M SeaMaster*, p. 62.

26. Piet and Raithel, *Martin P6M SeaMaster*, pp. 67–68; Status Report, Accident Investigation, Model XP6M-1 Aircraft Accident, December 7, 1955, 12 January 1956, box 48, file NOas 53-455, acc. no. 15392, Records of Divisions and Offices, Contract Records, 1940–60, BuAer Records, RG 72, NA.

27. Naval Communication, Rear Adm. J. S. Russell, BuAer, to BAR, Baltimore, 7 December 1955, box 554, file VP6M1/A25, "Unclassified" General Correspondence, 1955, BuAer Records, RG 72, NA; Piet and Raithel, *Martin P6M SeaMaster*, pp. 68–71.

28. XP6M-1 Accident Investigation, Volume 2, Analysis, April 1956, box 48; Special Aircraft Accident Investigation of Model XP6M-1 Potomac River, Maryland, December 7, 1955, vol. 33, box 46; both in file NOas 53-455, acc. no. 15392, Records of Divisions and Offices, Contract Records, 1940–60, BuAer Records, RG 72, NA. Piet and Raithel, *Martin P6M SeaMaster*, pp. 71–73.

29. Tim Rathbone, "The History and Development of the Strategic Mobile Striking Force, the Martin P6M Seamaster: A Study of Military Weapons Procurement in the 1950s," 1985, pp. 24–25 (courtesy of Stan Piet and Al Raithel); Navy Comptroller Reports to Top Management, 1 February 1956, box 13, Subject files, Navy Comptroller Reports, Double Zero Files, 1956, OANHC.

30. Staff Study Naval Aviation, OP-05—1 February 1956, pp. 1:3, 8, 10, 13, 17, 19, 25–26, 10:2, 9–10, 11:4–5, box 13, Subject files, Navy Comptroller Reports, Double Zero Files, 1956, OANHC.

31. C. T. Ray to Col. J. A. Gerath, BuAer, enclosure: "P6M-1 Basing and Support Concept," 17 April 1956, pp. 1–2, 5, 15, vol. 2A, box 93, file NOas 55-535, acc. no.

59-1789, Records of Divisions and Offices, Contract Records, 1940–60, BuAer Records, RG 72, NA.

32. *Aviation Week* 65 (1 October 1956): 26–27; Bugos, *Engineering the F-4 Phantom II,* pp. 19, 56–58; George M. Bunker to Chief, BuAer, 29 April 1954, vol. 14, box 22, file NOas 53-455, acc. no. 15491, Records of Divisions and Offices, Contract Records, 1940–60, BuAer Records, RG 72, NA.

33. Reminiscences of Vice Adm. Charles S. Minter Jr., 2 vols., June 1981, Naval Institute Oral History Collection, 1:1–2, 339; interview with Vice Adm. Charles S. Minter Jr., 11 June 2003, Annapolis, MD.

34. Reminiscences of Vice Adm. Charles S. Minter Jr., 2 vols., June 1981, Naval Institute Oral History Collection, 1:334–36, 345; interview with Vice Adm. Charles S. Minter Jr., 11 June 2003, Annapolis, MD.

35. Reminiscences of Vice Adm. Charles S. Minter Jr., 2 vols., June 1981, Naval Institute Oral History Collection, 1:338–39, 357; interview with Vice Adm. Charles S. Minter Jr., 11 June 2003, Annapolis, MD.

36. Reminiscences of Vice Adm. Charles S. Minter Jr., 2 vols., June 1981, Naval Institute Oral History Collection, 1:340–41; interview with Vice Adm. Charles S. Minter Jr., 11 June 2003, Annapolis, MD.

37. Edgar A. Parsons, "Needed—A Military Strategy of Mobility," U.S. Naval Institute *Proceedings* 82 (December 1956): pp. 1263–69.

38. Burke to DCNO (Air), 10 August 1956, Op-09D/js Ser 048PO9D (courtesy of Stan Piet and Al Raithel).

39. Memo, Rear Adm. William V. Davis Jr. to Asst. CNO (General Planning), 9 January 1958, Op-552/br Ser O5P552 (courtesy of Al Raithel); GAO, *Report: Additional Costs of P6M Seaplanes,* pp. 3, 14–15.

40. Office of Assistant Secretary of Defense, Research and Development, Ad Hoc Committee on Water-Based Aircraft Capabilities, "Water-Based Aircraft Capabilities," 1 December 1956, DTIC, AD141474, pp. 1–4; for Stack, see Hansen, *Engineer in Charge,* pp. 257–61, 271, 304.

41. XP6M-1 Seamaster Ship No. 2, Accident Investigation, vol. 1, Summary, January 1957, vol. 42, box 45, file NOas 53-455, acc. no. 59-1789, Records of Divisions and Offices, Contract Records, 1940–60, BuAer Records, RG 72, NA.

42. GAO, *Report: Additional Costs of P6M Seaplanes,* p. 22; Piet and Raithel, *Martin P6M SeaMaster,* p. 92.

## Chapter 8. Toward an Operational Force

1. Convair, "Hydrodynamic Demonstration Report: The XF2Y-1 Single-Ski Airplane," Report No. ZC-2-061, April 1956, DTIC, AD107872, pp. 3, 83, 99–100; memo, Abraham Hyatt, BuAer Research Div., to Director, Aircraft Div., 19 February 1954, Aer-RS-3, vol. 5, box 12, file NOas 51-527, acc. no. 62A-2988, Records of Divisions and Offices, Contract Records, 1940–60, BuAer Records, RG 72, NA.

2. Flight Test Operation Report, XF2Y-1 Test Program for the Period 9 January 1956 through 22 January 1956, 16 March 1956, vol. 48, box 13, file NOas 51-527,

acc. no. 59-1789, Records of Divisions and Offices, Contract Records, 1940–60, BuAer Records, RG 72, NA; Convair, "Hydrodynamic Demonstration Report: The XF2Y-1 Single-Ski Airplane," Report No. ZC-2-061, April 1956, DTIC, AD107872, pp. 57–58, 71–72, 83–84, 100–101, 107–8, 113–19; Long, *Convair Sea Dart,* pp. 29–32.

3. Long, *Convair Sea Dart,* pp. 41–47.

4. Rear Adm. David L. McDonald (by direction, CNO) to Chief, BuAer, 27 December 1955, Op-551D2/dl, Ser 0199P551, vol. 48, box 13, file NOas 51-527, acc. no. 59-1789, Records of Divisions and Offices, Contract Records, 1940–60, BuAer Records, RG 72, NA; Long, *Convair Sea Dart,* p. 59.

5. BuAer, Research Division, "A Preliminary Design Study of an Open Ocean Sonar Dunking Flying Boat," Report No. DR-1716, April 1955 (courtesy of Hal Andrews); P6Y (ASW) Seaplane History, CV 24 History (P6Y), Design Proposals/Seaplanes, GD/Convair, Convair Collection, Archives, SDAM.

6. Staff Study, Naval Aviation, OP-05-1, February 1956, box 13, Subject files, Navy Comptroller Reports, Double Zero Files, 1956, OANHC.

7. Wallace A. Helmuth, Martin Co., to Chief, BuAer, 24 April 1956, 1 January–30 June 1956, QM/Glenn L. Martin Co. folder, vol. 1, box 261; George M. Bunker to Rear Adm. James S. Russell, 11 February 1957, Aer 3 S2/15,1 January–31 March 1957, QM/Martin Co. folder, vol. 1, box 265; both in "Unclassified" General Correspondence, 1956, BuAer Records, RG 72, NA. P6Y (ASW) Seaplane History, CV 24 History (P6Y), Design Proposals/Seaplanes, GD/Convair, Convair Collection, Archives, SDAM; Piet and Raithel, *Martin P6M SeaMaster,* pp. 189–90; Proposal, "ASW Patrol Seaplane Class VP," August 1956, Report No. ZP-170, Design Proposals/Seaplanes, GD/Convair, Convair Collection, Archives, SDAM (courtesy of George Cully).

8. Memo, DCNO (Air) to SecNav, 20 March 1958, Op-50/cg Ser 08414P50, A1(1) file, box 1, Double Zero Files, 1958, OANHC; Long, *Convair Sea Dart,* pp. 59–60; Convair, "Combat Seaplane Configuration Study," Report No. ZP-181, December 1956, DTIC, AD301274; Convair, "Supersonic Attack Seaplane Configuration Study (Chemically Powered)," Report No. ZP-178, April 1957, DTIC, AD303544.

9. Piet and Raithel, *Martin P6M SeaMaster,* pp. 89–92, 178–80; C. T. Ray, Martin Co., to Chief, BuAer, 4 May 1956, 535-0236, vol. 3, box 93, file NOas 55-535, acc. no. 59-1789, Records of Divisions and Offices, Contract Records, 1940–60, BuAer Records, RG 72, NA.

10. R. H. Draut, project engineer, Martin Co., to Chief, BuAer, 30 December 1957, with route slip comments, 535-1475, vol. 34, box 35, file NOas 55-535, acc. no. 61A-3254, Records of Divisions and Offices, Contract Records, 1940–60, BuAer Records, RG 72, NA.

11. C. T. Ray, Martin Co., to Chief, BuAer, 6 December 1956, 535-0755, vol. 8, box 93, file NOas 55-535, acc. no. 59-1789, Records of Divisions and Offices, Contract Records, 1940–60, BuAer Records, RG 72, NA.

12. Memo, Rear Adm. David L. McDonald to Director, Aviation Plans Div., 13 May 1957, Op-55H/br Ser 076P55; CNO to Distribution List, Fleet Induction of

P6M Aircraft, 30 September 1957, Op-502C2 Ser 002034P50 (both courtesy of Al Raithel).

13. Reminiscences of Vice Adm. Charles S. Minter Jr., 2 vols., June 1981, Naval Institute Oral History Collection, 1:344; interview with Vice Adm. Charles S. Minter Jr., 11 June 2003, Annapolis, MD; U.S. Cong., House, *Congressional Record,* 85th Cong., 1st sess., vol. 103, pt. 6, p. 7615; GAO, *Report: Additional Costs of P6M Seaplanes,* p. 3.

14. Vice Adm. C. R. Brown to CNO, 14 October 1957, 6F/332/bs A16-1, Ser: 00184, A1 through A1(2), box 1, Double Zero Files, 1958, OANHC.

15. Piet and Raithel, *Martin P6M SeaMaster,* p. 93; R. H. Draut, project engineer, Martin Co., to Chief, BuAer, 30 December 1957, 535-1475, vol. 34, box 35, file NOas 55-535, acc. no. 61A-3254, Records of Divisions and Offices, Contract Records, 1940–60, BuAer Records, RG 72, NA; Glenn L. Martin Co., "History of the Flight Test Development of Aerodynamic Modifications to the YP6M-1 and P6M-2 Seamaster," ER 10942, November 1959, DTIC, AD315574, pp. 12–13.

16. Piet and Raithel, *Martin P6M SeaMaster,* p. 93; Joseph Lynn (by direction, Chief, BuAer) to Martin Co., 5 February 1958, Aer-AD-23, NOas-55-535, vol. 36, box 35, file NOas 55-535, acc. no. 61A-3254, Records of Divisions and Offices, Contract Records, 1940–60, BuAer Records, RG 72, NA.

17. W. J. J. Leary (by direction, Chief, BuAer) to Martin Co., 2 January 1958, NOas-55-535c 021, vol. 32, box 35; J. R. Brown (by direction, Chief, BuAer) to BAR, Baltimore, 2 October 1958, Aer-AC-541 NOas-55-535c, 012936, vol. 64, box 36; both in file NOas 55-535, acc. no. 61A-3254, Records of Divisions and Offices, Contract Records, 1940–60, BuAer Records, RG 72, NA. Piet and Raithel, *Martin P6M SeaMaster,* pp. 93–98.

18. S. R. Ours (by direction, Director, Aircraft Div., BuAer) to Director, Maintenance Div., BuAer, 4 August 1955, Aer-AC-541, vol. 16, box 20, file NOas 53-455, acc. no. 15491, Records of Divisions and Offices, Contract Records, 1940–60, BuAer Records, RG 72, NA. For detailed information on tests of the system, see vol. 35, box 46, and vols. 38, 39, box 45, file NOas 53-455, acc. no. 59-1789, Records of Divisions and Offices, Contract Records, 1940–60, BuAer Records, RG 72, NA.

19. Joseph Lynn (by direction, Chief, BuAer) to Martin Co., 24 March 1958, Aer-AV-3233; R. H. Draut, Martin Co., to Chief, BuAer, 21 April 1958; route slip notes on J. A. Wright, Martin Co., to Chief, BuAer, 23 April 1958; all in NOas-57-161, vol. 14, box 59, file NOas 57-161, acc. no. 61A-3254, Records of Divisions and Offices, Contract Records, 1940–60, BuAer Records, RG 72, NA. Piet and Raithel, *Martin P6M SeaMaster,* pp. 81, 102, 149.

20. Piet and Raithel, *Martin P6M SeaMaster,* p. 156; "Flight Test and Evaluation of the Minelaying-Navigational Set AN/ASQ-29, Phase II," PTR-AV-32013.1, Final Report, 1 April 1960, DTIC, AD317677, pp. 2–7.

21. GAO, *Report: Additional Costs of P6M Seaplanes,* pp. 8, 22–25; Reminiscences of Vice Adm. Charles S. Minter Jr., 2 vols., June 1981, Naval Institute Oral History Collection, 1:361.

22. H. C. Wieben, Martin Co., to Chief, BuAer, 29 October 1958, 535-1739, JAW:J-349, vol. 67, box 36, file NOas 55-535, acc. no. 61A-3254, Records of Divi-

sions and Offices, Contract Records, 1940–60, BuAer Records, RG 72, NA; Piet and Raithel, *Martin P6M SeaMaster,* p. 107.

23. Adm. Robert E. Dixon to Martin Co., 3 October 1958, Aer-SY-5, NOas-55-535-c, NOas-57-161, NOas-58-603K, vol. 64, box 36, file NOas 55-535; J. E. Dodson to Chief, BuAer, 6 October 1958, Aer-PD-1, NOa(s)57-161, vol. 32, box 59, file NOas 57-161; both in acc. no. 61A-3254, Records of Divisions and Offices, Contract Records, 1940–60, BuAer Records, RG 72, NA.

24. Adm. Robert E. Dixon to Martin Co., 3 October 1958, Aer-SY-5, NOas-55-535-c, NOas-57-161, NOas-58-603K, vol. 64, box 36, file NOas 55-535, acc. no. 61A-3254, Records of Divisions and Offices, Contract Records, 1940–60, BuAer Records, RG 72, NA.

25. Thomas Wildenberg, *Destined for Glory: Dive Bombing, Midway, and the Evolution of Carrier Airpower* (Annapolis, MD: Naval Institute Press, 1998), p. 81; Reynolds, *Admiral John H. Towers,* pp. 406; Pirie to Col. C. I. Kephart, 5 September 1962, file K—Op-05, Series I, box 8, #21, Personal and Official Correspondence, 1943–62, DCNO (Air) file, AHNHC; interview with Vice Adm. Charles S. Minter Jr., 11 June 2003, Annapolis, MD.

26. Robert J. Watson, *Into the Missile Age, 1956–1960,* vol. 4, *History of the Office of the Secretary of Defense* (Washington, DC: Historical Office, Office of the Secretary of Defense, 1997), pp. 143–46, 309–20; Friedman, *U.S. Aircraft Carriers,* pp. 279–80, 316–17; May–June 1958 entries, Vice Admiral Pirie Personal Log, May 1958–September 1960, box 12, nos. 22–27, Personal and Official Correspondence, 1943–62, DCNO (Air) file, AHNHC.

27. Entry for 25 August 1958, Vice Admiral Pirie Personal Log, May 1958–September 1960, box 12, nos. 22–27, Personal and Official Correspondence, 1943–62, DCNO (Air) file, AHNHC.

28. Entry for 26 August 1958, Vice Admiral Pirie Personal Log, May 1958–September 1960, box 12, nos. 22–27, Personal and Official Correspondence, 1943–62, DCNO (Air) file, AHNHC; memo, Pirie to CNO, 29 August 1958, A1(1) file, box 1, Double Zero Files, 1958, OANHC.

29. J. E. Dodson to Chief, BuAer, 6 October 1958, Aer-PD-1, NOa(S)57-161, vol. 32, box 59; Martin Co. Monthly Report of Progress, 1–31 December 1958, vol. 37, box 28; both in file NOas 57-161, acc. no. 61A-3254, Records of Divisions and Offices, Contract Records, 1940–60, BuAer Records, RG 72, NA. Memo, Burke to SecNav, 19 November 1958, Op-50C/cjj Ser 08490P50 (courtesy of Al Raithel); Rear Adm. R. E. Dixon (chief, BuAer) to Rep. Harry R. Sheppard (chairman, Subcommittee on Military Construction, House Appropriations Committee), 24 November 1958, Aer-124/440, file QM/Martin Company, vol. 6, June 1–, box 214, "Unclassified" General Correspondence, 1958, BuAer Records, RG 72, NA.

30. Piet and Raithel, *Martin P6M SeaMaster,* pp. 108–9.

31. BuAer, Research Division, "Technical Feasibility and Operational Analysis of P6M-Regulus II Weapon System," Report No. DR-1792, May 1957, DTIC, AD311690; BuAer, Research Division, "A Preliminary Design Study of an Air-to-Surface, Boost-Glide Missile System for the P6M Aircraft," Report No. DR-1811,

February 1958, DTIC, AD311806; Martin Co. to Chief, BuAer, 23 April 1958, vol. 19, box 59, file NOas 57-161, acc. no. 61A-3254, Records of Divisions and Offices, Contract Records, 1940–60, BuAer Records, RG 72, NA.

32. Piet and Raithel, *Martin P6M SeaMaster*, pp. 150–51.

33. Ibid., p. 152; Richard K. Smith, *Seventy-Five Years of Inflight Refueling* (Washington, DC: Air Force History and Museum Program, 1998), pp. 16, 32–33.

34. Martin Co., "Inflight Refueling for P6M Support," Report no. ER 8450, June 1956, pp. vi–vii, 3, 18–21, 23, vol. 4, box 93, file NOas 55-535, acc. no. 59-1789; Martin Co. to Chief, BuAer, Model P6M-2 Airplanes Tanker/Receiver Status, 3 February 1958, vol. 12, box 59, file NOas 57-161, acc. no. 61A-3254; both in Records of Divisions and Offices, Contract Records, 1940–60, BuAer Records, RG 72, NA.

35. Naval Air Test Center, Patuxent River, "Model P6M Tanker Air Refueling Formation, Investigation of," Report no. 1, 5 September 1958, DTIC, AD30220. Martin Co. to Chief, BuAer, Model P6M-2 Airplane Air Refueling Program, 17 October 1958, vol. 35, box 58; F. W. Brown (by direction, Chief, BuAer) to Martin Co., 26 July 1958, Aer-if-6211/58, vol. 25, box 59; both in file NOas 57-161, acc. no. 61A-3254, Records of Divisions and Offices, Contract Records, 1940–60, BuAer Records, RG 72, NA.

36. Martin Co. to Chief, BuAer, Model P6M-2 Tanker/Receiver Status Monthly Report, 6 July 1959, vol. 50, box 29; Martin Co. to Chief, BuAer, Model P6M-2 Tanker/Receiver Status Monthly Report, 5 August 1959, vol. 53, box 28; both in file NOas 57-161, acc. no. 61A-2232, Records of Divisions and Offices, Contract Records, 1940–60, BuAer Records, RG 72, NA.

37. Martin Co. to Chief, BuAer, 7 January 1959, vol. 39, box 28, file NOas 57-161, acc. no. 62-A-2232, Records of Divisions and Offices, Contract Records, 1940–60, BuAer Records, RG 72, NA; Piet and Raithel, *Martin P6M SeaMaster*, p. 113.

38. Piet and Raithel, *Martin P6M SeaMaster*, p. 114.

39. Martin Co. to Chief, BuAer, 7 January 1959, vol. 39, box 28, file NOas 57-161, acc. no. 62-A-2232, Records of Divisions and Offices, Contract Records, 1940–60, BuAer Records, RG 72, NA.

40. BAR, Baltimore, to Martin Co., 20 January 1959, 44-hm F2/P6M-2S; Martin Co. to Chief, BuAer, 1–31 January 1959, Monthly Progress Report; both in vol. 39, box 28, file NOas 57-161, acc. no. 62-A-2232, Records of Divisions and Offices, Contract Records, 1940–60, BuAer Records, RG 72, NA.

41. Martin Co. to Chief, BuAer, 1–28 February 1959, Monthly Progress Report, vol. 41, box 29, file NOas 57-161, acc. no. 62-A-2232, Records of Divisions and Offices, Contract Records, 1940–60, BuAer Records, RG 72, NA; Piet and Raithel, *Martin P6M SeaMaster*, p. 116.

42. Glenn L. Martin Co., "History of the Flight Test Development of Aerodynamic Modifications to the YP6M-1 and P6M-2 Seamaster," Report No. ER 10942, November 1959, DTIC, AD315574, pp. 2–3.

43. Ibid., pp. 2, 5–8; Martin Co. to Chief, BuAer, 1–31 May 1959, Monthly Progress Report, vol. 47, box 29, file NOas 57-161, acc. no. 62-A-2232, Records of

Divisions and Offices, Contract Records, 1940–60, BuAer Records, RG 72, NA; Piet and Raithel, *Martin P6M SeaMaster,* pp. 118–21.

44. Memo, J. R. Brown, director, Aircraft Div., BuAer, to Director, Airframe Design Div., BuAer, 2 January 1959, Aer-AC-541, file VP6M1/F1, box 325, "Unclassified" General Correspondence, 1959, BuAer Records, RG 72, NA; Piet and Raithel, *Martin P6M SeaMaster,* p. 109.

45. R. H. Draut, Martin Co., to Chief, BuAer, 5 March 1959, 535-0381, RHD:J383, vol. 79, box 13, file NOas 55-535, acc. no. 62A-2232, Records of Divisions and Offices, Contract Records, 1940–60, BuAer Records, RG 72, NA.

46. Ibid., with C. D. Kephart route slip comments; H. A. Romberg (BAR, Baltimore) to Chief, BuAer, 1 April 1959, 46-hm A9-8/1-1/P6MS 0465, vol. 79, box 13, file NOas 55-535, acc. no. 62A-2232, Records of Divisions and Offices, Contract Records, 1940–60, BuAer Records, RG 72, NA.

47. H. A. Romberg (BAR, Baltimore) to Chief, BuAer, 7 May 1959, 10:md L4-3/M55-535, L4-3/M57-161, 5689, vol. 81, box 13, file NOas 55-535, acc. no. 62A-2232, Records of Divisions and Offices, Contract Records, 1940–60, BuAer Records, RG 72, NA.

## Chapter 9. End of the Line

1. Rear Adm. R. E. Dixon to Martin Co., 15 May 1959, Aer-PD-203/1, vol. 81, box 13, file NOas 55-535, acc. no. 62A-2232, Records of Divisions and Offices, Contract Records, 1940–60, BuAer Records, RG 72, NA.

2. Memo, Rear Adm. R. E. Dixon to CNO, 6 March 1959, Aer-SY, vol. 2, March 1–31, file QM/Martin Company, box 195, "Unclassified" General Correspondence, 1959, BuAer Records, RG 72, NA.

3. Capt. Robert B. Greenwood, USN (Ret.), to Vice Adm. James S. Russell, 6 January 1986 (courtesy of Vice Adm. Charles S. Minter Jr.). Greenwood, an officer in BuAer at the time, is vague about the timing of the study and briefing, but his recollections coincide with other developments in early 1959.

4. Memo, Vice Adm. R. B. Pirie to CNO, 11 April 1959, Op-O5W/mt Ser 0013PO5W, file Navaer 00, box 11, Subject Files 7300 through 12000, Double Zero Files, 1959, OANHC.

5. Memo, Burke to Pirie, 19 May 1959, Op-00:ty Op00 Memo 187-59, file Navaer 00, box 11, Subject Files 7300 through 12000, Double Zero Files, 1959, OANHC; Harvey M. Sapolsky, *The Polaris System Development: Bureaucratic and Programmatic Success in Government* (Cambridge, MA: Harvard University Press, 1972).

6. Rear Adm. R. E. Dixon to Martin Co., 15 May 1959, Aer-PD-203/1, vol. 81, box 13, file NOas 55-535, acc. no. 62A-2232, Records of Divisions and Offices, Contract Records, 1940–60, BuAer Records, RG 72, NA.

7. Martin Co., "Comparison of Flight Test and Estimated Stability, Control, and Flying Qualities of the YP6M-1 and P6M-2 Seamaster," Report No. ER 10944, October 1959, DTIC, AD315261, p. 11.

8. Daily Flight Report, encl. in BAR, Baltimore, to Chief, BuAer, 25 May 1959, vol. 45; Daily Flight Report, encl. in BAR, Baltimore, to Chief, BuAer, 22 July 1959, vol. 50; all in box 29, file NOas 57-161, acc. no. 62A-2232, Records of Divisions and Offices, Contract Records, 1940–60, BuAer Records, RG 72, NA.

9. Vice Adm. R. B. Pirie to Op-00, 13 August 1959, Op-502E/cmf Ser 02104P50, file Navaer 00, box 11, Subject Files 7300 through 12000, Double Zero Files, 1959, OANHC; 11 August 1959 entry, Vice Admiral Pirie Personal Log, May 1958–September 1960, box 12, nos. 22–27, Personal and Official Correspondence, 1943–62, DCNO (Air) file, AHNHC.

10. Adm. James S. Russell to SecNav, 13 August 1959, Op-502E/cmf Ser 02104P50, file Navaer 00, box 11, Subject Files 7300 through 1200, Double Zero Files, 1959, OANHC.

11. F. A. Bantz to SecDef, 19 August 1959, file Navaer 00, box 11, Subject Files 7300 through 12000, Double Zero Files, 1959, OANHC.

12. Piet and Raithel, *Martin P6M SeaMaster,* p. 127; "SeaMaster Cancellation Announced," *Martin Service News* (September–October 1959), p. 6 (courtesy of Stan Piet and Al Raithel).

13. Memo, A. E. Paddock (by direction, Asst. Chief for Research and Development, BuAer) to Assistant Chief for Plans and Programs, BuAer, 8 September 1959, Aer-AC-541, vol. 86; Maintenance Plans Directive 18-59, F. E. Rogozienski to Heads, Branches, Sections and Units, Maintenance Div., BuAer, 15 September 1959, Aer-MA-21, vol. 86; J. E. Dodson, asst. chief for procurement, BuAer, to BAR, Baltimore, 4 November 1959, Aer-PD-1143/50, vol. 87; all in box 13, file NOas 55-535, acc. no. 62A-2232, Records of Divisions and Offices, Contract Records, 1940–60, BuAer Records, RG 72, NA.

14. H. W. Merrill to Chief, BuAer, 30 August 1957, A9-3/3-1/300, file QM/Martin Company, vol. 5, 1 September–31 October, box 256; E. D. Tarmey to Chief, BuAer, 30 April 1958, 162 0599 EDT:9073, file QM/Martin Company, vol. 5, 1 May–31 May, box 214; J. Glenn Beall to Thomas S. Gates, 29 November 1958, file QM/Martin Company, vol. 6, 1 June–, box 214; Rear Adm. L. D. Coates to George H. Fallon, 16 October 1959, Aer-124/295, file QM/Martin Company, vol. 3, 1 April–, box 196; telegram, J. Glenn Beall to Thomas S. Gates, 22 August 1959, file QM/Martin Company, vol. 3, 1 April–, box 196; all in "Unclassified" General Correspondence, 1959, BuAer Records, RG 72.

15. Piet and Raithel, *Martin P6M SeaMaster,* pp. 202–4, 109.

16. U.S. Cong., *Hearings before the Subcommittee on Defense Procurement of the Joint Economic Committee, Congress of the United States,* 88th Cong., 1st sess. (Washington, DC: GPO, 1963), n.p.

17. GAO, *Report: Additional Costs of P6M Seaplanes,* pp. 1–3, 6, 8–12, 16, 21–25, 28–33.

18. U.S. Cong., Senate, *Congressional Record,* 88th Cong., 2d sess., vol. 110, pt. 5, p. 6247; ibid., vol. 110, pt. 10, pp. 13625, 13631.

19. Benson, *Acquisition Management in the United States Air Force,* p. 26.

20. General Dynamics, San Diego, "Combat Seaplane Configuration Study," Report No. ZP-181, December 1956, DTIC, AD301274; General Dynamics, San Diego, "Supersonic Attack Seaplane Configuration Study (Chemically Powered)," Report No. ZP-178, April 1957, DTIC, AD303544; George Cully, "A Convair Preliminary Design Study for a Mach 4 Attack Seaplane," *Aerospace Projects Review* 2 (November–December 2000): 4–8.

21. Piet and Raithel, *Martin P6M SeaMaster,* p. 192; Martin Co., "Advanced Seaplane Design," Report No. ER 10832, March 1959, DTIC, AD313424.

22. Carolyn C. Jones, "The Politics of Extravagance: The Aircraft Nuclear Propulsion Project," *Naval War College Review* 53 (Spring 2000): 168; Staff Study, Naval Aviation, OP-05-1, February 1956, box 13, Subject files, Navy Comptroller Reports, Double Zero Files, 1956, OANHC.

23. Jones, "Politics of Extravagance," pp. 176–77, 179–80; "Navy Awards Contract to Martin to Study Nuclear Seaplane for ASW," News about Martin, 26 July 1959, AM-201680-01 file, Martin Seamaster Family, Library, NASM; Piet and Raithel, *Martin P6M SeaMaster,* pp. 193–97.

24. Reminiscences of Vice Adm. Charles S. Minter Jr., 2 vols., June 1981, Naval Institute Oral History Collection, 1:355; interview with Vice Adm. Charles S. Minter Jr., 11 June 2003, Annapolis, MD; Adm. James S. Russell to Capt. Charles B. Greenwood, USN (Ret.), 20 January 1986; Adm. James S. Russell to Capt. Charles B. Greenwood, USN (Ret.), 17 April 1986 (courtesy of Vice Adm. Charles S. Minter Jr.).

25. Reminiscences of Vice Adm. Charles S. Minter Jr., 2 vols., June 1981, Naval Institute Oral History Collection, 1:339, 359; Piet and Raithel, *Martin P6M SeaMaster,* p. 205.

26. Bugos, *Engineering the F-4 Phantom II,* pp. 205, 207, 219–20; Sapolsky, *Polaris System Development,* pp. 58–59, 94–130.

# List of Abbreviations

| | |
|---|---|
| ANP | aircraft nuclear propulsion |
| AOSS | submarine tanker |
| ASW | antisubmarine warfare |
| AV | seaplane tender |
| AVA | attack seaplane tender |
| AVL | light tender |
| AVO | refueler |
| BIS | Board of Inspection and Survey |
| BuAer | Bureau of Aeronautics |
| CAB | Civil Aeronautics Board |
| CINPAC | Commander-in-Chief, Pacific Fleet |
| CNO | Chief of Naval Operations |
| DCNO | Deputy Chief of Naval Operations |
| DVL | Deutsche Versuchsanstalt für Flugwesen Luftfahrt |
| ECM | electronic countermeasures |
| FRL | Flight Refueling, Ltd. |
| GAO | General Accounting Office |
| HSML | high-speed minelayer |
| JATO | jet-assisted takeoff |
| JCS | Joint Chiefs of Staff |
| l/b | length-to-beam |
| LSD | landing ship dock |
| MTOW | maximum takeoff weight |
| NACA | National Advisory Committee for Aeronautics |
| NPE | Navy Preliminary Evaluation |
| NSPS | Naval Strategic Planning Study |
| OPNAV | Office of the Chief of Naval Operations |
| RAE | Royal Aircraft Establishment |
| SSF | Seaplane Striking Force |
| STOL | short takeoff and landing |
| VAH | heavy-attack squadron |
| VP | flying boat |

# Bibliography

**Manuscript and Archival Material**

Defense Technical Information Center, Ft. Belvoir, VA:

Bureau of Aeronautics (BuAer), Preliminary Airplane Design Section. "A Comparative Study of Landplanes and Flying Boats as Long Range Bombers." ADR No. R-17, 23 April 1943, AD896810.

BuAer, Research Division. "A Preliminary Design Study of an Air-to-Surface, Boost-Glide Missile System for the P6M Aircraft." Report No. DR-1811, February 1958, AD311806.

BuAer, Research Division. "Technical Feasibility and Operational Analysis of P6M-Regulus II Weapon System." Report No. DR-1792, May 1957, AD311690.

Convair. "Combat Seaplane Configuration Study." Report No. ZP-181, December 1956, AD301274.

Convair. "Hydrodynamic Demonstration Report: The XF2Y-1 Single-Ski Airplane." Report No. ZC-2-061, April 1956, AD107872.

Convair. "Supersonic Attack Seaplane Configuration Study (Chemically Powered)." Report No. ZP-178, April 1957, AD303544.

"Flight Test and Evaluation of the Minelaying-Navigational Set AN/ASQ-29, Phase II." PTR-AV-32013.1, Final Report, 1 April 1960, AD317677.

General Dynamics Corp. "Combat Seaplane Configuration Study." Report No. ZP-181, December 1956, AD301274.

General Dynamics Corp. "Supersonic Attack Seaplane Configuration Study (Chemically Powered)." Report No. ZP-178, April 1957, AD303544.

Glenn L. Martin Co. "History of the Flight Test Development of Aerodynamic Modifications to the YP6M-1 and P6M-2 Seamaster." ER 10942, November 1959, AD315574.

Glenn L. Martin Co. "Water-Based Aircraft: An Analysis of Their Potential." ER 6600, 1 October 1954, AD056773.

Glenn L. Martin Co. "Water-Based Aircraft: An Analysis of Their Potential Attack Missions." ER 6602, 30 April 1955, AD063941.

Martin Co. "Advanced Seaplane Design." Report No. ER 10832, March 1959, AD313424.

Martin Co. "Comparison of Flight Test and Estimated Stability, Control, and Flying Qualities of the YP6M-1 and P6M-2 Seamaster." Report No. ER 10944, October 1959, AD315261.

National Advisory Committee for Aeronautics. "Results of a Power-on Flight of a 1/10-Scale Rocket-Propelled Model of the Convair XF2Y-1 Airplane." Research Memorandum. NACA TED No. 365, 28 September 1953, AD030940.

Naval Air Test Center. "Model P6M Tanker Air Refueling Formation, Investigation of." Report No. 1, 5 September 1958, AD30220.

Office of Assistant Secretary of Defense, Research and Development, Ad Hoc Committee on Water-Based Aircraft Capabilities. "Water-Based Aircraft Capabilities." 1 December 1956, AD141474.

Operations Evaluation Group. "A Comparison of the Economic Cost and Military Suitability of the High Performance Seaplane with Other Alternative Aircraft for Bombardment Missions." Study 384, 10 February 1950, ADA950177.

General Board of the Navy. Hearings before the General Board of the Navy, 1934. Vol. 1 (micro roll 10).

National Air and Space Museum (NASM) Library, Washington, DC. File AM-201680, Martin XP6M-1 Seamaster (Model 275). File AN 650052-01, Martin Seamaster Family.

National Archives and Records Administration (NARA):

Bureau of Aeronautics (BuAer). Aircraft Specification File. Record Group (RG) 72.

BuAer. Annual Report of the Chief of the Bureau of Aeronautics to the Secretary of the Navy, Fiscal Years 1952, 1953, 1955. RG 72.

BuAer. Contract Correspondence, 1926–39. RG 72.

BuAer, Patrol Design Branch. Correspondence, 1944–53. RG 72.

BuAer, Records of Divisions and Offices. Contract Records, 1940–60. RG 72.

BuAer, Records of Divisions and Offices, Office Services Division/Administrative Services. Secret Correspondence, 1921–38. RG 72.

BuAer. "Unclassified" General Correspondence, 1953, 1955, 1956, 1958, 1959. RG 72.

Chief of Naval Operations, Office of. Formerly Classified General Correspondence of the Deputy Chief of Naval Operations, 1948–51. Department of the Navy, General Records, 1947–. RG 428.

General Board Subject File. General Records of the Department of the Navy. RG 80.

Secretary of the Navy, General Records of Department of the Navy, 1798–1947. Formerly Confidential Correspondence, 1927–39. RG 80.

Secretary of the Navy, General Records of the Department of the Navy, 1798–1947. Formerly Secret Correspondence, 1927–39. RG 80.

U.S. Fleet, Scouting Force. General Correspondence, Naval Operating Forces. RG 313.

Naval Historical Center, Aviation History Branch. Personal and Official Correspondence, 1943–62. DCNO (Air) file.

Naval Historical Center, Operational Archives. Double Zero Files, 1947–59.
San Diego Aerospace Museum, Archives, Convair Collection:
  GD/Convair, Design Proposals/Fighters.
  GD/Convair, Design Proposals/Seaplanes.
  GD/Convair, Personnel.
  GD/Convair, Programs/F2Y.
  Hydro Research, Convair.
  Misc. files, Gillespie Field Annex.
  XP5Y-1 file.


## Public Documents

U.S. Cong. *Hearings before the Subcommittee on Defense Procurement of the Joint Economic Committee, Congress of the United States*. 88th Cong., 1st sess. Washington, DC: Government Printing Office (GPO), 1963.

U.S. Cong. House. *Congressional Record*. 85th Cong., 1st sess. Vol. 103, pt. 6.

U.S. Cong. House. *Hearings before the Committee on Armed Services: The National Defense Program—Unification and Strategy*. 81st Cong., 1st sess. Washington, DC: GPO, 1949.

U.S. Cong. House. *Navy Jet Aircraft Procurement Program: Hearings before a Subcommittee of the Committee on Government Operations*. 84th Cong., 1st sess., 24, 25, 27 October 1955. Washington, DC: GPO, 1956.

U.S. Cong. Senate. *Congressional Record*. 88th Cong., 2d sess. Vol. 110, pts. 5, 10.

U.S. Department of the Navy. *Annual Reports of the Secretary of the Navy, Fiscal Years 1935–1939*. Washington, DC: GPO, 1935–39.

U.S. General Accounting Office. *Report to the Congress of the United States: Additional Costs Incurred in the Procurement of P6M Seaplanes from the Glenn L. Martin Company, Baltimore, Maryland*. Washington, DC: Comptroller General of the United States, 1964.


## Books

Barlow, Jeffrey G. *Revolt of the Admirals: The Fight for Naval Aviation, 1945–1950*. Washington, DC: Naval Historical Center, 1994.

Benson, Lawrence R. *Acquisition Management in the United States Air Force and Its Predecessors*. Washington, DC: Air Force History and Museums Program, 1997.

Bugos, Glenn E. *Engineering the F-4 Phantom II: Parts into Systems*. Annapolis, MD: Naval Institute Press, 1996.

Builder, Carl H. *The Masks of War: American Military Styles in Strategy and Analysis*. Baltimore: Johns Hopkins University Press, 1989.

Christensen, Clayton M. *The Innovator's Dilemma: When New Technologies Cause Great Firms to Fail*. Boston: Harvard Business School Press, 1997.

Creed, Roscoe. *PBY: The Catalina Flying Boat*. Annapolis, MD: Naval Institute Press, 1985.

*Dictionary of American Naval Fighting Ships.* Vols. 1 and 3. Washington, DC: Naval Historical Center, 1991, 1968.

Friedman, Norman. *U.S. Aircraft Carriers: An Illustrated Design History.* Annapolis, MD: Naval Institute Press, 1983.

Friedman, Norman. *U.S. Naval Weapons: Every Gun, Missile, Mine and Torpedo Used by the U.S. Navy from 1883 to the Present Day.* Annapolis, MD: Naval Institute Press, 1982.

Ginter, Steve. *Convair XP5Y-1 and R3Y-1/2 Tradewind.* Simi Valley, CA: Steve Ginter, 1996.

Green, William. *The Warplanes of the Third Reich.* Garden City, NY: Doubleday, 1970.

Grossnick, Roy A., ed. *United States Naval Aviation, 1910–1995.* Washington, DC: Naval Historical Center, 1997.

Hansen, Chuck. *U.S. Nuclear Weapons: The Secret History.* Arlington, TX: Aerofax, 1988.

Hansen, James R. *Engineer in Charge: A History of the Langley Aeronautical Laboratory, 1917–1958.* Washington, DC: National Aeronautics and Space Administration (NASA), 1987.

Hattendorf, John B., and Robert S. Jordan, eds. *Maritime Strategy and the Balance of Power: Britain and America in the Twentieth Century.* New York: St. Martin's Press, 1989.

Hayward, John T., and C. W. Borklund. *Blue Jacket Admiral: The Navy Career of Chick Hayward.* Annapolis, MD: Naval Institute Press, 2000.

Hone, Thomas C., Norman Friedman, and Mark D. Mandeles. *American and British Aircraft Carrier Development, 1919–1941.* Annapolis, MD: Naval Institute Press, 1999.

Hudson, Alec. *"Up Periscope!" and Other Stories.* Annapolis, MD: Naval Institute Press, 1992.

Isenberg, Michael T. *Shield of the Republic: The United States Navy in an Era of Cold War and Violent Peace, 1945–1962.* New York: St. Martin's Press, 1993.

Kaplan, Fred. *The Wizards of Armageddon.* New York: Simon and Schuster, 1983.

Knott, Richard C. *The American Flying Boat: An Illustrated History.* Annapolis, MD: Naval Institute Press, 1979.

Knott, Richard C. *Black Cat Raiders of World War II.* Annapolis, MD: Nautical and Aviation Publishing Company of America, 1981.

Layton, Edwin T., with Roger Pineau and John Costello. *"And I Was There": Pearl Harbor and Midway—Breaking the Secrets.* New York: William Morrow, 1985.

Leyes, Richard A., II, and William A. Fleming. *The History of North American Small Gas Turbine Aircraft Engines.* Washington, DC: National Air and Space Museum and American Institute of Aeronautics and Astronautics, 1999.

Loftin, Laurence K., Jr. *Quest for Performance: The Evolution of Modern Aircraft.* Washington, DC: NASA, 1985.

London, Peter. *Saunders and Saro Aircraft since 1917.* London: Putnam, 1988.

Long, B. J. *Convair XF2Y-1 and YF2Y-1 Sea Dart Experimental Supersonic Seaplane Interceptors.* Simi Valley, CA: Steve Ginter, 1992.

Maurer, Maurer. *Aviation in the U.S. Army, 1919–1939.* Washington, DC: Office of Air Force History, 1987.

Meilinger, Philip S., ed. *The Paths of Heaven: The Evolution of Airpower Theory.* Maxwell Air Force Base, AL: Air University Press, 1997.

Miller, Edward S. *War Plan Orange: The U.S. Strategy to Defeat Japan, 1897–1945.* Annapolis, MD: Naval Institute Press, 1991.

Miller, Jerry. *Nuclear Weapons and Aircraft Carriers.* Washington, DC: Smithsonian Institution Press, 2001.

Palmer, Michael A. *Origins of the Maritime Strategy: American Naval Strategy in the First Postwar Decade.* Washington, DC: Naval Historical Center, 1988.

Piet, Stan, and Al Raithel. *Martin P6M SeaMaster.* Bel Air, MD: Martineer Press, 2001.

Prados, John. *Combined Fleet Decoded: The Secret History of American Intelligence and the Japanese Navy in World War II.* New York: Random House, 1995.

Reynolds, Clark G. *Admiral John H. Towers: The Struggle for Naval Air Supremacy.* Annapolis, MD: Naval Institute Press, 1991.

Rosenberg, David A., and Floyd D. Kennedy Jr. *History of the Strategic Arms Competition, 1945–1972.* Supporting study: *US Aircraft Carriers in the Strategic Role, Part I—Naval Strategy in a Period of Change: Interservice Rivalry, Strategic Interaction, and the Development of Nuclear Attack Capability, 1945–1951.* Falls Church, VA: Lulejian and Associates, 1975.

Sapolsky, Harvey M. *The Polaris System Development: Bureaucratic and Programmatic Success in Government.* Cambridge, MA: Harvard University Press, 1972.

Sapolsky, Joel J. *Seapower in the Nuclear Age: The United States Navy and NATO, 1949–80.* Annapolis, MD: Naval Institute Press, 1991.

Smith, Richard K. *Seventy-Five Years of Inflight Refueling.* Washington, DC: Air Force History and Museum Program, 1998.

Swanborough, Gordon, and Peter M. Bowers. *United States Military Aircraft since 1909.* Washington, DC: Smithsonian Institution Press, 1989.

Swanborough, Gordon, and Peter M. Bowers. *United States Navy Aircraft since 1911.* 3d ed. Annapolis, MD: Naval Institute Press, 1990.

Watson, Robert J. *Into the Missile Age, 1956–1960.* Vol. 4: *History of the Office of the Secretary of Defense.* Washington, DC: Historical Office, Office of the Secretary of Defense, 1997.

Wegg, John. *General Dynamics Aircraft and Their Predecessors.* Annapolis, MD: Naval Institute Press, 1990.

Werrell, Kenneth P. *The Evolution of the Cruise Missile.* Maxwell Air Force Base, AL: Air University Press, 1985.

*Who's Who in American Aeronautics, 1928.* New York: Aviation Publishing, 1928.

Wildenberg, Thomas. *All the Factors of Victory: Adm. Joseph Mason Reeves and the Origins of Carrier Airpower.* Washington, DC: Brassey's, 2003.

Wildenberg, Thomas. *Destined for Glory: Dive Bombing, Midway, and the Evolution of Carrier Airpower.* Annapolis, MD: Naval Institute Press, 1998.

## Articles

Bradley, Robert E. "Convair Post World War II Seaplane Studies, Part One." *Aerospace Projects Review* 2 (July–August 2000): 11–18.

Bradley, Robert E. "Convair Post World War II Seaplane Studies, Part Two." *Aerospace Projects Review* 2 (September–October 2000): 13–20.

Cully, George. "A Convair Preliminary Design Study for a Mach 4 Attack Seaplane." *Aerospace Projects Review* 2 (November–December 2000): 4–8.

Dorr, Robert F. "Convair R3Y Tradewind." *Wings of Fame* 18 (2000): 4–15.

Grove, Eric, and Geoffrey Till. "Anglo-American Maritime Strategy in the Era of Massive Retaliation." In John B. Hattendorf and Robert S. Jordan, eds., *Maritime Strategy and the Balance of Power: Britain and America in the Twentieth Century.* New York: St. Martin's Press, 1989. Pp. 271–303.

Hansen, Chuck. "Nuclear Neptunes: Early Days of Composite Squadrons 5 and 6." *American Aviation Historical Society Journal* 24 (Fourth Quarter, 1979): 262–68.

Jones, Carolyn C. "The Politics of Extravagance: The Aircraft Nuclear Propulsion Project." *Naval War College Review* 53 (Spring 2000): 158–90.

Jordan, Robert S. "The Balance of Power and the Anglo-American Maritime Relationship." In John B. Hattendorf and Robert S. Jordan, eds., *Maritime Strategy and the Balance of Power: Britain and America in the Twentieth Century.* New York: St. Martin's Press, 1989. Pp. 1–20.

Martin, Glenn L. "The Case for the Flying Boat." *Aero Digest* 46 (1 September 1944): 78–79.

McSurely, Alexander. "Design for a Supersonic Flying Boat?" *Aviation Week* 55 (23 October 1950): 14.

Mets, David R. "The Influence of Aviation on the Evolution of American Naval Thought." In Philip S. Meilinger, ed., *The Paths of Heaven: The Evolution of Airpower Theory.* Maxwell Air Force Base, AL: Air University Press, 1997. Pp. 115–49.

Parsons, Edgar A. "Needed—A Military Strategy of Mobility." U.S. Naval Institute *Proceedings* 82 (December 1956): 1263–69.

"SeaMaster Cancellation Announced." *Martin Service News,* September–October 1959, p. 6.

Smith, Richard K. "The Intercontinental Airliner and the Essence of Airplane Performance, 1929–1939." *Technology and Culture* 24 (July 1983): 428–49.

Stout, Ernest G. "Bases Unlimited." *Aeronautical Engineering Review* 14 (June 1955): 42–55.

Stout, Ernest G. "Development of High-Speed Water-Based Aircraft." *Journal of the Aeronautical Sciences* 17 (August 1950): 469–80.

Stout, Ernest G. "Development of Precision Radio-Controlled Dynamically Similar Flying Models." *Journal of the Aeronautical Sciences* 13 (July 1946): 335–45.

Stout, Ernest G. "Experimental Determination of Hydrodynamic Stability." *Journal of the Aeronautical Sciences* 8 (December 1940): 55–61.

Stout, Ernest G. "High-Speed Water-Based Aircraft." *Aircraft Engineering* 25 (February 1953): 43–50.

## Periodicals

*Aviation Week*
*New York Times*
*Washington Post*


## Interviews and Oral Histories

Interview with Vice Adm. Charles S. Minter Jr. Annapolis, MD, 11 June 2003.
Reminiscences of Vice Adm. Charles S. Minter Jr. June 1981. Naval Institute Oral History Collection. 2 vols.


## Unpublished Papers

BuAer, Research Division. "The Attack Seaplane Task Force vs. the Attack Carrier Task Force: A Preliminary Comparison." Report No. DR-1700, 1 November 1954.
BuAer, Research Division. "A Preliminary Design Study of an Open Ocean Sonar Dunking Flying Boat." Report No. DR-1716, April 1955.
Glenn L. Martin Company. "A Plan for Seaplane Handling for the United States Navy." ER 5612, July 1953.
"The Last Great Act of Defiance: The Memoirs of Ernest C. Simpson, Aero Propulsion Pioneer." 1 June 1987. Aero Propulsion Laboratory, Air Force Wright Aeronautical Laboratories, Wright-Patterson AFB, Dayton, OH.
NASA Biographical Data Sheet. "George Simpson Trimble Jr." N.d. NASA Manned Spacecraft Center, Houston, TX.
Rathbone, Tim. "The History and Development of the Strategic Mobile Striking Force, the Martin P6M Seamaster: A Study of Military Weapons Procurement in the 1950s." 1985.
Rodney, George A. "The P6M Seamaster." Undated speech. File AM-201680-0, Martin Seamaster Family. National Air and Space Museum Library, Washington, DC.
Russell, James S. "Sea Master—P6M: The Last of the Navy's Flying Boats." 1986.

# Index

# About the Author

William F. Trimble is Professor and Chair of the Department of History at Auburn University in Alabama. He received his Ph.D. from the University of Colorado, Boulder, in 1974. His book *Jerome C. Hunsaker and the Rise of American Aeronautics* won the 2003 Gardner-Lesser Award presented by the American Institute of Aeronautics and Astronautics for the best book in the history of aeronautics over a five-year period. Among his other published books are *Wings for the Navy: A History of the Naval Aircraft Factory, 1917–1956* (Naval Institute Press, 1990) and *Admiral William A. Moffett: Architect of Naval Aviation* (Naval Institute Press, 1994).

From 1999 to 2000, Professor Trimble held the Charles A. Lindbergh Chair of Aerospace History at the National Air and Space Museum in Washington, D.C. In 1996, the Northeast Aero Historians named him Historian of the Year.